Hedge
Funds

Founded in 1807, John Wiley & Sons is the oldest independent publishing company in the United States. With offices in North America, Europe, Australia, and Asia, Wiley is globally committed to developing and marketing print and electronic products and services for our customers' professional and personal knowledge and understanding.

The Wiley Finance-Series includes books written specifically for finance and investment professionals as well as sophisticated individual investors and their financial advisors. Topics range from portfolio management to e-commerce, risk management, financial engineering, valuation, and financial instrument analysis, as well as much more.

For a list of available titles, please visit our web site at www.Wiley Finance.com.

Hedge Funds

Definitive Strategies and Techniques

Edited by
KENNETH S. PHILLIPS
and
RONALD J. SURZ, CIMA

WILEY

John Wiley & Sons, Inc.

Published by John Wiley & Sons, Inc., Hoboken, New Jersey
Published simultaneously in Canada

Limit of Liability/Disclaimer of Warranty: While the publisher and author have used their best efforts in preparing this book, they make no representations or warranties with respect to the accuracy or completeness of the contents of this book and specifically disclaim any implied warranties of merchantability or fitness for a particular purpose. No warranty may be created or extended by sales representatives or written sales materials. The advice and strategies contained herein may not be suitable for your situation. You should consult with a professional where appropriate. Neither the publisher nor author shall be liable for any loss of profit or any other commercial damages, including but not limited to special, incidental, consequential, or other damages.

For general information on our other products and services, or technical support, please contact our Customer Care Department within the United States at 800-762-2974, outside the United States at 317-572-3993 or fax 317-572-4002.

Wiley also publishes its books in a variety of electronic formats. Some content that appears in print may not be available in electronic books.

For more information about Wiley products, visit our web site at www.wiley.com.

Library of Congress Cataloging-in-Publication Data:
Phillips, Kenneth S.
   Hedge funds : definitive strategies and techniques, IMCA / Kenneth S. Phillips, Ronald J. Surz.
        p.   cm. — (Wiley finance series)
     ISBN 0-471-46309-4 (hard : alk. paper)
     1. Hedge funds. I. Title: Definitive strategies and techniques, IMCA. II. Surz, Ronald. III. Title. IV. Series.
   HG4530.P47   2003
   332.64'5—dc21   2003006622

Printed in the United States of America
10 9 8 7 6 5 4 3 2 1

Contents

PREFACE   VII

ACKNOWLEDGMENTS   XI

CHAPTER 1
Hedge Funds: Overview and Regulatory Landscape   1
The Managed Fund Association

CHAPTER 2
Alpha-Generating Strategies   10
Thomas Schneeweis and Richard Spurgin

CHAPTER 3
Funds of Hedge Funds: Definitive Overview of Strategies and Techniques   25
Thomas Zucosky

CHAPTER 4
Investing in Hedged Equity Funds   49
Brian A. Wolf, CFA

CHAPTER 5
Arbitrage   65
Alfredo M. Viegas

CHAPTER 6
Global Macro Funds   82
Gary Hirst

CHAPTER 7
Managed Futures   94
Frank Pusateri

CHAPTER 8

Manager Searches and Performance Measurement   112
Meredith A. Jones and Milton Baehr

CHAPTER 9

Risk Management for Hedge Funds and Funds of Funds   139
Leslie Rahl

CHAPTER 10

Structured Products—Then and Now   159
John Kelly and Kirt Strawn, CFA, CIMA

APPENDIX A

The Hedge Fund Difference   176
Todd Goldman

APPENDIX B

Some Helpful Links   180

APPENDIX C

Value at Risk and Probability of Loss   181

RESOURCES   183

GLOSSARY OF TERMS   192

CONTRIBUTORS   195

INDEX   205

Preface

Since the downturn in the U.S. and global equity markets in 2000, investors and their advisors have begun seriously questioning many of the asset allocation and portfolio diversification assumptions that had influenced their policies and decisions. Several theories that had previously been considered unquestionable, and which had served as the cornerstones of their asset diversification strategies, were increasingly being challenged. As a result, investment policy and strategy saw significant shifts, both at the institutional and high-net-worth investor levels. A broader segment of institutional and private investors began embracing alternative investment strategies, private equity, venture capital, and a range of sophisticated hedge fund strategies.

To be sure, many investors had already embraced the notion of alternative investment strategies during the 1990s, while equity and fixed-income returns were experiencing historic bull market appreciation. But the majority of investors, experiencing substantial investment success, showed little interest in changing their strategic investment policies. Infact, many investors abandoned all sense of discipline, expecting equity returns to simply continue to rise.

Times are changing and the returns of the global capital markets over the 5 years ending December 2002 have encouraged investors to question many of their most basic investment theories. Beginning with the "efficient market" theory, investors learned that although markets may prove efficient over the long term, there may be incredibly large short-term inefficiencies, and tactical and strategic asset diversification strategies should be managed accordingly. Investors that had shifted from value equities to growth equities in the latter part of the 1990s as a result of the poor *relative* performance of value managers, for example, found their decision to be one of the worst they could have made. Similarly, the more recent "flight to quality" from equities to fixed-income investments during the tandem decline in equity valuations and interest rates could potentially result in similar investor losses should the U.S. economy recover and experience a rapid or sustained rise in interest rates. On a similar note, investors have begun questioning the notion that stocks always outperform fixed-income investments—the notion of risk-premium-related return expectations. Over the short term, this theory is as threatened as the efficient market theory, from which it was initially derived. As recent times have demonstrated, markets are not efficient over short-term periods, stocks don't necessarily always outperform bonds, and prices don't always rise!

Unfortunately, during this difficult period many investors also learned that their portfolio mangers were poorly equipped to protect them from declining markets. Traditional equity strategies—and their managers— whose prior selection had been based upon their *relative* performance versus *unmanaged* indices and/or peer groups with similar strategies, experienced significant *absolute* losses. When compared on a relative basis these absolute losses appeared understandable and perhaps acceptable. However, on an absolute basis, these losses were dramatic and significant for most. Fortunately for some, while most investors were experiencing substantial losses, a growing group had already begun embracing a completely different paradigm of investing—a paradigm of absolute returns.

The term "absolute return" refers to a broad range of investment strategies that seek to profit from all market conditions. Rather than employ investment strategies that are closely correlated to the performance of the broad equity and fixed-income markets, managers of absolute-return strategies attempt to employ noncorrelated, skill-based strategies with the intention of delivering consistent, positive returns in all market conditions. These managers, in general, don't measure or compare their returns on a relative basis against passively managed indices—such as the S&P 500— although such comparisons are often useful. Instead, these managers are held to a different standard—the standard of generating positive returns irrespective of the direction of the markets or the behavior of the rest of the world.

The funds (and managers) that operate in this world are often referred to as hedge funds, largely because their strategies attempt to hedge various investment risks. Loosely regulated when compared with mutual funds— which are registered with the SEC and generally targeted toward smaller, retail investors—hedge funds are private partnerships that are generally unregistered and are available only to accredited investors—those investors who are, by definition, already wealthy and/or experienced. Limited in the number and types of investors that can be accepted into these partnerships, and often limited by the dollar capacity of their various strategies, hedge fund managers employ a broad range of skill-based strategies that are comparatively uncorrelated with the performance of the broad markets.

Uncorrelated returns, however, do not mean risk-free returns. And hedge fund strategies, which by definition are nontraditional, generally expose investors to a broad range of risks that are also nontraditional, and that should be fully understood prior to investing. In fact, the ability of a hedge fund manager to generate consistent positive returns is often accomplished through the use of investment strategies and securities that, in themselves, may expose investors to a substantial range of unique risks—risks that are not market-related but, instead, are security- or strategy-specific. Some of these many risks may include, but are certainly not limited to, the liberal use of leverage (margin debt); short selling; hedging with complex derivative securities, which often expose an investor to a range of nonsymmetrical return characteristics (tail risk); and the use of complex futures, commodities, currencies, and option strategies.

In recent years, and largely in response to investors' disappointment with their traditional portfolios' returns, institutional and wealthy private investors have begun showing greater interest in the hedge fund world of absolute returns. An increasing number of consultants and financial advisors have begun to regularly include hedge funds and funds of hedge funds in their asset allocation and diversification strategies. Many well-known and highly regarded institutional investors have allocated upward of 60 or 80% of their entire portfolio to the world of alternative investments (including private equity, venture capital, oil and gas, timber, real estate, and other such investments).

The entire subject of alternative investing is very broad, so the editors of this book have elected to focus on the most liquid—and perhaps most popular—sector of alternative investing: hedge funds. Our goal, in creating this book, has been to demystify the subject of hedge fund investing by inviting industry experts to explain the strategies they employ in the management of their funds. This book has not been targeted to the consultant or investor with many years of hedge fund investment experience. At the same time, the book has not been targeted to inexperienced advisors or their clients. Instead, the editors have attempted to create an understandable and straightforward handbook, which can be used as a desk reference or primer for experienced advisors and investors seeking to broaden their horizons.

The handbook's two editors have more than 50 years of combined experience as consultants to large institutional and individual investors. Additionally, in recent years both have devoted substantial time to the study of hedge fund strategies, their risks, opportunities, and potential benefits. We hope you find the handbook useful and valuable as you consider your future investment strategies and portfolio allocations. And we hope this book helps you develop the same enthusiasm for this area of investing that we have. We believe hedge fund investing will continue to grow in the years to come. We also believe that there will be increased regulation and that such regulation will eventually contribute to increased accountability and professionalism in this quiet, very private, and often misunderstood sector of our industry.

The future growth of the hedge fund industry will ultimately be greatly influenced by the investment consulting industry and its leading professional organization, the Investment Management Consultants Association (IMCA). The editors are proud to have been associated with IMCA for many years and greatly appreciate the opportunity to prepare this book for its members and the general investment community.

KENNETH S. PHILLIPS
RCG Capital Partners, LLC
New York, NY

RONALD J. SURZ, CIMA
PPCA, Inc.
San Clemente, CA

Acknowledgments

The editors, Ken Phillips and Ron Surz, would like to acknowledge our contributor: The Managed Funds Associates; Thomas Schneeweis; Richard Spurgin; Thomas Zucosky; Brian A. Wolf, CFA; Alfredo M. Viegas; Gary Hirst; Frank Pusateri; Meredith A. Jones; Milton Baehr; Leslie Rahl; John Kelly; and Kirk Strawn, CFA, CIMA. The editors also acknowledge and thank the following for their time and editorial assistance: Sohaila Abdulali, Eileen Swinehart, and, most importantly, Evelyn Brust.

CHAPTER 1

Hedge Funds: Overview and Regulatory Landscape

The Managed Fund Association

Too many people believe that hedge funds are unregulated investment vehicles. This is not so at all. In fact, this has been a hot topic in recent years—do they need more regulation? Less? None? This chapter does not take a position either way. It attempts to illuminate the United States' current regulatory framework as of the Spring, 2003. It first describes hedge funds and then addresses the relevant regulations.

WHAT IS A HEDGE FUND?

A hedge fund is an investment vehicle. A.W. Jones launched the first modern hedge fund in the late 1940s. Some investment historians place the roots of hedge funds in the 1930s. Regardless of the specific date, hedge funds are rather new concepts in the investment world. Since their advent, they have varied dramatically in terms of scope, strategy, and philosophy. Their heterogeneity makes definitions difficult. People's misconceptions about them get in the way of a clear understanding.

The most famous as well as most misunderstood hedge fund was probably Long Term Capital Management (LTCM), which first shot to fame due to its "all-star" cast of founders. It plunged to infamy through its near default on a massive portfolio in 1998. So was born the modern view of hedge funds as maverick, risky, and aggressive investment vehicles.

This view does a great disservice to the hedge fund industry. LTCM had unique players who made unique plays. Most hedge funds are much smaller, and use much less leverage. After LTCM's failure, the President's Working Group on Financial Markets (PWG) undertook a prolonged study of the issues. Fortunately, the PWG issued a positive definition of a hedge fund: A pooled investment vehicle that is privately organized, administered by a professional investment management firm (the hedge fund manager), and not widely available to the public.

Most importantly, hedge funds offer investors innumerable investment alternatives for diversifying portfolios. They are not meant to be anyone's sole investments. They increase market liquidity, provide shock absorption in volatile markets, mitigate price swings, and reduce bid/ask spreads.[1]

These pooled investment vehicles are often organized as private partnerships that reside offshore for tax and regulatory reasons. The managers frequently receive fees based on performance. They are generally unregistered investment vehicles whose advisors may or may not be registered. This is why people believe that hedge funds are unregulated. There is a difference between "unregistered" and "unregulated." The regulatory landscape is perpetually changing, so it is quite difficult to create a simple snapshot. This chapter tries to include anticipated changes that could affect the market.

HEDGE FUNDS: UNREGISTERED, BUT NOT UNREGULATED

Paul Roye, the director of the Division of Investment Management of the U.S. Securities and Exchange Commission (SEC), recently stated: "Hedge funds generally are referred to as unregulated investment pools. This may conjure up images of some maverick managers doing as they please. However, hedge fund managers who take this attitude do so at their peril." This discussion will focus first on which hedge funds and hedge fund managers are exempt from registration, and seconds, on the regulations they do face.

Hedge Funds and Registration

Hedge funds can bypass many regulations by avoiding registration under the Investment Company Act of 1940 (Investment Company Act), the Investment Advisors Act of 1940 (Investment Advisors Act), the Securities Act of 1933 (Securities Act), and the Securities Exchange Act of 1934 (Exchange Act). Exemption from one category does not necessarily exempt them from others. And while hedge funds are free from registration with the SEC, those that use futures and trade commodities are registered with the Commodity Futures Trading Commission (CFTC), which wields great power under the Commodity Exchange Act (CEA). Hedge fund managers must

---

[1]For more information on the nature of hedge funds and the uniqueness of LTCM, see *Hedge Funds: Issues for Public Policy Makers*, published by Managed Funds Association, April 1999.

also pay attention to the securities and investment advisor laws of their states and the states and countries where their investors may reside.

Investment Company Act

Investment companies have to register under the Investment Company Act and abide by its regulations. This Act delineates a number of exceptions to the definition of an investment company, thereby exempting such entities from some, but not all, regulations. Hedge funds can qualify for one of two major exceptions to the definition of an investment company by limiting either the number or type of investors so long as the fund is not proposing to make a public offering of its securities.

Section 3(c)(1) of the Investment Company Act A hedge fund is not an investment company for the purposes of the Investment Company Act if it has less than 100 beneficial owners and does not publicly offer its securities. Before 1997, if a company owned less than 10% of a hedge fund's securities, that company was considered one beneficial owner of that fund; otherwise, the Investment Company Act would have "looked through" that company to all its respective investors so that each investor in the company would be considered an individual owner of the fund for purposes of 3(c)(1). Since 1997, after the National Securities Market Improvement Act of 1996, a company can own more than 10% of a hedge fund's securities and still be considered one beneficial owner of the fund, so long as the value of that company's securities in the fund is less than 10% of the company's total assets.

Section 3(c)(7) of the Investment Company Act A fund that limits its sales only to "qualified purchasers" and does not publicly offer its securities is also excluded from being considered an investment company. Qualified purchasers include an individual (or an individual and his or her spouse, if they invest jointly) with at least $5 million in investments; specified family-owned companies with at least $5 million in investments; trusts established and funded by qualified purchasers, so long as a qualified purchaser makes the trust's investment decisions; and any person acting for his or her account or the account of other qualified purchasers who own and invest more than $25 million.

Investment Advisors Act

Hedge fund managers are investment advisors as defined by the Investment Advisors Act. Most large investment advisors are required to register with the SEC. They must follow myriad regulations, such as extensive record-keeping requirements and restrictions on performance-based fees. Some hedge fund advisors register under the Investment Advisors Act, but many avoid it with the private advisor exemption under Section 203(b)(3).

Section 203(b)(3) exempts advisors who have fewer than 15 clients and who neither hold themselves up as investment advisors nor act as investment advisors to an investment company registered under the Investment Company Act or a company that has elected treatment as a "business development company" under the Investment Advisors Act. For the purposes of Section 203(b)(3), the SEC promulgated Rule 203(b)(1)-1, which defines a limited partnership or a limited liability company as a single client, so long as that partnership or company is investing for its own benefit rather than the individual benefits of its owners. Rule 203(b)(1)-1 allows many hedge fund managers to enjoy an exempt status.

Securities Act

Section 5 of the Securities Act mandates that securities be registered with the SEC before they are sold, unless they are exempt. Most hedge funds qualify for exemption under Section 4(2) of the Securities Act, which exempts "transactions by an issuer not involving any public offering." A similar concept is found in Sections 3(c)(1) and 3(c)(7) of the Investment Company Act. Section 4(2) is confusing, and in 1982 the SEC adopted Regulation D to provide a safe harbor for certain offerings. Regulation D offers two ways for an issuer to use the safe harbor. First, the issuer cannot use any general solicitation, such as newspaper articles, advertisements, seminars, or circulars. Web sites can be used to attract solicitation if certain procedures are used.[2] The second way involves the nature of purchasers. Issuers relying on Regulation D cannot offer or sell securities to more than 35 non-accredited investors.

Exchange Act

Any person who is "engaged in the business of effecting transactions in securities for the account of others" qualifies as a broker–dealer who must register with the SEC under Section 3(a)(4)(A) of the Exchange Act. People who receive transaction-related compensation and/or hold themselves out as brokers, or as assisting others in completing securities transactions, must register as broker–dealers under Section 15(a) of the Exchange Act, and follow all its rules. Hedge funds are able to avoid those regulations by

---

[2]See *IPONET*, SEC No-Action Letter (July 26, 1996). The SEC issued 2 no-action letters to Lamp Technologies, Inc. (May 29, 1997 and May 29, 1998) that bring the use of websites for broad solicitation by hedge funds under Regulation D's safe harbor, if the hedge funds had previous relationships with the potential investors solicited.

taking advantage of the broker–dealer exemption under Section 3(a)(5)(C) for entities trading securities solely for their own accounts and by not holding themselves out to the public as broker–dealers.

Commodity Exchange Act ("CEA")

If a hedge fund trades futures and options contracts on a futures exchange, the CEA considers the fund a commodity pool. The operator of that pool, the hedge fund manager, is then subject to regulation as a commodity pool operator (CPO) under the CEA. The CEA has no registration-exemption scheme equivalent to those under the Investment Company Act, the Investment Advisors Act, or the Exchange Act. Although the hedge fund operators who qualify as CPOs are required to register, they may be exempt from some disclosure and reporting requirements, depending on the nature of their investors.

State Securities Laws

Most states have their own regulatory structures for investments and investment services offered within their borders. Hedge fund operators need to know the regulatory schemes of each state in which they operate, because exemption at the federal level does not necessarily equate to exemption at the state level. Some states are adopting the federal government's exemption model. California, for example, has recently adopted regulations that incorporate a "private advisor" registration exemption similar to the federal exemption in Section 203(b)(3) of the Advisors Act.

HEDGE FUND REGULATION

Registered securities, investment companies, and investment advisors must follow many rules that most hedge fund operators would view as burdensome and prohibitive to conducting their business. However, hedge funds are subject to other regulations, such as antifraud provisions. Plus, after the tragedy of September 11, 2001, hedge funds, among others, face mandated antimoney-laundering programs for the first time.

Hedge fund regulation can be put into five categories: antifraud provisions, antimoney-laundering requirements, CFTC regulations, Employee Retirement Income Security Act of 1974 (ERISA), and other miscellaneous legal considerations.

Antifraud Provisions

Hedge funds and hedge fund managers, both registered and unregistered, are subject to the extensive antifraud provisions of the Securities Act (Section 17), the Exchange Act (Section 10 and Rule 10b-5 promulgated thereunder) and the Advisors Act. The antifraud provisions apply to any offer, sale or purchase of securities, or any advisory service of such offer, sale or purchase. Furthermore, hedge funds must not engage in activities detrimental to market integrity, such as market manipulation and insider trading.

Antimoney-Laundering Requirements

In the wake of the terrorist attacks on America, Congress began work on the Uniting and Strengthening America by Providing Appropriate Tools Required to Intercept and Obstruct Terrorism Act of 2001 (USA PATRIOT Act), which President Bush signed into law on October 26, 2001. Revelations that some of the terrorist activity was funded by money that had been laundered through a variety of financial vehicles resulted in Title III of the USA PATRIOT Act, entitled the "International Money Laundering Abatement and Anti-Terrorist Financing Act of 2001," which required all financial institutions to establish an antimoney-laundering program by April 24, 2002. Section 352 of the USA PATRIOT Act states that each program should include at least internal policies; procedures and controls; a compliance officer; an ongoing employee training program; and an independent audit function.

As defined in the USA PATRIOT Act, the term "financial institution" includes, among other things, any entity that is "an investment company,"[3] and any entity that is registered (or required to register) as a CPO or a commodity trading advisor (CTA) under the Commodity Exchange Act.[4] Although it is not entirely clear whether the reference to an investment company could be construed to include a hedge fund excepted from the definition of investment company under the Investment Company Act, the Treasury Department has suggested that hedge funds are covered by the USA PATRIOT Act, and they must adopt and implement antimoney-laundering programs.

---

[3]The reference to "an investment company" in this definition is not expressly limited to registered investment companies; as a result, it is unclear whether the definition is intended to include unregistered, private investment funds, i.e., funds excepted from the definition of "investment company" under the Investment Company Act of 1940. This ambiguity may be resolved by the investment company study to be undertaken by the Secretary of the Treasury, the Federal Reserve Board, and the Securities and Exchange Commission by October 26, 2002, pursuant to Section 356(c) of the USA PATRIOT Act. This requires these agencies to report on recommendations for effective regulations to apply the currency reporting and related requirements of the Bank Secrecy Act to registered investment companies as well as certain funds excepted from the definition of "investment company."

CFTC Regulations

Regulation of hedge funds under the Commodity Exchange Act applies to the hedge fund managers, not the funds. So, only CPOs and CTAs need comply.

Hedge Fund Managers as CPOs   Under the CEA, a CPO is any person engaged in the business of soliciting or accepting funds from others for the purpose of trading commodity futures contracts in connection with a commodity pool, which is any investment trust, syndicate, or similar entity that invests its pooled funds in commodity interests. Most hedge fund managers who use futures and options on futures qualify and must register. However, the CFTC has adopted three rules that relieve hedge funds from the requirements of disclosure, reporting and recordkeeping. The manager must file notice to apply these. In addition to this existing relief, Managed Funds Association (MFA)[5] is promoting a new rule (Proposed Rule 4.9) that would provide CFTC registration relief for certain funds.

Disclosure Relief   CFTC Rule 4.7 relieves a hedge fund manager registered as a CPO from the requirement of providing a CPO Disclosure to each customer, so long as the offering memorandum is not misleading. To qualify for the exemption under Rule 4.7, the hedge fund manager can sell ownership in the fund only to Qualified Eligible Participants (QEPs) and must file a simple exemption form with the CFTC. Rule 4.7 defines QEPs as, among others, registered commodities and securities professionals; accredited investors under the Securities Act who have an investment portfolio of at least $2,000,000, $200,000 on deposit as commodities margin, or both; and non-U.S. persons.

A registered CPO primarily involved in securities might consider seeking disclosure relief under Rule 4.12(b), which concerns disclosure, particularly

---

[4]Section 321 of the USA PATRIOT Act expands the definition of "financial institution" in the Bank Secrecy Act to include "any futures commission merchant, commodity trading advisor, or commodity pool operator registered or required to register under the Commodity Exchange Act." As a result, any CPO or CTA managing a hedge fund would be required to comply with Section 352 of the USA PATRIOT Act.

[5]MFA, located in Washington, D.C., is a membership organization dedicated to serving the needs of the professionals who specialize in the global alternative investment industry—hedge funds, funds of funds, and private and public managed futures funds. MFA has over 600 members, which represent a significant portion of the $500 billion invested in alternative investment vehicles around the world. MFA members, including many of the largest international financial services conglomerates, are based in the U.S. and Europe.

performance information, to investors. Under this rule, the hedge fund manager need not disclose any performance information. However, he or she must file with the CFTC and provide prospective investors a disclosure document. Managers often can use the offering memorandum for nonaccredited investors in accordance with Regulation D to satisfy the CFTC requirements; otherwise, the manager might need to supply a CFTC supplement.

Reporting Relief   Rule 4.7 also provides an exemption for the required certified annual report under Rules 4.22(c) and (d). In lieu of the extensive reporting requirements of Rules 4.22(c) and (d), managers under 4.7 need only supply an uncertified annual statement to the CFTC and the National Futures Association (NFA). This must contain at least a Statement of Financial Condition as of the close of the fiscal year and a Statement of Income (Loss) for that year. Hedge fund managers seeking disclosure relief under Rule 4.12(b) cannot avail themselves of the annual report relief under Rule 4.7.

Recordkeeping Relief   CPOs qualifying for relief under CFTC Rule 4.7 are exempt from the extensive recordkeeping requirements of Rule 4.23.

Proposed Rule 4.9   Currently, unlike any SEC relief, no registration relief exists for CPOs with the CFTC. Proposed Rule 4.9 would provide CFTC registration relief for CPOs who operate funds only with qualified investors.

Hedge Fund Managers as CTAs   The Commodity Exchange Act defines a CTA as anyone who, for profit, advises others about trading in commodity futures and options on futures. At least two exemptions exist for them. First, under Rule 4.14(a)(4), managers only provide trading advice to the pool or pool for which they are registered; they are exempt from registering as CTAs. Second, they need not register as CTAs if they have fewer than 15 clients in 12-month period and do not advertise themselves as CTAs. This is of limited use because each investor in each fund is counted as a client.

ERISA

If at least 25% of a fund's assets consist of ERISA assets, the entire fund is considered "plan assets" under ERISA. It is subject to numerous restrictions and prohibitions under ERISA. Most hedge funds simply ensure that their ERISA assets remain below the 25% level.

Other Miscellaneous Legal Considerations

Antifraud provisions, antimoney-laundering programs, CFTC regulations, and ERISA requirements are the four major categories of regulation affecting unregistered hedge funds and hedge fund managers. Hedge fund managers must be vigilantly aware of other regulations and restrictions that could affect them.

State Securities Laws All exemptions from registration or regulation by the SEC and the CFTC are the result of federal laws. Every state has developed and promulgated its own system of regulation for hedge funds that conduct business or offers securities within its borders. While many states have adopted structures that mirror the federal system, each has its own nuances.

The Exchange Act Aside from antifraud provisions, the Exchange Act has other regulations that might affect hedge funds and managers. For example, they might be subject to the beneficial ownership requirements of Section 13(d) of the Exchange Act, which affects any person who is the beneficial owner of more than five percent of any class of voting securities registered under the Exchange Act. If a hedge fund or manager qualifies as such a beneficial owner, he or she must file reports with a number of entities, including the SEC, and report all positions that meet the five percent threshold. Some of the specific reporting requirements can be found under SEC Rule 13d-1.

Taxes All hedge funds, hedge fund managers, and hedge fund investors must consider the tax burden based on the structure of the fund. For example, funds structured as limited partnerships are not considered taxable entities, but the partners in the funds must consider income, deductions, and realized gains and losses from the partnership, even if they don't receive any income from the partnership. Many funds are based offshore for tax benefits.

CONCLUSION

Hedge fund managers cannot assume that their unregistered status equals an unregulated one. The regulatory framework provides specific parameters in which each hedge fund must conduct its business if it is to be an unregistered fund. The laws specifically dictate who must or must not register. It is not voluntary. Critics of hedge funds should understand that unregulated hedge funds don't exist. Of course, hedge funds and hedge fund managers do receive great benefits from registration exemptions. These give them tremendous ability to operate the funds in a much more effective and productive manner. However, no matter what their status in the industry, all hedge funds have restrictions and limitations.

CHAPTER 2

Alpha-Generating Strategies

Thomas Schneeweis
Richard Spurgin

INTRODUCTION

Alternative investments are investments that provide unique risk and return properties not easily found in traditional stock and bond investments. Alternative investments include more traditional, less liquid alternatives, such as private equity and real estate, and more modern, more liquid alternatives, such as hedge funds.[1] The recent growth in alternative investments has happened partly because investors are becoming increasingly aware of the benefits of a wide range of alternative investments. These benefits include both unique diversification benefits as well as unique return opportunities. For instance, hedge fund strategies are called alpha-generating strategies because they are seen as actively managed asset strategies that have shown the ability to provide superior market performance—alpha—rather than a commonly accepted performance benchmark.

Some hedge fund strategies are called absolute return strategies since they are designed to provide positive returns in all market environments. Since these strategies' goal is to provide consistent positive returns, they often use the risk-free Treasury bill as a comparison benchmark. Necessary in this book context. This is generally misguided. The Treasury bill rate is truly without risk while even low-risk hedge fund strategies have variable returns.

In recent years, people have questioned bond- and stock-based mutual fund investments' ability to produce consistent alpha. Hedge funds have been increasingly marketed as providing positive alpha. This chapter briefly reviews various hedge fund strategies' alpha-generating properties relative to comparable risk traditional stock and bond portfolios. The following section

---

[1]Goldmen Sachs/Frank Russell report (2002).

looks at alternative ways of alpha determination. Simple variance-based (e.g., Sharpe), beta-based (CAPM), or risk-free rate (zero beta) models of alpha determination are often incomplete. Section 3 describes the basis for potential alpha returns to trading in various hedge fund strategies. Section 4 shows analytical evidence of the ability of stock and bond funds as well as hedge funds to provide alpha-generating returns.

Results indicate that, relative to traditional stock and bond funds, hedge funds have shown a greater ability to provide positive alpha. However, the level of reported alpha depends on the completeness of the corresponding benchmark model, and historical evidence of relative performance is not necessarily reflective of future relative performance. In short, both academic theory and empirical results indicate potential for hedge funds to provide excess return relative to simple investment in similar risk strategies. However, the results also show, as expected, that hedge fund alphas are not easily attained and are not as large as some hedge fund managers would like to maintain. Also, individual hedge fund managers are not as consistent in outperforming other managers as simple historical representations might indicate.

SOME BACKGROUND ON ALPHA DETERMINATION

At alternative investment seminars and conferences, most hedge fund managers are intent on proving their ability to produce alpha. Each manager and investor has his or her own unique take on what alpha is or how it should be measured. It should come as no surprise, therefore, that academics have weighed in on the central question of this issue: What is alpha and what is the best way to measure the alpha of an investment strategy?

The term alpha comes from statistics. In linear regression, the equation that relates an observed variable y to some other factor x is written as:

$$y = \alpha + \beta x + \varepsilon$$

The first term, α (alpha), represents the intercept; β (beta) represents the slope; and ε (epsilon) represents a random error term. In finance, it is generally assumed that returns to some asset have a linear relationship to the returns to one or more factors or performance benchmarks. The alpha term is important in finance because it represents the return that the investor would receive if the benchmark had a zero return. As such, it is a proxy for manager skill. Rearranging the previous formula (and ignoring the error term for now), the equation can be restated to focus on the alpha:

$$\alpha = y - \beta x$$

It is better to think about returns that are net of the risk-free rate, so both the asset and the benchmark returns are adjusted downward by the risk-free rate of interest. Consider these definitions: R_i = Return on Fund i; R_f = Return on a risk-free asset, such as Treasury bills; and R_M = Factor or benchmark, such as the SP500, the MSCI, or a CTA Index. The equation that relates return on an asset to a benchmark (the familiar CAPM equation) becomes:

$$(R_i - R_f) = \alpha + \beta(R_M - R_f).$$

When rearranged to measure alpha, it is $\alpha = (R_i - R_f) + \beta(R_M - R_f)$.

While the academic community prefers this equation, there are a number of variations on the theme. It is not one purpose to give a complete statistical and theoretical review of alpha determination or to attempt to re-educate the entire investment community brought up on Modern Portfolio Theory and the Capital Asset Pricing Model. In the world of academics, alpha is generally defined as the excess return to active management, appropriately adjusted for risk. It is the return adjusted for the risk of a comparable risky asset position or portfolio. Therefore, the questions are how do we define the expected risk of the manager's investment position, and how do we obtain the return on a comparable risk position or portfolio?

ALTERNATIVE INVESTMENTS: SOURCE OF ALPHA

Alternative investments tend to have better access to alpha. Private equity, private debt, and venture capital derive their returns from the same general source (economic growth) as stocks and bonds, albeit with risk premiums for illiquidity and informational costs. Similarly, many hedge funds that hold primarily long positions in stocks or bonds may have a claim on economic growth. In contrast, several alternative investment strategies, such as market-neutral equity, fixed income arbitrage, or commodity trading advisors (e.g., systematic global macro) may not have claims on natural returns due to long-term economic growth, and instead may hold essentially market-neutral positions or trade in what may be regarded as zero sum game markets. This refers to the fact that derivatives markets reallocate uncertain cash flows among market participants without enhancing aggregate cash flows in any way.

However, the existence of a single market neutral investment position, or zero sum game futures and option markets, does not restrict certain hedge fund strategies and futures- and options-based investment strategies from offering positive expected rates of return.

First, market-neutral hedge funds, while reducing the risk of single or multimarket exposures, may still remain exposed to a series of systematic risk-based factors. For investors who trade only futures and option markets, the costs of carry and put/call parity models ensure that futures and options can be used to create investment positions that are similar, if not identical to, the underlying cash instruments. Moreover, given the lower transaction costs of trading in futures and options markets, these trading strategies may be superior to the underlying cash markets for comparable long positions.

Second, institutional characteristics and differential carry costs among investors may allow managed fund traders to take advantage of short-term pricing differences between theoretically identical stock, bond, futures, options, and cash market positions. Thus, managed fund traders have opportunities for arbitrage profits under a number of varying market conditions, unlike traditional stock fund managers, who are restricted by convention or regulation from taking short or arbitrage positions.

Arbitrage profits and risk/return positions, which replicate the underlying cash markets, are not the only potential positive risk/return strategies of market-neutral strategies or managed futures that trade in zero sum markets. In cash and futures/options markets, speculative positions are often required to meet the risk management or hedging demands of cash-market participants. This hedging demand may create investment situations in which hedgers are required to offer speculators a risk premium for holding open long or short positions even in a world of arbitrage traders. This may result in positive rates of return in various cash markets as well as the underlying futures and options markets. This return to traders for hedgers' liquidity may exist not only in futures markets, but also in a wide range of derivative and cash market products.

For instance, option traders may be able to create positions that offer a risk premium for holding various options contracts when cash market participants increase purchases of options to protect themselves in markets with trending prices or volatility. This return (e.g., convenience yield) can be earned simply by buying and holding a derivative portfolio and is, arguably, the basis for the positive long-term return in various futures markets based on publicly available commodity index products (e.g., Goldman Sachs commodity indexes).

The return to various hedge funds and managed futures funds as well as private equity can also stem from the ability of managers to exploit imperfections in the markets for futures and options, as well as the markets for the underlying cash instruments. Research on traditional investment vehicles (e.g., stocks, bonds, and currency) indicates that investors may underreact to information. This creates trends in various financial prices. In addition, except in the case of purely unexpected information releases, market prices may incorporate market or security information before it is public. Lastly, research has shown that impending government intervention in interest rate and currency markets may result in trending currency and interest rate markets. Similarly, various rigid risk management approaches may result in security trading, which may create short-term market trends. Trading techniques based on capturing these price trends can be profitable.

Since various alternative investment strategies, providing access to economic factors similar to those in traditional stock and bond markets (albeit with differential returns due to exposure to additional risk factors, such as illiquidity, etc.), replicate many of the investments available in the spot market more cheaply (e.g., replication of cash indexes), and provide exposure to some techniques that cannot be easily achieved in spot markets (e.g., ability to short), *ex ante* hedge fund risk and return models must be based not only on factors that explain traditional asset class returns, but also on the factors unique to trading opportunities of managed funds' traders. Simply put, managed futures, hedge funds, real estate, commodity, and private equity funds may offer risk/return patterns that differ from underlying traditional cash markets. Specifically, the differing investment styles and investment areas enable investors to create asset-allocated portfolios that offer expected positive returns in various market cycles and market conditions not easily available through traditional stock or bond market investments.

TRADITIONAL STOCK AND BOND FUNDS AND HEDGE FUNDS AS ALPHA-GENERATING INVESTMENTS

Traditional investments are often classified according to investment style (for example, growth, value). Within each style category, funds are then classified according to the underlying markets traded. For example, within the relative value-style classification, there are a number of subgroups, including large, small, etc. Considerable academic research has focused on the ability of active stock and bond fund managers to provide alpha—return in excess of a passive benchmark of similar investments. As shown in Tables 2.1 and 2.2, there is little evidence that active stock and bond managers can provide alpha when compared to passive indexes with similar risk. Table 2.3 (see page 16) shows alternative benchmarks for hedge fund performance. Table 2.4 (see page 17) and Figure 2.1 (see page 18) show measured alpha for each of the benchmarks listed in Table 2.3. The measured alpha is a function of the benchmark used. Most significantly, multifactor or total risk-based measures of expected return result in the lowest reported alpha.

TABLE 2.1 Equity Fund and S&P Equity Index Performance Comparison (1996–2001)

Lipper Mutual Fund Index	Annual Return	Annual StDev	S&P Benchmark	Annual Return	Annual StDev
Lipper Lg-Cap Core IX	10.0%	16.3%	S&P 500	11.6%	16.7%
Lipper Lg-Cap Growth IX	8.3%	21.4%	S&P 500 Growth	11.8%	19.3%
Lipper Lg-Cap Value IX	10.2%	14.2%	S&P 500 Value	10.7%	16.1%
Lipper Mid-Cap Core IX	12.9%	21.4%	S&P MidCap	17.3%	19.3%
Lipper Mid-Cap Growth IX	8.2%	30.0%	S&P MidCap Growth	17.6%	24.8%
Lipper Mid-Cap Value IX	12.0%	15.1%	S&P MidCap Value	16.1%	17.1%
Lipper Sm-Cap Core IX	12.5%	20.5%	S&P SmallCap	12.6%	20.0%
Lipper Sm-Cap Growth IX	10.0%	29.9%	S&P SmallCap Growth	8.8%	23.9%
Lipper Sm-Cap Value IX	13.5%	15.6%	S&P SmallCap Value	15.9%	18.2%

FUTURE OF ALPHA DETERMINATION

Hedge funds have often been promoted as absolute return vehicles. They are investments that have no direct benchmark, or that make money in a wide variety of market conditions (beta (S&P 500) = 0). Estimates of excess return must be relative to a representative benchmark. Alpha determination problems have been widely discussed in the literature (Schneeweis, 1998). Table 2.5 (see page 19) shows how differences in the cited benchmark can result in large differences in reported alpha.

The lack of a clear hedge fund benchmark does not indicate an inability to determine expected return for a hedge fund strategy. Hedge fund strategies within a particular style often trade similar assets with similar methodologies and are sensitive to similar market factors. Now a book. While we do not aim to cover all issues relative to passive benchmark tracking and return forecasting for hedge funds it's worth noting that Kazemi and Schneeweis (2001) explore passive indexes created to track underlying hedge fund returns. Two ways to establish comparable portfolios are to use a single- or multifactor-based methodology, or to use

TABLE 2.2 Bond Fund and Lehman Bond Index Performance Comparison (1996–2001)

Lipper Mutual Fund Index	Annual Return	Annual StDev	Lehman Benchmark	Annual Return	Annual StDev
Lipper General Bond Fd	6.1%	3.4%	Lehman Aggregate Bond	6.6%	3.5%
Lipper General US Govt Fd	5.7%	3.8%	Lehman Gov-Credit Bond	6.5%	3.9%
Lipper Global Inc. Fd	3.9%	4.5%	Lehman Global Aggregate	3.6%	4.8%
Lipper Hi Yield Bond Fd	3.3%	7.9%	Lehman Hi Yield Credit Bond	4.6%	7.0%

TABLE 2.3 Alternative Return Forecast Methods

Return Relationships (1990–2000)	Historical Return	Volatility	Sharpe	Beta	R-Square Market Model	R-Square Multifactor	CAPM Estimate Return	Multifactor Estimate Return	Sharpe Estimate Return
HFRI Convertible Arbitrage Index	11.4%	3.4%	1.92	0.09	0.12	0.19	5.9%	6.4%	7.7%
HFRI Distressed Securities Index	14.6%	6.6%	1.48	0.19	0.15	0.26	7.0%	7.3%	10.3%
HFRI Emerging Markets (Total)	15.3%	16.4%	0.63	0.67	0.32	0.36	12.5%	14.2%	18.4%
HFRI Emerging Markets: Asia Index	10.1%	14.5%	0.36	0.49	0.22	0.23	10.4%	11.5%	16.8%
HFRI Equity Hedge Index	21.2%	9.3%	1.75	0.41	0.37	0.37	9.5%	11.4%	12.5%
HFRI Equity Market Neutral Index	11.0%	3.3%	1.87	0.05	0.05	0.03	5.5%	6.4%	7.6%
HFRI Equity Non-Hedge Index	19.2%	14.4%	0.99	0.78	0.56	0.60	13.7%	16.4%	16.7%
HFRI Event-Driven Index	16.1%	6.4%	1.75	0.27	0.35	0.47	8.0%	8.7%	10.1%
HFRI Fixed Income (Total)	10.9%	3.7%	1.62	0.11	0.17	0.22	6.1%	6.4%	7.9%
HFRI Fixed Income: Arbitrage Index	8.7%	4.9%	0.78	−0.03	0.01	0.00	4.6%	4.4%	8.9%
HFRI Fixed Income: High Yield Index	9.9%	6.9%	0.72	0.21	0.17	0.33	7.2%	6.9%	10.6%
HFRI Fund of Funds Index	11.5%	6.3%	1.05	0.19	0.17	0.19	7.0%	7.7%	10.0%
HFRI Fund Weighted Composite Index	16.4%	7.3%	1.58	0.35	0.45	0.50	8.9%	10.1%	10.9%
HFRI Macro Index	17.9%	9.3%	1.41	0.29	0.19	0.24	8.2%	8.3%	12.5%
HFRI Market Timing Index	14.8%	6.9%	1.43	0.32	0.42	0.41	8.5%	10.1%	10.5%
HFRI Merger Arbitrage Index	13.2%	3.9%	2.15	0.11	0.16	0.28	6.1%	6.7%	8.0%
HFRI Relative Value Arbitrage Index	13.4%	4.0%	2.12	0.10	0.12	0.20	6.0%	6.3%	8.2%
HFRI Sector (Total)	23.9%	14.2%	1.34	0.50	0.24	0.27	10.6%	12.1%	16.5%
HFRI Statistical Arbitrage Index	11.1%	3.8%	1.66	0.14	0.27	0.26	6.5%	7.8%	8.0%

TABLE 2.4 Excess-Return Determination

Alpha Determination (1990–2000)	Historical Minus Risk Free	Historical Minus CAPM	Historical Minus Multifactor	Historical Minus Volume Adjusted
HFRI Convertible Arbitrage Index	6.1%	5.6%	4.8%	3.7%
HFRI Distressed Securities Index	9.3%	7.7%	7.2%	4.3%
HFRI Emerging Markets (Total)	10.0%	2.8%	0.9%	−3.1%
HFRI Emerging Markets: Asia Index	4.8%	−0.3%	−1.6%	−6.7%
HFRI Equity Hedge Index	15.9%	11.7%	9.4%	8.7%
HFRI Equity Market Neutral Index	5.7%	5.5%	4.6%	3.4%
HFRI Equity Non-Hedge Index	13.9%	5.5%	2.2%	2.4%
HFRI Event-Driven Index	10.8%	8.1%	6.8%	5.9%
HFRI Fixed Income (Total)	5.6%	4.8%	4.5%	3.0%
HFRI Fixed Income: Arbitrage Index	3.4%	4.1%	4.4%	−0.2%
HFRI Fixed Income: High Yield Index	4.6%	2.6%	2.5%	−0.7%
HFRI Fund of Funds Index	6.2%	4.5%	3.6%	1.4%
HFRI Fund Weighted Composite Index	11.1%	7.5%	6.0%	5.5%
HFRI Macro Index	12.6%	9.7%	9.4%	5.4%
HFRI Market Timing Index	9.5%	6.2%	4.7%	4.2%
HFRI Merger Arbitrage Index	7.9%	7.0%	5.8%	5.1%
HFRI Relative Value Arbitrage Index	8.1%	7.4%	7.1%	5.2%
HFRI Sector (Total)	18.6%	13.4%	11.6%	7.4%
HFRI Statistical Arbitrage Index	5.8%	4.6%	3.3%	3.1%

optimization to create tracking portfolios with similar risk and return characteristics.[2] In that analysis, passive indexes that track the return of the hedge fund strategy are created from actual securities or factors that underlie the strategy as well as financial instruments used in the strategy. In these cases, active hedge fund management showed positive alpha relative to cited tracking portfolios.

ISSUES IN DETERMINING ACTIVE MANAGER INDEX

Active manager-based indexes are generally determine hedge fund alpha inaccurately. While one can use a peer index of similar managers to capture the expected return of a particular strategy, that index itself will contain, in its construction, both strategy and manager alpha. Previous studies of hedge fund performance were often based on various existing active manager-based hedge fund indexes and sub-indexes. Each hedge fund index has

---

[2]Additional academic research on the use of factor-based means of tracking hedge fund return includes Fung and Hsieh (2000).

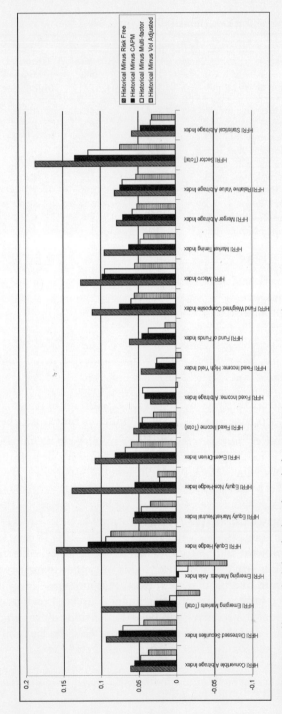

FIGURE 2.1 Differential alphas by benchmark determination.

TABLE 2.5

Funds of Funds	Alpha Determination	Alpha
Benchmark	Model (R_i-Expected Return)	
T-Bill:	R_i-R_f	5.26%
CAPM	R_i-(R_f+($R_{(S\&P)}$-R_f)B_i)	4.32%
Historical Var.	R_i-(R_i from Sharpe Ratio=.66)	0.68%
Factor Index	(R_i-R_f)-(b_o+b_i(S_r-R_f)+b_i(BR-Rf)+biCCP+biCTP+ biCBV+biCSV+biCVix)[a]	.03%

[a]The C in front of CCP, CTP, CBV, CSV, and CVIX stands for change (i.e., change in credit premiums, change in term premiums, change in intermonth bond volatility, change in intermonth stock volatility, and change in Vix).

its own methodology. Previous research has analyzed the actual tracking error between various hedge fund indexes (McCarthy and Spurgin, 1998) as well as various weightings (e.g., value versus equal), survivor bias, selection bias, and other effects in the use of various hedge fund indexes (Fung and Hsieh, 2000d).

Active or passive indexes themselves are used as surrogates for hedge fund performance, based on the simple assumption that the indexes themselves reflect the actual return process inherent in the funds used by investors. The problem of using existing indexes to track a universe of hedge funds has been addressed in academic research (Fung and Hsieh, 2000). Fung and Hsieh point out that the indexes that are value-weighted reflect the weights of popular bets by investors, since the asset values of the various funds change due to asset purchases as well as price. An investor would have a hard time tracking such indexes. Equally weighted indexes may better reflect potential diversification of hedge funds and funds designed to track such indexes. However, the cost of rebalancing may make these indexes likewise difficult to create in an investable form. Hedge fund indexes that are themselves investable have only recently been created, as have indexes with the expressed goal of tracking a non-investable index (Zurich Hedge Fund Indexes, 2001).

In brief, while overall market indexes may provide an indication of current market return (on an equal-weighted or value-weighted basis), the concept of a single, all-encompassing active manager or passive hedge fund index reflecting the returns to one's own portfolio may not be realistic. In fact, as shown in Figure 2.2, one may wish to create one's own hedge fund index from existing indexes to track one's own risk/return profile.

Fund of Funds

Annual Mean	10.68%
Annual Std Deviation	7.59%
Correlation with S&P500	32.80%
Correlation with LB Bond In	16.25%

Hennessee Macro		**HFRI F of F**		**EACM 100**	
Annual Mean	9.70%	Annual Mean	9.34%	Annual Mean	11.85%
Annual Std Deviation	8.68%	Annual Std Deviation	7.03%	Annual Std Deviation	4.86%
Corr with S&P500	50.71%	Correlation with S&P500	53.30%	Correlation with S&P500	47.88%
Corr with LB Bond Index	21.17%	Correlation with LB Bond Ind	1.30%	Correlation with LB Bond Index	8.29%

Portfolio 1	**Weights**	**Portfolio 2**	**Weights**	**Portfolio 3**	**Weights**
Hennessee Macro	87.37%	HFRI F of F	79.35%	EACM 100	60.04%
S&P500	0.00%	S&P500	20.65%	S&P500	39.96%
LB Aggregate Bond	0.79%	LB Aggregate Bond	0.00%	LB Aggregate Bond	0.00%
T-Bill	11.84%	T-Bill	0.00%	T-Bill	0.00%
Mean Ret on the Portfolio	9.12%	Mean Ret on the Portfolio	11.36%	Mean Ret on the Portfolio	14.76%
Std. Deviation of the Portfolio	7.59%	Std. Deviation of the Portfolio	7.59%	Std. Deviation of the Portfolio	7.59%
Corr with S&P500	50.72%	Corr with S&P500	78.31%	Corr with S&P500	94.13%
Corr with LB Bond Index	21.63%	Corr with LB Bond Index	10.96%	Corr with LB Bond Index	22.54%

Portfolio 4	**Weights**
Hennessee Macro	59.6%
HFRI F of F	40.4%
EACM 100	0.0%
S&P500	0.0%
LB Aggregate Bond	0.0%
T-Bill	0.0%
Mean Ret on the Portfolio	9.55%
Std. Deviation of the Portfolio	7.59%
Corr with S&P500	54.5%
Corr with LB Bond Index	14.9%

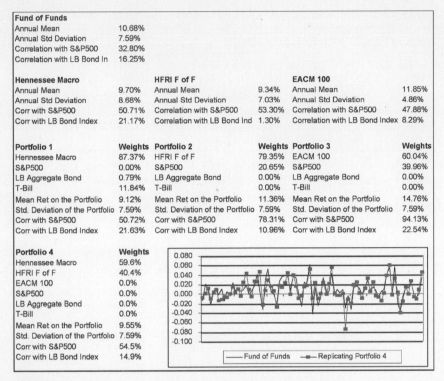

FIGURE 2.2   Replicating portfolios created from existing indexes.

PORTFOLIO CREATION WITH ALPHA-GENERATING STRATEGIES

The previous sections show hedge funds' ability to provide alpha, at least at the strategy level. Is there a simple way for individual investors to decide how best to allocate alpha-generating strategies? Hedge fund strategies have often been grouped into four basic categories: relative value (equity market neutral, bond hedge, convertible hedging, rotational or multiprogram), event (merger arbitrage, distressed, bankruptcy), hedged equity (U.S., European, global, sector), and global asset allocators (macro traders, such as commodity trading advisors who trade primarily in futures and option markets). Each of these strategies is typically presented as offering low correlation with stock and bond portfolios.

One reason for the supposedly low correlation and potential diversification benefit is that hedge funds often describe themselves as employing skill-based investment strategies that do not explicitly attempt to track a particular index. Since their goal is to maximize long-term returns independently of a proscribed traditional stock and bond index, they emphasize absolute returns and not returns relative to a predetermined index. It is important to realize, however, that while hedge funds do not emphasize benchmark tracking, this does not mean their entire return is based solely on manager skill, or is independent of underlying stock, bond, or currency markets. Hedge fund managers often track a particular investment strategy or investment opportunity. When appropriately grouped, these hedge fund strategies have been shown to be driven by common market factors, such as changes in stock and bond returns or market volatility.

HEDGE FUND ADDITIONS TO TRADITIONAL ASSET PORTFOLIOS: A RISK DIVERSIFIER OR RETURN ENHANCER

Hedge fund classification basically groups hedge funds according to the markets they invest in or the trading strategies they employ. However, classification fails to emphasize that hedge funds are generally regarded as additional investments to an existing stock and bond portfolio. As a result, the real risk and return benefits of a particular hedge fund has less to do with its stand-alone performance than with its performance relative to an investor's existing portfolio.

A logical next step in the effort to classify hedge funds is to group them based on the impact a particular fund would have on an existing stock/bond portfolio. In short, is the strategy a "return enhancer" (high return, high correlation with stock/bond portfolio) or a "risk reducer" (lower return, low correlation with stock/bond portfolio)?

Table 2.6 provides a simplified hedge fund classification based on relative returns and correlations with an equally weighted stock and bond portfolio. For different asset portfolios (e.g., stand-alone stock or bond portfolios), the strategy classification of a particular hedge fund would depend on its correlation with that asset portfolio.

TABLE 2.6 Performance: EACM Hedge Fund Strategies, Zurich CTA$ and Traditional Assets (1/1990–12/2001)

	Return	Stdev	Sharpe Ratio	Minimum Monthly	Corr/S&P&Lehman Port.
Relative Value	10.2%	3.3%	1.43	−6.1%	0.06 Risk Diversifter
Event Driven	12.8%	5.2%	1.43	−7.5%	0.44 Return Enhancer
Equity Hedge	17.6%	10.3%	1.18	−9.8%	0.57 Return Enhancer
Global Asset Allocators	16.7%	10.2%	1.10	−5.4%	0.15 Risk Diversifier
Zurich CTA$	11.2%	10.3%	0.56	−6.0%	−0.02 Risk Diversifier

TABLE 2.7　Strategic Asset Allocation

| | Balanced Portfolio (1990–2000) | | | | | |
| | Stock & Bond | | | Stock, Bond & Hedge Funds | | |
	Annualized Return	Standard Deviation	Weight Limits	Weight Limits	Same Risk	Same Return
Lehman Bond	7.84	3.82	50.0%	40.0%	40.0%	40.0%
Russell 1000	15.47	14.02	50.0%	40.0%	42.4%	40.0%
Relative Value	9.81	3.38				12.3%
Event	12.72	5.23				
Equity Hedge	18.62	10.50			17.6%	
Global Macro	17.11	10.51				4.1%
CTA$	11.75	10.41				3.6%
Annualized Return			11.66		12.97	11.66
Standard Deviation			7.93		7.93	6.49

In brief, if an investor wished to keep his or her existing level of volatility, but increase expected return, the investor would reduce stock and bond allocations and add an allocation to "return enhancer" hedge funds. If an investor wished to keep the current level of return, but lower risk level, the investor would reduce stock and bond allocations and add an allocation to "risk diversifier" hedge funds Table 2.7 shows that if an investor starts with an equal allocation to a stock and bond portfolio and wants to re-weight the portfolio to include a portion of hedge funds without changing risk, the investor adds return enhancer hedge funds. Conversely, if an investor re-weights the portfolio to include a portion of hedge funds with the goal of keeping current returns while reducing risk, then the investor adds risk diversifer hedge funds.

CONCLUSIONS

This chapter briefly reviewed various hedge fund strategies' alpha-generating properties relative to comparable risk traditional stock and bond portfolios. Alpha generation depends on the benchmark used, but after considering a more modern multi-factor model of return determination, hedge funds continue to provide evidence of manager skill in addition to the natural return coming from the strategy itself. Results also show that an investor can use traditional asset allocation methodology (e.g., mean/variance optimization) to evaluate hedge funds as additions to a stock and bond portfolio. Investors wishing to concentrate on increasing expected return should focus on return enhancing strategies, while those who wish to reduce volatility should concentrate primarily on risk-reducing strategies.

REFERENCES

Agarwal, Vikas, and Narayan Y, Naik, 2000a. "On Taking the Alternative Route: Risks, Rewards, and Performance Persistence of Hedge Funds." *Journal of Alternative Investments,* 2, No. 4: pp. 6–23.

Agarwal, Vikas, and Narayan Y. Naik, 2000b. "Performance Evaluation of Hedge Funds with Option-based and Buy and Hold Strategies." Working paper, London Business School.

Asness, Clifford, R. Krail, and J. Liew, 2001. "Do Hedge Funds Hedge?" *Journal of Portfolio Management.* Forthcoming.

Bodie, Z., M. Kane, and A. Marcus, 2000. Np.: *Investments.*

Brealey, R.A, and E. Kaplanis, 2000. "Changes in Factor Exposures of Hedge Funds." Working paper, Bank of England and Institute of Finance and Accounting, London Business School.

Brown, Stephen J., William Goetzmann, and Roger G. Ibboston, 1999. "Offshore Hedge Funds: Survival and Performance 1989–95." *Journal of Business,* Vol. 72, pp. 91–117.

Brown, Stephen J., William Goetzmann and J. Park, 1997. "Conditions for Survival: Changing Risk and the Performance of Hedge Fund Managers and CTAs." *Review of Financial Studies,* Vol. 5, pp. 553–580.

Brown, Stephen J., and William N. Goetzmann, 2001. "Hedge Funds With Style." Working paper, New York University and Yale School of Management.

Fung, W., and D. A. Hsieh, 1997a. "Empirical Characteristics of Dynamic Trading Strategies: The Case of Hedge Funds." *Review of Financial Studies,* Vol. 10, pp. 275–302.

Fung, W., and D. A. Hsieh, 1997b. "Survivorship Bias and Investment Style in the Returns of CTAs." *Journal of Portfolio Management* Vol. 24 (No. 1), pp. 30–41.

Fung, W., and D. A. Hsieh, 1999a. "A Primer on Hedge Funds." *Journal of Empirical Finance* Vol. 6, pp. 309–331.

Fung, W., D. A. Hsieh, and K. Tsatsaronic. 1999b. "Do Hedge Funds Disrupt Emerging Markets?" In Brookings–Wharton Papers on Financial Services. Forthcoming.

Fung, W., and D. A. Hsieh, 2000a. "The Risk in Hedge Fund Strategies: Theory and Evidence from Trend Followers." In *Review of Financial Studies.* Forthcoming.

Fung, W., and D. A. Hsieh, 2000b. "Performance Characteristics of Hedge Funds and CTA Funds: Natural Versus Spurious Biases." In *Journal of Financial and Quantitative Analysis.* Forthcoming.

Fung, W., and D. A. Hsieh, 2000c. "Measuring the Market Impact of Hedge Funds." *Journal of Empirical Finance,* Vol. 7, No. 1, pp. 1–36.

Fung, W. and D. A. Hsieh, 2000d. "Benchmarks of Hedge Fund Performance: Information Content and Measurement Biases. *Financial Analysts Journal.* Forthcoming.

Kazemi, Hossein, and Thomas Schneeweis, 2001. "Traditional Asset and Alternative Asset Allocation." CISDM/SOM. Working paper, University of Massachusetts.

Liang, Bing, 1999. "On the Performance of Hedge Funds. *Financial Analysts Journal,* July/August, pp. 72–85.

Liang, Bing, 2000. "Hedge Funds: The Living and The Dead." In *Journal of Financial and Quantitative Analysis.* Forthcoming.

Liang, Bing, 2001. "Hedge Fund Performance: 1990–1999." *Financial Analysts Journal,* January/February, pp. 11–18.

McCarthy, D., and Richard Spurgin, 1998. "A Review of Hedge Fund Performance Benchmarks." *Journal of Alternative Investments,* Summer, pp. 18–28.

Schneeweis Partners, 2001. *A Review of Alternative Hedge Fund Indexes.* N.p.

Schneeweis, Thomas, 1998. "Evidence of Superior Performance Persistence in Hedge Funds: An Empirical Comment." *The Journal of Alternative Investments,* Fall, pp. 76–80.

Schneeweis, Thomas, 1999. "Alpha, Alpha . . . Who's Got the Alpha?" *The Journal of Alternative Investments,* Winter, pp. 83–85.

Schneeweis, Thomas, and Hossein Kazemi, 2001. "Alternative Means of Replicating Hedge Fund Manager Performance." CISDM/SOM, University of Massachusetts.

Schneeweis, Thomas, and Richard Spurgin, 1998. "Multifactor Analysis of Hedge Fund, Managed Futures and Mutual Fund Return and Risk Characteristics." *Journal of Alternative Investments,* Fall, pp. 1–24.

Schneeweis, Thomas, and R. Spurgin, 1999. "Quantitative Analysis of Hedge Fund and Managed Futures Return and Risk Characteristics." In *Evaluating and Implementing Hedge Fund Strategies,* Edited by P. Lake 2 ed.

Schneeweis, Thomas, and Joseph Pescatore, eds., 1999. *The Handbook of Alternative Investment Strategies: An Investor's Guide.* Np. Institutional Investor.

Schneeweis, Thomas, and R. Spurgin, 2001. "Trading Factors and Location Factors in Hedge Fund Return Estimation." CISDM/SOM, University of Massachusetts.

Zurich Hedge Fund Indexes, 2001. Zurich Capital Markets, NYC.

CHAPTER 3

Funds of Hedge Funds: Definitive Overview of Strategies and Techniques

Thomas Zucosky

PREFACE

Over the past few years, hedge funds have gained enormous popularity among institutional and super-high-net-worth investors. This is largely because the funds are seen as a panacea for an otherwise volatile and directionless group of capital markets. While hedge fund investing can be beneficial, particularly in the context of traditionally allocated portfolios, there are many potential pitfalls. This chapter seeks to explain the hedge fund phenomenon, with a specific focus on funds of hedge funds, and to juxtapose the opportunities for consultants and their investor clients with the risks of this investment style. To properly discuss funds of hedge funds, we must first introduce hedge funds generally.

HEDGE FUNDS

While subsectors of this broadly diverse group—i.e., equity long/short and global macro—are fairly independent of one another, a few of the general characteristics of this class of investment include its ability to use financial instruments not normally allowed in U.S.-regulated investment programs, mutual funds, and the hedge fund's historic freedom from many forms of regulatory oversight and compliance. As a result, investors are generally required to demonstrate a sophisticated understanding of investing, as well as a high net worth or assets under management prior to investing.

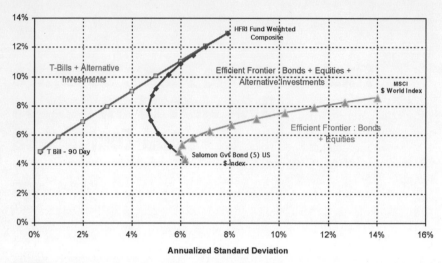

FIGURE 3.1   Risk-return chart (from 1994 to 2001).

Why has the collective investment consciousness about hedge funds apparently undergone a massive shift from apathy to great interest? Studies suggest that 80% of the return from traditional equity investing comes from the overall market. In fact, the correlations of most traditional domestic equity strategies suggest this number is conservative. Hedge funds, on the other hand, can generate returns that are uncorrelated to major market movements because they extract performance in a fundamentally different way. The manager's skill (alpha), rather than movements in the underlying markets (beta), determines hedge fund performance.

It has been suggested that the term "hedge funds" has taken on a negative connotation related to sensationalist investment stories. While commonly referred to as hedge funds, other terms for this investment activity are gaining acceptance. These include "hedged strategies" and "marketable alternatives." Some serious industry professionals and sophisticated investors prefer these terms.

Academic research illustrates the advantages of placing a portion of a portfolio's assets into alternative investment strategies, such as hedge funds. With return streams often uncorrelated to equity and bond markets, marketable alternative investments can enhance and smooth overall portfolio performance. Figure 3.1 depicts the advantage of investing in alternative instruments in addition to traditional instruments, such as Treasury bills, bonds, and/or equities.

Most institutional investors have played a relative return game since 1982, but a number of challenges are shaking the beliefs of pension asset allocators, consultants and investment advisors everywhere. Challenges facing traditional asset allocation include:

1. increased complexity of financial markets and instruments;
2. increased globalization of financial markets;
3. heightened volatility of global financial markets; and
4. persistently high valuations for many individual stocks.

One other important, but subtle, reason for the interest in hedge funds is that from August 1982 through March 2000, the markets experienced an historical bullish trend that significantly challenged managers' ability to add skill over and above market movements. During this period, passive investment strategies were prevalent. There was no need to hedge. In fact, the conventional wisdom was that not only should an investor be totally long in the markets, but also leveraged long. This market psychology created indexed mutual funds that became the largest investment pools in the world. However, since the Internet bubble burst in the spring of 2000, active portfolio management has become more important for investors needing to achieve positive return assumptions. Hedge fund strategies represent the ultimate in active management. Therefore, the interest in hedge funds has a demand-driven underpinning creating a major long-term trend that can persist for years.

As a style of investment (not an asset class), hedge funds are distinctive for a number of reasons. For example, market timing is not as essential as it is in other capital market strategies. Hedge funds have historically tended to increase a portfolio's reward-to-risk ratio and they provide at least the opportunity to take advantage of worldwide market inefficiencies that are not available to larger, less flexible capital pools. The hedge fund provides investors with access to some of the most entrepreneurial, analytic, and managerial talent in the investment management industry, people who are attracted to complex investment themes, niche and contrarian opportunities. Interestingly, hedge fund managers tend to be master gamesmen—at bridge and chess, for example. Furthermore, most hedge fund managers will limit the size of their funds—closing their funds to new investors and often returning money to existing investors—once their funds reaches a size that may negatively impact the liquidity or capacity of their trading strategies.

FUNDS OF HEDGE FUNDS

Funds of hedge funds (FoHF) are the current preference for institutional investors and family wealth seeking to enter the marketable alternatives investment arena (see Table 3.1). This parallels the path of Japanese institutions in

TABLE 3.1   Traditional Investments vs. Hedged Strategies

Traditional Investments	Hedged Strategies
• Separate accounts or registered funds	• Unregistered funds (currently)
• Relative performance-oriented	• Absolute return-oriented
• Returns largely derived from beta of the underlying asset class or benchmark (e.g., U.S. equities or S&P 500)	• Returns largely derived from alpha, or skill of the manager
• High correlation with markets	• Low correlation with markets
• Instrument limitation	• Diverse range of instruments
• No leverage	• May use leverage
• Typically asset-based fee only	• Asset-based and performance fee
• Manager typically not a significant investor in program or fund	• Manager invests side-by-side with client and is often a significant investor

the early 1990s as they entered the managed futures field, deciding first to invest in commodity pools (multimanager funds), thereby learning from the experts and intending to later invest directly themselves. This process of knowledge transfer is an important concept as large investors become interested in new investment themes or styles. Recently, private U.S. investors in funds of hedge funds create their own multimanager portfolios and have begun offering these pools to peers for coinvestment.

In their simplest form, funds of hedge funds (see Table 3.2), like multimanager pools offered by traditional asset management firms, spread investments among different fund vehicles and strategies. For the investor, selecting a fund of hedge funds simplifies the overall investment process because of the reduction of alpha decisions (the need to determine who are

TABLE 3.2   Fund of Hedge Funds

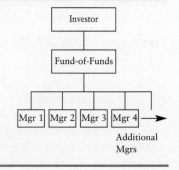

PROS
• Professional asset allocation, manager research/selection
• Access to potentially closed managers
• Increased diversification (10–100 funds)
• Single point of client services
• Consolidated reporting/monitoring

CONS
• Additional layer of fees associated with fund management and administrative services

the most skillful managers available). For now, investors know that they want an allocation to low or negatively correlated investments emphasizing absolute, rather than relative, returns. This is a simple decision that seeks to be expressed in a broad allocation decision and certainly not in making many minor alpha decisions by identifying and vetting numerous single-manager hedge funds.

In panel discussions and speeches, the question has been raised, "How many managers are optimal for a multimanager portfolio?" "One, if you know the future," is obviously correct. If you knew which strategies or sectors would outperform, certainly you would use them and not dilute that insight with less sure ideas. In reality, the blending of multiple strategies, sectors, and managers aims to decrease the risk of mistakes in any of these areas. However, the blending of these elements has the additional benefit of creating a different return characteristic from general capital markets and their associated investment strategies, generally resulting in lower volatility portfolios.

Often overlooked as a serious investment effort, managing a quality FoHF actually requires significant experience, insight and skill. Typically, the investment manager or asset allocator of a fund of hedge funds selects and invests in multiple hedge funds—from as few as 5 to as many as 100 or more. The investor receives the pooled returns of the constituent funds, minus fees paid to the individual hedge fund managers, service providers (accountants, lawyers, auditors), and the fund of hedge funds manager, who provides numerous ongoing services.

While funds of hedge funds may be structured differently to achieve a variety of targets, the main objective is the reduction in risk and volatility achieved through diversification. Funds of hedge funds can be widely diversified with respect to specific hedge fund strategies. They can be diversified, multistrategy funds or they might be concentrated on specific strategies, geographies, or industry sectors, such as an equity long/short fund, a technology or healthcare fund, or an Asian or European fund.

The type of a fund of hedge funds is defined by the performance objective, volatility (see Figure 3.2) and mix of strategies.

Advantages of Funds of Hedge Funds

- The investor can access a well-diversified hedge fund portfolio employing a broad range of investment strategies with a smaller investment than the minimum often required by each individual hedge fund.
- The investor benefits from the expertise of the asset allocator who has analyzed the underlying hedge funds' strategies, designed a balanced allocation strategy, constructed the portfolio, and who continually monitors the managers, the changes in the investment environment, and the fund of funds' performance.

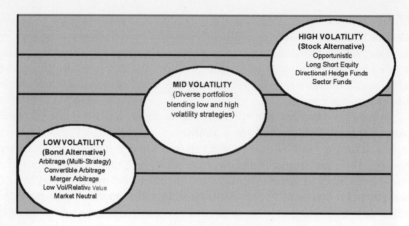

Lower

Standard Deviation   Higher

FIGURE 3.2   Relative risk
Source: Altvest.

- Because of the inherent diversification in funds of hedge funds, the investor presumably incurs less risk than investing in individual funds.

Disadvantages of Funds of Hedge Funds

- The asset allocator and fund administrator charges an additional layer of fees, similar to those charged by a traditional investment consultant or advisor.
- Depending on the asset class, there can be limits on investment liquidity in funds of hedge funds that require a minimum investment period of 6 months, 1 year, or more.
- As a result of diversification, returns tend to be more modest than those of top-performing single hedge funds.

Ultimately, one has to ask whether funds of hedge funds add value. Over-diversifying with a group of subfunds is not value added. On the other hand, dynamically matching top talent with client needs can create a rewarding investment vehicle.

ANALYZING FUNDS OF HEDGE FUNDS

Because of low barriers to entry, some in the funds of hedge funds business are, in reality, hobbyists and marketing organizations, while others approach this activity as a genuine form of investment management. The hedge fund industry is inherently inefficient as information on managers is not available for all; therefore, the quality FoHF manager has a competitive advantage to add value relative to less expert single investors. When implemented as an investment management function, the process of selecting managers, managing portfolios of hedge funds and monitoring risks is an intricate, multi-faceted challenge.

Listed here are some of the strategies from which funds of hedge funds asset allocators typically choose.

Equity Hedge

Equity hedge strategies invest in equities and equity derivatives both on the long and short side, and the outcome is somewhat more correlated with movements in financial markets. Stock selection techniques are extremely varied and utilize fundamental analysis, technical analysis, quantitative programs, and macro and/or sector approaches, among others. The focus may be on global stock markets, country- or region-specific markets, individual industries, different capitalization classes within the same market, etc. Sample position: unrelated longs and shorts, i.e., long Exxon Mobil, short Citigroup.

Merger/Risk Arbitrage

Merger/Risk Arbitrage is the purchase of the equity instruments of a company to be acquired, and the offsetting short sale of the equity instruments of the acquiring company (if it offers its own shares in exchange for the shares of the company to be acquired). If the acquiring company offers cash, no offsetting short position in the equity of the acquiring company is necessary. In normal circumstances, there will be a discount between the value of the package offered in exchange for the shares in the company to be acquired and the stock's actual market price. Sample position: long Compaq, short Hewlett–Packard.

Event-Driven

In addition to merger arbitrage, other events, such as recapitalizations, restructurings, or other corporate reorganizations may create situations in which there is a perceived differential between the value to be received upon successful consummation of the transaction and the current market price. In many such opportunities, offsetting positions are taken in related assets, and in all cases the investment risk is actively managed. A typical position is a series of hedged or unhedged positions in individual stocks, i.e., short Hong Kong Telecom in anticipation of a spin-off.

Convertible Securities/Capital Structure Arbitrage

Convertible Securities/Capital Structure Arbitrage involves the simultaneous purchase of a difficult-to-value security believed to be undervalued (the convertible bond), and sale of other securities of the same issuer that are believed to be relatively overvalued. A long position in a convertible debt instrument (or preferred stock or warrant) is typically established, and an offsetting short position in the underlying equity security may be established at the same time (mainly on a delta neutral basis). Sample position: long Liberty Media Convertible bonds (BBB+) (convertible into Motorola stock), short Motorola stock.

Relative Value

Relative Value managers attempt to exploit temporary price inefficiencies or discrepancies between securities or markets using fixed income, equities or derivatives. Strategies tend to be more or less market-neutral since managers typically do not speculate concerning market direction. Sample position: long Dell, short Gateway.

Global Macro

Under the Global Macro strategy, specific investment ideas are generated by a top-down, global (or regional) macro economic outlook that implies certain market directional movements (up or down) that can then be exploited. Markets include a wide range of equities, fixed income, financial and commodity derivatives, and other asset categories. Although hedging may be utilized, managers will generally have market exposure. Sample position: long the euro.

The Fixed Income Arbitrage strategy generally engages in matched purchase and sale, or sale and purchase transactions in the same or similar instruments. Trading techniques and strategies include basis trading, calendar spreads trading, yield curve arbitrage, and intermarket spread trading for example mortgage-backed securities (MBS) arbitrage. MBS arbitrage involves the purchase of difficult-to-value mortgage-backed security pools believed to be undervalued, and overlaying various hedges with regard to interest-rate risk and prepayment risk, to lock in the attractive current yields for the anticipated holding period. Sample position: long 10–year Treasury Note, short 5–year Treasury Note.

Distressed Securities

The Distressed Securities strategy involves the purchase of debt-related instruments of a company which has become financially distressed and operates under bankruptcy or insolvency laws. But the purchase is made only if the manager is convinced that a restructuring or reorganization is likely to be successfully completed, and that the value of the new securities, cash, and/or other consideration received will exceed the current value of securities purchased. Distressed debt-related instruments include traded debt securities (normally with fixed interest rates) and bank loans (floating-rate debt) for which an active secondary market exists. Distressed securities are not interest-rate sensitive in principle, and their valuation depends on the successful restructuring and emergence from bankruptcy or insolvency. To the extent that such securities are often collateralized, the value of the underlying assets also serves to hedge risk. Sample position: Buy Global Crossing bonds.

Futures Trading

In Futures Trading, commodity trading advisors (CTAs) seek to capture trends (up or down) in specific, highly liquid markets on a diversified basis using a fundamental or systematic analysis of market historical patterns and expected future movements. Futures and other highly liquid derivatives are the principal asset class utilized, and managers will have market exposure. Sample position: Long Treasury bond futures contract.

Short Selling

Short selling is used to take advantage of an anticipated price decline. The seller borrows securities from a third party and sells them to the purchaser. The seller returns the borrowed securities to the lender by purchasing them back in the open market. If he can buy it back at a lower price, a profit results. If the price is higher, a loss results. A short-seller must generally pledge other securities or cash with the lender in an amount equal to the market price of the borrowed securities. Sample position: Short Enron.

It is helpful to think of FoHF as micro versions of large Wall Street investment banks, i.e., Goldman Sachs or Lehman Brothers, which achieve much of their profitability from proprietary trading activities, which have not traditionally been available to clients. Funds of hedge funds investment managers are also self-contained companies and should be evaluated as such. Individuals with a background in investment consulting, corporate analysis, accounting, law, and, interestingly, journalism, tend to approach the FoHF manager analysis process best. Some of the basic corporate attributes of a FoHF to be analyzed include legal structure; ownership and capital size of the company; investment team–background and personality of key executives, adequacy of team size; business plan; financial statements; back-up capabilities; insurance coverage; and conflicts of interest.

TABLE 3.3 Hedge Fund Market Size

Buyer Segment		United States HF's	HFoF's	Europe HF's	HFoF's	Japan & Asia HF's	HFoF's
Institutional Market	Corporate Pensions	35	6				
	Public Pensions	28	5				
	Endowments/ Foundations	21	5	10	2		
	Insurance Companies	5	1				
High Net Worth		261	50	68	13		
Totals		350	67	78	15	22	10

Source: Barra Strategic Consulting Group (2001).
All numbers are in billions of US dollars.

Hedge funds (see Table 3.3) and funds of hedge funds are merely investment vehicles consisting of a network of service-provider relationships.

Service providers for funds of hedge funds and/or single-manager hedge funds include fund manager, fund administrator, custodian, broker/dealer, and sponsor, if any. The oversight of service providers at all levels, in addition to the fund manager, increases shareholder security and risk avoidance for the fund of funds investor.

Fund Manager*

- Due Diligence Issues
    - Statistical analysis of historic returns
    - Persistence of performance relative to style benchmarks
    - Geographic, sector and security-specific concentrations
    - Restrictions on investments, particularly with regard to illiquid investments
    - Buy and sell disciplines
    - Attribution of returns by internal trading strategies
    - Historic use of leverage
    - Risk-control procedures
    - Portfolio Transparency Policies

- Compliance Issues
    - Review of private placement memorandum
    - Review of prior independent audits and exception reports
    - Compliance structure for U.S. money-laundering and Patriot Act reporting

- Availability of books and records
- Regulatory history and reputation

- Business-Related Issues
  - Size and history of the fund
  - Employee turnover
  - State, country or regional charter of the organization
  - Registrations
  - Financial strength of organization
  - Is the fund large enough to support its financial overhead structure?
  - Do the fund and its management have sufficient operating experience?

* The details of individual manager analyses are complex enough to be the subject of a separate report. This outline is by no means complete; it is meant to be a launching point for hedge fund due diligence.

Fund Administrator

- Onshore and/or offshore capabilities
- Experience with similar fund structures
- Specific product expertise
- Back-office software platform
- Processing capacity
- Back-up systems, frequency, and redundancy of data storage
- Periodicity of reporting
- Accuracy of reporting (accuracy reports and exception reporting)

Custodian

- Is the custodian independent?
- Legal domicile of custodian
- Financial strength of custodian
- Does the named custodian hold the assets?
- How are securities registered?
- Is all processing done according to the fund's legal domicile?

Broker/Dealer

- Is the account properly registered?
- Who is authorized to make cash payments from the account?
- Can the account be used as collateral by an unrelated entity?

Whether for fund investments or for a managed account, investors should understand the manager's perception of the investment mandate. The rule of thumb, "Don't invest in things you don't understand," applies. The typical legalese in offering documents to "achieve long-term appreciation and protect capital" is too broad; many funds are not clear enough with regard to their mandate.

While much is made of position transparency in the hedge fund industry, for funds of hedge funds the structure and investment guidelines are key to understanding the risk management of the fund. However, guidelines are rarely absolute and ignoring guidelines often leads to losses. On the other hand, there are always reasons for an exception to rules, e.g., to make an extra-large allocation in a fund because it is closing, or to overleverage for a short period to meet redemptions. Some general FoHF investment guidelines include maximum individual position sizes, maximum strategy sizes, minimum diversification, maximum leverage, and maximum exposure to markets.

Many institutional investors believe that all funds of hedge funds are created equal. These investors may not have an appreciation for the process of allocating assets to hedge funds, and therefore believe that they should allocate to the groups that have the most assets under management and the largest teams (see Figure 3.3). Performance and qualitative analysis suggest this could be an incorrect assumption.

Constituent manager identification processes for many funds of hedge funds look the same with regard to sourcing funds, filtering the manager universe and conducting manager reviews. The difference between multi-manager groups in these areas is not so much the process, but the way it is implemented.

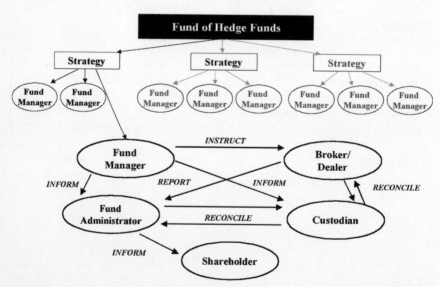

FIGURE 3.3 The structure of a fund of hedge funds.

However, various FoHF managers often address important aspects differently, particularly with regard to portfolio allocation. The main differences in portfolio allocation are linked to top-down/strategic allocation versus bottom-up/fund-picking procedures. Emphasizing strategic allocation first, the portfolio manager determines optimal allocation per strategy, based on a macro analysis and then finds managers to express this view. Conversely, emphasizing fund-picking first, the portfolio manager selects the best managers whatever their strategies. Funds of hedge funds often focus their marketing message on an ability to pick the right managers (see Figure 3.4) rather than on their approach to asset allocation and portfolio construction. When analyzing performance attribution, however, strategic allocation (or errors in strategic allocation) drives performance significantly.

If allocation decisions are primary drivers of returns, it is important to understand how the manager makes these decisions. Even if it is only a two-member team, a structured-investment committee assures that process is followed. Factor to consider are the composition and role of the investment committee; committee voting procedures—simple majority versus unanimity; and implementation of allocation decisions.

PERFORMANCE 3 YEARS (1999-2001) BY ASSETS UNDER MANAGEMENT			
ASSETS UNDER MANAGEMENT	Nb of Funds	3 Years Annualized Performance	3 Years Annualized Standard Deviation
Less than 50	32	15.16%	7.33%
50 to 100	108	11.49%	9.23%
100 to 500	53	14.93%	7.09%
500 to 1000	16	14.40%	6.06%
More than 1000	8	13.78%	7.27%
All funds	217	13.17%	8.12%

There is no evidence that size has an influence on performance

Little relationship exists between inception date and performance

PERFORMANCE 3 YEARS (1999-2001) BY INCEPTION DATE			
INCEPTION	Nb of Funds	Annualized 3 years performance	Annualized 3 years Standard Deviation
Before 1990	24	14.67%	8.43%
1991	9	13.61%	7.21%
1992	18	11.95%	11.81%
1993	13	11.69%	11.20%
1994	25	13.66%	8.44%
1995	33	12.91%	6.24%
1996	35	14.94%	9.49%
1997	35	10.16%	7.89%
1998	40	15.63%	9.54%
All funds	249	13.47%	8.60%

FIGURE 3.4 Size and experience do not explain performance.
Source: Altvest (Dec 2001), funds of hedge funds.

Additional issues to bear in mind when considering funds of hedge funds include:

- Liquidity—The liquidity of hedge funds is perceived as an advantage relative to other alternative investment strategies. Historically, hedge funds and funds of hedge funds have had monthly liquidity. This is mostly because investors (originally offshore) who were not completely sure of the managers' strategies, wanted to know that they could at least get out at month-end. In today's environment, investors and managers alike value longterm investment horizons. As a result, few new funds have less than quarterly liquidity, and an increasing number are featuring semiannual and annual redemption procedures. Often, liquidity policies are related to the strategy employed by the fund.

  It is also important to consider the match-up of the liquidity of the FoHF and its constituent funds. There will be those FoHF managers who have mismatched strategy and/or instrument liquidity with the liquidity of their funds. A fund of hedge funds with monthly liquidity, but with mostly quarterly liquid constituent funds, is bound to face a crisis at some point.

- Fees—When new investment styles are introduced to the marketplace, fees are relatively high, and as they become more commonplace, fees come down. However, because extraordinary manager skill is such a rare commodity, hedge fund fees for quality individual managers probably will not drop much if at all from the current average of 1% management and 20% incentive fees. FoHF fees are a slightly different consideration because of the perception that alpha is less inherent in these structures. Also, institutionally oriented funds that are designed to accept larger asset pools, may introduce lower fees. However, investors should be aware that if a manager (single manager or FoHF) is really skillful, he or she will not give away precious capacity for below-market fee structures—unless there is some strategic rationale for doing so.

  Investors should note that smaller, newer funds of hedge funds tend to have higher "all in" fees as a percentage of capital; this is caused by start-up costs, such as legal, offering, and administrative expenses.

- Volatility—Due to diversification, for the most part, funds of hedge funds are less volatile than individual hedge fund allocations. However, one should not assume that this is true in every case. For example, a broadly diversified fund that focuses on equity long/short managers could very well be much more volatile than a single-manager, market-neutral fund.

- Principal Protection and Principal Guarantee — This is addressed comprehensively in the chapter on structured products. Funds of hedge funds are increasingly offering principal protection options for their investors. Although there are many structural approaches to principal protection, they are generally designed to guarantee the return of the investor's initial principal at some future time.

- Portfolio Leverage—Although not often fully understood by investors, funds of hedge funds may employ leverage from time to time, often as a core strategy. When employed, this leverage may be used simply to provide short-term liquidity for fund redemptions from time to time or, at a more aggressive level, it may be used to amplify the returns of hedge funds that themselves may already be substantially leveraged. Because well diversified FoHFS often have very low volatility, applying leverage to these investments can be very attractive, particularly in the context of an overall risk budget.

- Domicile—Tax havens are under intense scrutiny. Offshore venues are attractive to ERISA plans for UBTI (unrelated business taxable income) purposes. However, percentage allocation limits are currently muzzling what might otherwise be much greater interest. Funds of hedge funds are challenged to create institutionally acceptable vehicles that can manage the regulatory demands of investors and constituent fund managers. Expert counsel should be sought before considering structures that seem to address these investor needs.

- Registered Funds—Because the creation of publicly offered vehicles is gaining momentum, hedge fund managers can hope to gain the blessing of regulators, and smaller investors can play the game with the big boys. This trend is a concern to some, since hedged strategies were never intended for the masses. However, one needs to take a broader perspective and realize that this trend toward wider acceptance of hedge funds is really a paradigm shift, in which old beliefs, such as "Shorting stocks is un-American," will fade as investors who do not believe that Social Security will be there for them when they retire take matters into their own hands. The broad acceptance of hedged strategies is more than a fad—it is a fundamental change in the way people invest. Once the regulatory dust settles, registered funds will be another vehicle for investors to gain access to marketable alternative investments (see Figure 3.5).

While fund of hedge funds products have seen 90% of their growth from individuals, it is expected that institutions will utilize these vehicles for their entrée into the hedge fund industry, thereby dramatically modifying the landscape.

In his fine report on funds of hedge funds, "The Search for Alpha Continues" (2001), UBS's Alexander Ineichen states that successful fund of hedge funds management "involves qualitative processes and projections.

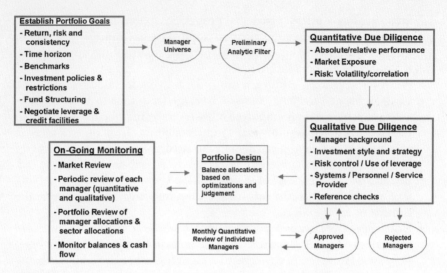

FIGURE 3.5 Typical fund of hedge funds investment management process.

In addition, it requires the knowledge, insight, and experience of getting a qualitative interpretation of the quantitative analysis. The whole process is iterative because there is no beginning or end to the process of manager selection, portfolio construction, risk monitoring, and portfolio rebalancing."

As with any form of investing, in selecting a fund of hedge funds, a fully implemented due diligence process should allow the investor to understand whether:

1. the company is solid and well staffed;
2. the fund has a suitable structure and treats all investors equitably;
3. the investment mandate suits the investor needs;
4. the manager has a concrete process to generate performance in line with the mandate;
5. the investment process has a good probability of achieving performance goals.

A PARTIAL LIST OF HEDGE FUND RELATED RISKS

If playing a word association game, typically, when the term "hedge fund" is used, the immediate response is "risky." While there are all sorts of risk issues related to hedge funds that must be addressed, it is wrong to assume that the funds are inherently risky. Typically, the majority of any risks associated with hedge funds are related to the structure of the vehicle. Listed here are some of the risks, and how they are typically addressed, either by the investor, fund of hedge funds manager, or hedge fund manager:

- ■ Business risk
  - – Many hedge funds are start-up firms with new infrastructure and/or new investment teams.
  - – *Mitigated through thorough, proper due diligence.*

- ■ Credit risk
  - – Potential loss due to a downgrade in rating or default of a particular issuer.
  - – *Mitigated by setting investment parameters, with, among other things, minimum ratings and concentration limits.*

- ■ Counterparty risk
  - – Potential loss due to the failure of a trading partner to meet obligations.
  - – *Mitigated by setting exposure limits; calculating market exposure by counterparty, probability of expected loss and unexpected loss.*

- ■ Liquidity risk
  - – Lender refuses to extend additional credit; margin calls must be met (particularly a risk for managers utilizing high leverage).
  - – *Mitigated by ample cash reserves and diversification.*

- ■ Market risk
  - – Potential loss due to the movement in market-based risk factors.
  - – *Mitigated through understanding the manager's strategy, setting parameters, and monitoring; also by calculating risk using sophisticated risk tools.*

- ■ Operational risk
  - – Potential loss due to the failure in processes or systems relating to accounting, paying, and receiving, or other support functions.
  - – *Mitigated by researching operational capability of managers and their use of independent fund administration.*

- ■ Personnel risk
  - – Quality of individual investment professionals is important because most return comes from manager alpha.
  - – *Mitigated with thorough due diligence and by regular manager monitoring.*

- Short squeezes
  - Security lender demands return of the asset; manager must cover the short position inopportunely.
  - *Mitigated by using "easy-to-borrow" stocks and limiting size of individual short positions.*

- Structure risk
  - Risk relating to suitability, legal, and tax issues of the investment.
  - *Mitigated via independent tax and legal advisors, fiduciary due diligence and suitability, and a detailed investment policy statement.*

MAJOR HEDGE FUND INDUSTRY CHALLENGES

Several major challenges face the hedge fund industry. Investors and consultants should familiarize themselves with them. What follows is a brief description of some of these challenges/trends, and some possible outcomes.

The Institutionalization of Hedge Funds

The popularity of hedge funds among large, sophisticated investors of all types and the resultant asset allocations to these strategies has created one of the major trends in the history of investment. Today, one cannot look at a serious financial journal, nor have a discussion about investment management, without seeing or hearing about hedge funds.

It is not exactly clear what "institutionalization" means in this context. As Mark Anson of CalPERS has said, "We do not necessarily mean the incarceration of these individuals." The term institutionalization suggests the creation of standards for the marketable alternatives industry, including funds of hedge funds. As with their traditional asset management brethren, marketable alternatives require performance standards, benchmarks, risk measurement standards, and professional standards. These are well established and respected in the traditional asset category; however, the opposite must be said of the marketable alternatives arena.

In funds of hedge funds, the marketplace is maturing quickly as a result of the enormous growth of this style of investment. Traditionally, the least structured and professional in an already entrepreneurial industry, FoHFs must make a concerted effort to improve standards applied to their attendant activities, such as manager selection, client services, portfolio allocation, fund monitoring, and risk management.

As ultra-high-net-worth and institutional investors clamor for information about and exposure to hedge funds, traditional money managers are responding by creating hedged strategies products, circumventing the traditional entrepreneurial route of marketable alternatives managers. In so doing, they also hope to keep their talented managers in house. The jury is still out on this development's success; it's simply too early. Many believe that the bureaucratic nature of large firms is too stifling for the creation of alpha generators.

Capacity

It is important to understand that the hedge fund industry was never designed to absorb high levels of assets or intense scrutiny. While it is true that many managers in the field are dazzled by the prospect of marquee investor names and the long-horizon nature of institutional assets, many are deeply concerned about the potentially deteriorating effects of large and demanding assets on what has until now been a cottage industry. Of course, some strategies are less size-constrained than others. Nonetheless, it is too late to go back now. The compelling appeal of hedge funds has a full head of steam and will forever change not only the hedge fund industry, but the investment business as well.

In its excellent report, "Funds of Hedge Funds – Rethinking Resource Requirements" (2001), Barra Strategic Consulting Group states: "There is considerable debate about the future of the marketable alternatives industry and opportunities. Many expect that the flood of assets will diminish returns because market inefficiencies will become more fully arbitraged." This is certainly a major consideration. The numerous influences at work constitute a multifaceted equation that is difficult to monitor and impossible to predict with accuracy. Not fully appreciated, however, is the inherent need for large asset pools to seek either very liquid hedged strategies requiring deep markets or long-duration (private equity-like) strategies with extended gestation periods. Both are less likely to see inefficiencies easily "arbed out."

The marketable alternatives arena is by its nature inventive and adaptable. Managers will create strategies that more readily handle the asset flood. It is probably also true that there will be some loss of alpha as managers refine strategies to absorb more assets. On the other hand, the longer term nature of the institutional investor will give rise to special products that seek to capitalize on market inefficiencies in a manner and time frame that has not previously fit the shorter term focus of the traditional hedge fund investor.

In a growing trend, in-house managers are tempted to leave their jobs, effecting a "brain drain" from traditional asset management. We frequently see talented investment managers at major organizations with a desire to create or join entrepreneurial hedge fund shops. They are not targeting traditional asset management entities. The reasons for this trend are fairly simple:

- Rich margins are to be had if one is any good. The truly skillful in any field will be able to garner incredible compensation.
- The markets seem to require a more flexible response that at least has the chance to profit in bullish and bearish markets while lowering portfolio volatility.
- Wall Street players need a place to direct risk assumption, since they are forced by their public status and quarterly reporting periods to pass on what has historically been a rich source of return on capital. Hedge funds are the natural beneficiary of this transformation.

Serious hedge fund investors are concerned about the issue of capacity. Large amounts of capital are coming into the hedge fund field, at the same time that large numbers of managers are beginning hedge funds. Meanwhile, there continues to be extreme risk and uncertainty in the world. This is a recipe for great change. No doubt there will be bumps in the road to the future of this industry. Clearly, the road is leading to a much different place in the coming years. Markets will deepen, regulators will become increasingly involved, smaller investors will press for a seat at the table, and financial engineers will devise new instruments. No one can predict how this business will actually evolve, but the contrast between considerable pools of assets in search of alpha and mounting numbers of managers seeking investors will force evolution.

Hedge Funds have historically been utilized by sophisticated, high-networth investors (see Figure 3.6). It will take some time for institutions to catch up to the assets allocated by individuals. However, significant growth is expected in the funds of hedge funds field, and geographically outside the U.S.

Transparency

It is understandable that hedge fund managers have been hesitant to share the intimate details of their portfolio positions with their investors. However, institutional investors have a completely different mind-set. They are fiduciaries that are bound by strict regulatory environments. They also tend to have comparatively long investment time horizons.

Transparency is a word that is used by both investor and manager, but has different meanings for each. Managers feel that transparency means a regularly available listing of all positions. However, to investors, transparency tends to mean risk transparency or information about exposure to

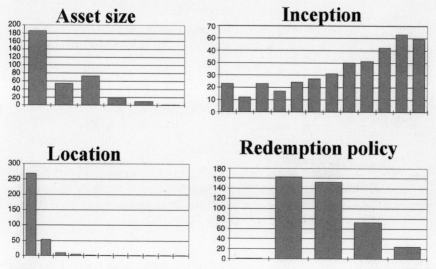

FIGURE 3.6 Fund of funds is a diverse industry.
Source: Altvest (December 2001).

such things as market capitalizations, industry groups, short sales, derivatives, and leverage.

Since many, if not most, institutions are investing in, or contemplating entering, hedge funds through investments in funds of funds, it then falls to these pooled vehicles to address the transparency issue. Over the past few years, several risk management firms have begun working closely with the hedge fund community in an attempt to provide a solution to transparency demands. Typically, these firms will (pursuant to a strict nondisclosure agreement) gain access to hedge fund position statements, on a daily and/or monthly basis, by receiving electronic data transmissions from the hedge fund's custodian and/or administrator. In turn, comprehensive risk-management reports are provided which, although lacking disclosure of the specific holdings by name, will reveal a robust set of data with respect to numerous risk-exposure factors. These reports allow the to HF Manager to closely monitor changes within each of the individual hedge funds, as well as the aggregate fund, and analyze such factors as security concentrations, portfolio leverage, tail-risk exposure, VaR, and numerous others.

Complaints of foul play by investors who feel that hedge funds at large are a closed society are really the misunderstandings caused by hedge funds, historically a cottage industry. This has not lessened the intense curiosity each party has about the other, as investors attempt to identify hedge fund managers, and hedge fund managers try to gain access to institutional investors.

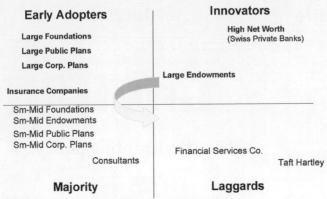

FIGURE 3.7 Segmentation/adoption rates: Where's the opportunity?

Benchmarks

Institutional investors require benchmarks against which to compare their investments. For hedge funds, creating indices that act as benchmarks is difficult because it requires classification for a style of investment that is by its nature iconoclastic. To be useful, benchmarks must be unequivocal and replicable. Because returns are driven by individual manager skill, there is little agreement about how to classify hedge fund investment styles and exactly who belongs in which style. The advent of multistrategy managers has compounded this confusion. Absolute return benchmarks, such as Treasury bills plus some premium, help establish hurdle rates of return, but do not adequately represent styles (see Figure 3.7). In order for an index to be most representative and comparable, it should be investable, non biased in its selection of holdings, and comprehensive in its representation of the asset loss. Because of wide diversity of strategies and the idiosyncratic nature of hedge funds, no one has satisfactorily accomplished this feat. However, serious work is being done and one should expect that a convergence of ideas will occur to create standards in hedge fund indices.

CONSULTANTS

Consultants are perceived as being late with respect to investor interest in hedge funds. However, ultra-high-net-worth and institutional investor dependence on consultants will catapult them redundant to the forefront.

Consultants will have an increasing role in hedge fund allocations, but are currently behind the curve. A 2002 analysis conducted by InvestorForce indicates several interesting trends:

- 80% of the 200 consultants surveyed indicate an interest in hedge funds. However, only 5% are currently active in the category.
- Of the 200, 50 consulting firms were identified as seeking a way to access information on funds of hedge funds.
- At the time of the survey, 2 of the top 5 U.S. institutional consultants offered no guidance on hedge funds for their clients.
- 87% of institutions investing in hedge funds use a consultant in some capacity.

CONCLUSION

In general, funds of hedge funds represent an important trend in investment management that is in its infancy. This under-appreciated form of asset management has gained in popularity because it has delivered on the promise of lower volatility than investing directly in hedge funds and low correlation to the stock market. Some findings:

- In studies conducted with various hedge fund databases, over varying time periods, the average fund of hedge funds delivers good returns with greater consistency when compared to various hedge funds indices and stock market benchmarks, despite the additional layer of fees. Presumably, this is because the fund of hedge funds asset allocator adds alpha in selecting funds relative to nondiscretionary indices.
- Funds of hedge funds offer a wide spectrum of alternatives from which investors can choose: small boutiques versus large organizations, experienced teams versus new groups, and liquid (monthly) redemptions versus more illiquid (quarterly/annual) redemption vehicles.
- Funds of hedge funds are not homogeneous, but need to be segmented into groups in order to properly compare them: diversified versus focused and low volatility versus aggressive.
- Funds of hedge funds' performance may range widely, not only due to different mandates but also due to different allocator skills.

Some investors and consultants have resisted hedge fund investments because of fear of presumed career risk and headline risk associated with this investment style. However, groups that are compared with the performance of their peers might want to ask themselves, "What's the risk of not investigating hedge funds?"

It is clear that the marketable alternatives world is growing and changing rapidly. Investors and consultants alike must be prepared for the

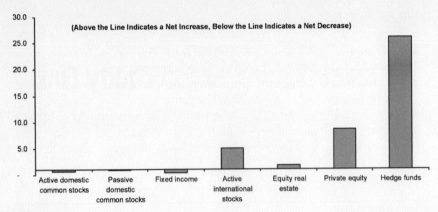

FIGURE 3.8 Institutions expectations to change asset allocations: increase-to-decrease ratio.

increasing complexity of strategies and instruments traded by hedge funds, not to mention the increase in the number of managers. All of this makes it daunting to know which are the right funds for a given investor, the prospect of which makes funds of hedge funds an attractive alternative for the informed consultant.

The Greenwich Associates study, "Hedge Fund Investing in the Upscale Institutional Marketplace" (2002), found 130 institutions expecting to increase allocations to hedge funds while only 5 expected a decrease (see Figure 3.8). According to Mercer, 21% of plans with more than $500 million in assets intend to hire an alternative manager in the next 2 years.

Thomas Zucosky would like to thank Christophe Olivier, Alison Cohen, and Kenneth Phillips for their invaluable contributions to this chapter.

CHAPTER 4

Investing in Hedged Equity Funds

Brian A. Wolf, CFA

INTRODUCTION

Hedge funds likely originated in 1949 with the hedged equities strategy. Alfred Winslow Jones is most commonly credited with being the first person to have combined long and short equity positions and leverage in a single investment portfolio. He attempted to create an investment vehicle whose performance would be a function of his stock-picking skills, and not of the general direction of the U.S. equity markets. By maintaining both long and short position, the Jones portfolio was less affected by broad market fluctuations than a traditional, long-only portfolio would have been. Profits were instead derived from his ability to select long investments that would outperform his shorts. Jones then utilized leverage to magnify returns, with stock positions typically in excess of 150% of the equity capital in his fund. The strategy proved highly successful and, following a 1966 article about Jones in *Fortune* magazine, many people adopted similar approaches.

A great deal of the appeal of the strategy was (and remains today) the ability to insulate investment performance by some degree from that of the overall market. Absolute return-oriented strategies, as they grew to be known, offered less uncertainty and lower levels of volatility to investors while still offering return potential on par with the long-term returns achieved by long-only equity investors. The time period for the absolute return has varied; some fund managers sought to earn a target return each calendar year while others looked to compound capital at a target rate over a multiyear period or a full market or economic cycle.

Today, hedged equity investing remains the most widely practiced of all hedge fund strategies, with an estimated 4,000 funds employing strategies born from the original Jones model. Despite their common origin and the fact that nearly all of today's funds have investment models centered on some type of fundamental analysis, perhaps the single most distinguishing characteristic of this hedge fund strategy is the diversity of approaches employed by the funds' portfolio managers. As a result, the alpha derived from hedged equity programs tends to be highly manager-specific, in a marked contrast to other hedge fund strategies, in which alpha tends to be more strategy-specific.

One way to bring order to the disparate universe of hedged equity managers is to classify them along 3 primary lines: differences in the broad investment strategy or mandate; differences in the research process, and differences in portfolio management. This chapter will describe the differences in these 3 areas and discuss the evaluation of managers in the hedged equity strategy.

BROAD INVESTMENT STRATEGY DIFFERENCES

Sector Specialists versus Generalists

There are innumerable ways to parse the universe of hedged equity funds by strategy. One useful method is to separate managers focusing on specific sectors from those who have a generalist mandate. Sector funds are built on the premise that focusing on a limited number of companies in a specific industry will give a manager an informational or analytical edge over other market participants. Typically, the manager has specialized experience in a chosen sector—perhaps only as an investment professional, but also often as an industry professional, such as a doctor, engineer, product manager, etc. Most sector funds focus on 1 of the following industries: technology, healthcare/biotech, financials, consumer, or energy. Some managers utilize a sector approach, but focus on 2 or 3 areas, such as technology and healthcare or consumer and financials.

The specialization of sector funds offers investors 3 distinct advantages. First, investor get a manager who, due to prior experience and a focus on a limited universe of companies, may provide expertise beyond that of other market participants. Second, they receive a mandate, which allows the investor to make the sector allocation decision, and thus may make it easier for the investor to underwrite. Three, investor put their money into an investment whose performance is easier to benchmark due to its limited mandate.

While sector specialization can be theoretically appealing, these funds offer a unique set of risks that must be considered. Foremost among them is cyclicality. Specialization quite frequently results in managers who become myopic in their areas of coverage. These managers may lack the ability to distinguish the attractiveness of opportunities in their areas of expertise relative to opportunities elsewhere. What often transpires is an inherent long bias, often accompanied by a fear of missing the next bull move. Some managers think that not fully participating in a rally in their specialty area is a sign of inferiority. Similarly, some managers view their mandate as giving their investor base intelligent exposure to a particular sector, rather than earning an absolute rate of return. This phenomenon can be exacerbated, because in some industry sectors, long and short positions, despite their fundamental differences, tend to exhibit a relatively high degree of correlation. In all these cases, performance of sector funds may show signs of a relative-return orientation, effectively transferring the sector timing decision from the manager to the investor. Thus, sector funds that view their mandate as utilizing specialized expertise about a universe of stocks to earn an attractive absolute rate of return are preferable.

While a generalist approach has distinct advantages, most notably the flexibility to invest where opportunities are most attractive and the ability to maintain long and short portfolios with very little correlation, it also has its own unique set of challenges resulting from a broadened mandate. Here, an investor must underwrite the manager's evaluation and investment skills in multiple industries as well as the ability to make timely sector allocations—a daunting task. With a broad mandate, one must also ask whether an investment team has sufficient expertise across the industries in which a manager may invest. Small funds with a limited number of investment professionals may be particularly challenged. The lack of focus relative to sector specialists often results in difficulty in identifying a generalist's edge. However, since most hedged equity funds employ a generalist approach, it is imperative to take advantage of investment opportunities with such managers.

Geographic Mandate

It is also useful to divide managers by their geographic mandates. Typical mandates include U.S. and Canadian stocks only, Western Europe, Japan, Asia ex-Japan, and Emerging Markets. Global mandates, which encompass all of the above or various subsectors, are also common. Obviously, as managers broaden their mandates, their opportunity sets and requisite skill levels increase. Such managers may be well served by maintaining offices in the regions in which they invest and by having investment professionals on staff who speak the native languages of countries whose stocks make up a meaningful percentage of the portfolio. Differences in accounting treatment, legal restrictions, heightened sociopolitical and currency risks, and cultural differences make investing outside a manager's domestic market a challenge. Regionally focused managers pose the same risks as sector specialists—their limited focus may obscure their judgment and result in an inherent long bias. In addition, some strategies, such as those focused on emerging markets, may be directional because less-developed countries do not have the infrastructure to sell stocks short.

Exposure Bias

Another valuable manager classification method is that of typical exposure bias. Directional and long-only managers occupy one end of the spectrum, followed by long-biased managers, neutral managers, and short-biased managers; short-only managers are at the opposite end. Opportunistic managers, whose net exposure may change frequently and vary widely, are a separate classification, off the spectrum. Since an overwhelming majority of hedged equity managers are long-biased, additional gradations between degrees of long bias may be necessary. One thing to consider is how frequently and to what degree exposure may vary. Some managers rarely exceed a defined range of net and gross exposure and change this exposure incrementally while others stick to a typical range, but may briefly have exposure far outside their USUAL parameters or change their net or gross invested position quickly. Determining whether a manager is comfortable being net short can be useful in determining a manager's exposure bias. Categorizing managers by a common risk factor, such as typical net equity exposure, can make comparisons easier.

Other Broad Strategy Differences

Other important differences in broad investment strategy include investment style and market capitalization biases, the degree of liquidity with which a manager is comfortable, the use of index instruments and derivative securities, and the inclusion of quasi-equity strategies—such as private equity or distressed debt—within the fund's investment mandate. In addition, some managers tend to favor certain investment themes (e.g., turnarounds, spin-offs, asset plays), while others traffic in (or avoid) stocks with some common element (e.g., binary outcome stocks, such as those in the biotech sector; product-driven companies; or "story stocks" whose earnings and cash flow are negative).

DIFFERENCES IN THE INVESTMENT RESEARCH PROCESS

The research processes of managers in the hedged equity strategy can differ greatly, even among those managers with similar investment styles. A focus on several core functional areas of the research process can help illustrate this variety.

Idea Generation

Knowledge regarding how investment ideas are generated can offer significant insights into potential risks and better enable an investor to assess a manager's risk/reward profile. Additionally, such knowledge can assist the investor in assessing correlation risk among managers. Below are some common ways that ideas are generated.

Screens

Whether their style is pure value, pure growth, or somewhere in between, virtually all managers use screens to develop investment ideas. Screens are frequently used via some type of software program or through a device such as a Bloomberg terminal. They are more commonly used by generalists or by managers with broad investment mandates; these managers may not be able to dynamically monitor all of the companies in their respective universes, and use screens to alert them to potential investment opportunities. Using screens, value-oriented managers may search for long ideas, such as low multiples of cash flow or earnings, relative or absolute cheapness based on a dividend discount model, net assets in excess of equity, "hidden" assets (such as overfunded pension liabilities), share prices that are making new lows, and companies showing improvement in one or more areas after a period of underperformance. Growth managers typically screen for such factors as accelerating top-line growth or growth in cash flow, earnings, revenue, or earnings before income tax, depreciation and amortization (EBITDA).

While screening is quite commonly utilized (especially among smaller firms) to generate long ideas, it is employed more frequently in the short-sale research process. This happen largely because there are far fewer sources touting short ideas relative to longs. Managers are typically more secretive about the shares which they are shorting, because of the risks of shorts being "squeezed" (the rapid run-up in share prices attributed to long players in the stock attempting to force managers to cover their shorts, i.e., losing the ability to borrow the shares sold short), being bought-in, or losing access to corporate management teams. Therefore, they can be less likely to share short ideas with others. Common short candidate screens include high or increasing levels of day's sales outstanding; receivables and/or inventories; deferred revenues; unbilled receivables; the capitalization of items which similar companies are expensing; notable or growing differences between cash flow and reported earnings, and the reverse of long-idea screens.

Screening's primary strength is its ability to cut quickly through the reams of data available on publicly held companies and identify companies whose characteristics fit a manager's particular investment style. However, a considerable number of variables are relevant to an investment's attractiveness (quality of management, industry attractiveness, etc.), which cannot be effectively screened. Screens are a valuable starting point for further due diligence. Screening is rarely relied upon as the primary supporting evidence behind an investment thesis; however, managers inexperienced in short selling may, at times, lean too heavily on screens to generate investment ideas.

Such sources as investment periodicals and journals, mutual fund managers, and sell-side analysts can be grouped together, since mutual fund managers and sell-side analysts often provide the ideas for articles in the trade press. Quality ideas can be found in investment periodicals and/or the sell side, but the signal-to-noise ratio is often quite poor. Some managers find sell-side opinions highly valuable as a gauge of investor sentiment; situations in which a manager's opinion differs greatly from that of the Street are of particular interest to these managers. Other managers never talk to the sell side, as they feel this adds little value and may cloud the independence of their own analysis.

These sources of information can provide opinions from experts with focused coverage on a limited universe of companies. Specialized publications, like *Outstanding Investor Digest* (a popular journal among value investors) or *CFRA* (a widely read publication offering write-ups of companies whose accounting practices are being questioned), may also offer high-quality ideas. However, conflicts of interest present at sell-side firms (such as the pressure on analysts to write favorable recommendations to boost their firms' investment banking business potential) may diminish the objectiveness of analyst recommendations. This also explains the dearth of sell-side short sale recommendations. Ideas from investment periodicals may also be stale and offer less compelling opportunities than those from more proprietary sources. Few managers profess to generate a large percentage of their ideas from these sources.

Trade Journals Trade Shows, CEOs, Field Contacts

These sources offer ideas from outside the investment community and may be favored by managers because of their more proprietary nature. Often, managers attempt to use their limited partner base or even recruit limited partners who can offer strategic value to generate ideas of this nature. Trade publications and contacts outside the investment community can also be quite valuable in generating short ideas, as these sources are more likely to have a neutral or negative bias toward a company than others. However, reliable sources with access to relevant information are difficult to identify. Unlike sell-side analysts, who may earn commission revenues in return for information, industry sources may feel they have nothing to gain by sharing information, and therefore may be reluctant to do so.

Other Hedge Fund Managers

An understanding of a manager's network is a critical element of the due diligence process. The sharing of ideas among hedge fund managers has increased dramatically; while this provides opportunities, it also poses several risks. Managers may benefit from their peers' ideas, particularly when other funds have a full position but a stock continues to appear undervalued. In addition, managers who invest in similar companies may be more effective at accessing management, sharing research costs, and contributing advice to management. Prominent risks include the possibility that common short positions can become crowded, creating liquidity problems, borrowing difficulty, and call risk. Managers may also, at times, perform little or no original research, and simply buy another manager's idea(s). In this case, a manager may have to rely on others to determine when to exit a position, to the detriment of his or her investors. Managers may be skilled at articulating a story they have heard elsewhere, but may perform little additional proprietary research.

Other Sources

Corporate filings, corporate events (such as spin-offs, restructurings, etc.), conversations with professionals in the debt markets and news services, such as Bloomberg and Reuters, are also important sources of investment ideas. Corporate filings or events may signal inflection points in a company's fundamentals and provide investment opportunities. Investment professionals in the debt markets frequently possess divergent views about a company's fiscal health relative to their professional counterparts in the equity markets, which may also generate opportunities. News services provide up-to-the-minute information, which can be valuable for sourcing short-term trading opportunities and for generating long-term investment ideas.

Information-Gathering

Information-gathering is the core of the investment research process. An informational advantage over other market participants can provide managers with a true research edge. The type of information sought or deemed most relevant may also provide valuable insight into a manager's investment philosophy, strengths, weaknesses, and work ethic.

Financial statement analysis is one important mode of gathering information. Financial statements are the most comprehensive set of information an investor has about a company's fiscal health; the ability to understand and interpret them is critical to a manager's success. A fair number of hedge funds have built their investment process around the analysis of a company's financials, and virtually every manager performs some level of analysis in this area. However, financial statements tend to lag behind economic reality and may have limited usefulness in assessing a company's future prospects. Few firms rely entirely on them to make investment decisions.

Another important method is "channel checking," or conversations with a potential investment candidate's customers, suppliers and ultimate end users as well as with competitors and current and former employees. This grassroots research may be more likely to create a proprietary informational edge than financial statement analysis. In some cases, managers even employ "secret shoppers," who, for example, visit retail outlets and collect information on which products are selling and which are seeing markdowns in their prices.

Visits to a company's management and tours of a company's facilities are considered by some managers to be extremely beneficial; these managers typically cite the ability to observe body language and the willingness of management teams to divulge more or better information in a face-to-face setting as the primary reasons why such visits are useful. Others elect to never visit management teams, feeling such visits provide little useful information that isn't already publicly available. Regulation FD (for "fair disclosure"), which specifies that companies may not selectively disclose information to certain investors, went into effect in the fall of 2000, and has made management visits somewhat less relevant in the U.S. In Japan and some other countries, management visits are considered much more valuable.

Managers may also use outside consultants and private investigators. Consultants can be especially helpful to smaller firms with generalist mandates, allowing them to gain a deeper understanding of industries in which they may be less experienced. Private investigators are most typically used in the short-sale research process, in which the negatively biased nature of the information being sought typically makes the information more difficult to uncover.

Both the information a manager looks for and the method employed in the search are closely related to the typical investment horizons on a manager's long and short positions. For example, financial statement analysis, management visits, and outside consultant work are typically more useful in formulating a longer term investment thesis while trading-oriented managers with briefer investment horizons may use channel checks more frequently.

Valuation Approaches

Approaches to company valuations differ among managers, but most use some form of discounted cash flow analysis to compute a company's intrinsic value. Most managers build earnings models, but considerable differences may exist about the level at which the model is truly proprietary versus an adaptation of Street research. Within this framework, a subset of managers looks at the valuation issue from a private equity perspective, determining what a company would be worth to private equity investors or another public company in an acquisition. Others may try to gauge the potential for increased institutional ownership and/or multiple expansion. While numerous managers use Wall Street earnings models in whole or in part, truly proprietary models are preferable.

View Toward Short Selling

Hedged equity fund managers have differing views on short selling, and these may or may not be consistent with views held by hedge fund investors. Short selling tells one a lot about a manager's investment philosophy and helps to assess a fund's true absolute return potential. Successful shorting of stocks is generally regarded as harder than long investing, for several reasons, including the increased difficulty in obtaining negatively biased information or bad news; the more limited return potential of shorts (i.e., 100% is the maximum possible return); the infinite loss potential (versus maximum loss potential of 100% for longs); the difficulty of correct timing, because shorts that do not work become larger positions, and stock borrow and call issues combined with the uptick rule, which make execution more difficult. Because far fewer managers are talented at short selling (relative to those who are skilled long investors), assessing short-selling skills may be valuable as a "litmus test" to quickly determine whether a manager is worth pursuing.

Although most managers profess to be absolute return-oriented, many view their short portfolio as a hedge (as opposed to a profit center) and are uncomfortable with, or unwilling to have, a net short position. Viewing short positions as a hedge lowers the bar on the quality of the ideas in which a manager will invest and results in a portfolio that will probably provide less alpha. Alpha may be further reduced when a manager uses index instruments, such as S&P 500 futures or exchange-traded funds (e.g., SPYders, QQQs), to obtain short exposure as opposed to individual stock shorts—although it can be a good idea to use such instruments to quickly alter net exposure in the short term.

How a manager sizes short positions should be another of the investor's concerns. Because of their unlimited loss potential, their characteristic of becoming larger positions if they do not work, and the fact that shorts frequently exhibit higher volatility than long positions, the sizing of short positions can have a material impact on a fund's volatility and potential loss. Smaller short positions are preferable, but require managers to find more ideas to create an adequate level of short exposure. Investors should assess a manager's ability to source short-sale ideas with his or her ability to endure volatility and drawdowns.

A final issue to consider when evaluating a manager's short-selling ability is how positions are timed. Some managers prefer taking small positions and being early, when stock borrow is easier but risk is higher. Others seek to short "the middle of the move," a lower risk proposition that is more difficult to execute. Managers may also differ regarding their attitudes as to what constitutes a crowded short and on their ability to borrow stock without getting called. Obtaining the names of managers' large short positions (which is often quite challenging) and a review of common short-sale idea sources (the aforementioned *CFRA*, newsletters such as *Short Alert, Short on Value*, etc.) as well as commonly published data on short interest and short interest ratios can alert investors to possible "crowded shorts." They can be problematic in that concurrent short-covering by multiple managers may reduce liquidity and, consequently, result in share prices that can rise quickly. Prime brokerage relationships can also provide clues about managers' borrow problems or how often they have short positions called away.

Other Considerations

The investment research process may also differ with regard to a position's hurdle rate, investment horizon, and the degree to which a manager is willing to become active to spur realization of intrinsic value. Managers have widely varying investment horizons and ROI (return on investment) hurdle rates. Short positions typically have lower hurdle rates and investment horizons which are briefer than longs. Some managers may seek to add value by becoming active. Such activity ranges from writing letters to management and/or other shareholders to waging proxy fights and seeking board representation. Other managers are passive investors; some may even choose to invest without any contact with company management. Because of the greater time commitment involved, managers' portfolios generally show a higher concentration level as they become more active in the research process.

DIFFERENCES IN PORTFOLIO MANAGEMENT

A third prominent area of differentiation among hedged equity managers is portfolio management. A manager's approach to portfolio management may provide greater insight into a fund's risk/reward profile than a review of the broad strategy or research process. A talented portfolio manager can add a lot of value. Conversely, the hedge fund graveyard is littered with the ruined careers of competent analysts who started new funds, but lacked the portfolio management skills to maintain their businesses.

Funds' portfolio concentration levels show considerable variation. Some managers limit positions to as little as 2%, while others are comfortable with an occasional position greater than 20%. Most managers, however, have different sizing disciplines for long and short positions, with shorts almost always being sized much smaller, because they are viewed as higher risk and/or more volatile. Some managers may determine a position's attractiveness as a function of upside potential to downside risk, while others focus on sizing positions by either return potential or possible loss, but not both. Still others pair one or more long positions with one or more shorts and assess the attractiveness of the positions in aggregate. More concentrated portfolios offer better return potential, but at the expense of higher volatility and greater risk of drawdown. Less concentrated portfolios may offer less risk, but may also have lower return potential because of the dilution of the best investment ideas.

Managers may use formal position limits as well as limits on gross and net exposure to industry groups, sectors, or geographical regions. These limits are useful, but often set wide parameters and require investors to inquire about typical position sizes, exposure limits, and historical maximums and minimums. Aside from position limits, it is also useful to know and track the typical percentage of equity in the top 10 or 20 positions. Position sizing, concentration, and exposure limits can provide investors with useful information about the risks a manager has taken or is willing to take.

Stop-loss rules, both formal and informal, are typically utilized to some degree by managers and may provide valuable insight regarding a manager's risk appetite. Stop-loss rules may also have relevance in a discussion of how positions are built. Position-building styles can vary from a contrarian approach, in which a manager adds to positions as they decline (on weakness), to a momentum-oriented approach, in which a manager closes positions as they decline and adds to them as they are appreciating (on strength). It's useful to know if a manager "legs" in and out of positions slowly or chooses to initiate or close them quickly. Ensuring that a manager is a talented and timely "seller" is as important as being comfortable with a manager's ability to buy shares at attractive prices.

Investors should also assess a manager's willingness to expand or reduce net and gross exposure. Managers who expand their balance sheets and increase their exposure when ideas are working and reduce gross and net exposure when money is being lost have typically provided less volatile results and have incurred less severe drawdowns than managers who take the opposite approach.

Perhaps the 2 most critical factors in a hedged equity program are the manager's accurate assessment of company fundamentals, and an environment in which, fundamentals are the primary driver of share prices. When short-term macro events or crises trump fundamentals, or a manager is just out of synch, it is usually preferable to see gross and net exposure reduced. There is a range of differing approaches to the exposure/leverage issue, with some managers choosing to maintain approximately the same exposure at all times, while others take an active interest in timing industry and market cycles, and thus alter their exposure frequently. As mentioned earlier, even those managers whose typical portfolios consist only of individual stock positions may use derivatives to quickly adjust exposure.

How managers' views on macroeconomic conditions affect decisions also plays a role in defining their portfolio management styles. Allocation decisions may be driven entirely by a top-down view on the broad equity markets, or by such views on geographic regions or industry sectors. In other cases, macro views shape the portfolio in a more oblique manner through the presence of themes that permeate the long and short portfolios. Many managers, however, profess to be completely agnostic with regard to top-down views and make allocation decisions entirely based on a bottom-up assessment of the attractiveness of individual ideas.

Trading frequency is also an important element of a manager's portfolio management style. Portfolio turnover rates are a good staring point, but they do not always accurately reflect a manager's willingness to trade, and can be measured differently. Some managers choose to actively trade their core positions, adding and reducing to existing allocations as prices fluctuate, in an attempt to add incremental profits while waiting for theses to play out. Other managers may either directly elect to, or give their traders discretion to, put on extremely short-term positions and/or maintain a separate profit-and-loss account for the trading desk.

How allocation decisions are made also merits careful analysis. Is there a single portfolio manager or are there multiple managers? Are decisions made by consensus or does each manager maintain a separate "book"? Do any analysts have "carve-outs" or pools of capital over which they have discretion? How is the team incentivized? Is a greater portion of total compensation based on the performance of the fund as a whole or on the performance of an investment professional's individual ideas?

Finally, some firms maintain a risk management function outside the area of portfolio management. An investment professional not involved in portfolio decisions or an operations person may have the authority to trim or liquidate positions, based on a predetermined set of rules. Such arrangements can give investors some level of comfort, but it is important to understand the level of true authority the risk manager has and how that authority may change.

Manager Evaluation

The sheer size and wide-ranging diversity of the hedged equity manager universe can make the evaluation process challenging. Different strategies and processes require different methods of evaluation. Proper due diligence always requires detailed quantitative and qualitative analysis as well as extensive reference checking. The evaluation process should be centered on an attempt to understand the manager's strategy, investment process, and potential edge, and to accurately assess the risk/reward profile of the fund. The investor should evaluate risk-adjusted, not absolute, performance, and should note whether or not the process yields consistent, sustainable results or whether it is designed to exploit an opportunity with a limited duration. Managers should be able to articulate an intelligent, structured investment program and explain how and why they expect superior investment performance.

Quantitative Analysis

Both the breadth and depth of data that managers provide to prospective investors are improving, and offer an excellent starting point when screening for new managers. An area of focus should be on the types and levels of risk a manager has incurred, or "the story behind the numbers." Particular data useful in this regard include a manager's average returns and betas in months when the S&P 500 (or other relevant index) has declined (and conversely, in just the months when it has appreciated); the monthly gross long and short exposure, industry, and geographic exposure information; the return on invested capital of the long and short portfolios; and the ratio of profitable-to-unprofitable positions (winners-to-losers) for both longs and shorts. Calculating the manager's peak-to-trough drawdown and studying the period in which it occurred will likely provide clues as to which risk factors affect the manager's performance. Correlation analysis with various indices, commodity prices, changes in interest rates, etc., may also be useful in determining potential risks to a manager's strategy.

Studying a manager's returns (and beta) in just the months when a relevant equity index has declined, or in a period of market stress, is one true test of a manger's absolute return potential. Very few managers exhibit the ability to compound capital at positive rates of return in both advancing and declining markets, and therefore cannot be counted on as true absolute-return vehicles. Measuring up- and down-market returns relative to the index being used (i.e., a manager's return in months when the S&P 500 has declined versus the returns of the S&P 500 in those months) reveals where the manager is adding alpha and can be useful to the investor when considering the risk/reward profile of the portfolio being constructed. For example, a manager who, on average, provides 50% of the appreciation in the S&P 500 in rising months and suffers 10% of the index's decline in falling months may be more interesting to a conservative investor but less so to a more aggressive investor than a manager who is capturing 110% of the market's advances and 70% of its declines.

Details on the attribution of profits and losses are also an essential part of the quantitative due diligence effort. Attribution between longs and shorts, between industry sectors, and geographic regions, and from large positions is typically available. Attribution information can help an investor gauge the quality of returns. It is preferable to see a manager who is consistently profitable on both long and short positions or across all areas in which investment occurs. Reliance on one part of the portfolio to carry performance may be indicative of luck or of a limited opportunity, and typically yields less consistent results.

It is important to consider how often a manager adjusts the fund's net and gross exposure. Managers who make frequent significant changes must have their skills in market timing more closely evaluated than managers whose exposure changes less often. Also, as a manager utilizes greater leverage, the impact of dual losses from both the long and short portfolios increases. This requires investors to more carefully assess the potential mismatch in betas, industry and geographic exposure, market cap, relative P/Es, and other factors between the longs and the shorts.

Qualitative Analysis

The qualitative evaluation process spans a wide range from the abstract to the concrete. One needs to make subjective and judgmental assessments about a manager's character, integrity, work ethic, and risk appetite, while details about a manager's experience, investment philosophy, and individual positions are factual in nature. It can be particularly useful to talk about individual positions during this phase of due diligence. Such discussions help illuminate a manager's work ethic, risk appetite, and investment philosophy. It is instructive to talk about fresh ideas in which a manager's thesis has not yet played out, as well as past mistakes.

It is also imperative to meet with the other professionals in a manager's organization—outside of the portfolio manager(s). Meeting with analysts and noninvestment professionals, such as the CFO, can give one valuable information about the depth and quality of the firm's infrastructure. It can help one understand potential problems, and learn whether or not the other team members understand and agree with the firm's investment philosophy. Often, a portfolio manager is quite skilled at giving presentations and/or ticking off all the right answers while other team members, who are less experienced in such matters, offer more candid responses.

Reference checking should be performed during all phases of the due diligence process. Early reference checks can ring alarm bells and alert a potential investor to managers not worthy of further consideration. Reference checking in the middle to later stages of the due diligence process can be used to see if the manager's past record is consistent with the program being articulated. Checks should be performed with many people with whom the manager has a relationship. They should include current investors, other hedge fund managers (especially some whose names were not provided by the manager), past colleagues and employers, and the manager's prime broker, who can verify where and in what the manager is investing and the level of net and gross exposure used. It may also be worthwhile to speak with individuals from the companies with whom the manager has invested or currently invests.

Noninvestment due diligence is also important. Background checks, a detailed document review (including a manager's audited financial statements), and a thorough review of a manager's back office and infrastructure should all be part of the normal due diligence process. Too often, managers, as well as investors, do not pay enough attention to non-investment issues.

An investment firm's size and rate of growth should also be studied. Larger firms may have built their track records utilizing the advantages of a smaller capital base. In addition, over time, senior management may have migrated from a role of analyst and portfolio manager to that of portfolio manager alone. Understanding factors, such as who was responsible for investment decisions in the past, what staff turnover has occurred, and how infrastructure has been built to keep pace with growth, should be a part of the qualitative evaluation process. A firm's rate of growth should also be studied with an eye to understanding how a larger capital base affects a manager's investable universe, research process, and ability to sell short, as well as how a manager's risk-adjusted performance has changed with capital growth. Managers should be able to articulate some vision with regard to the capacity of their investment strategy.

Each hedged equity fund is unique and in the end, there is no formula or checklist to effectively assess an investment program's attractiveness. Investors should look for evidence of a well-thought-out program with a definable structure, evidence of an edge, and investment principals who show a clear and consistent understanding of what the program is, how and why it works, and its primary risks or weaknesses. These elements do not guarantee success, but they increase the chance that a manager will produce consistent and sustainable investment results.

CONCLUSION

Investing in the hedged equities strategy poses a unique set of challenges and opportunities. The aggregate capitalization of the global equity markets relative to total hedged equity fund assets suggests little in the way of a strategy-level capacity constraint. However, the manager-specific nature of the alpha generated from hedged equity programs makes the evaluation and selection process critically important. Because of the burgeoning interest in hedge fund programs and the fact that a finite number of superior managers exists, it is crucial for investors to be able to quickly distinguish those candidates who may be suitable for investment from those who are not.

Studying a manager's broad investment strategy, research process, and portfolio management is a useful three-step process in evaluating a manager. The investor must be able to build a high level of conviction in his or her understanding of a manager's risk/reward profile. This requires a detailed knowledge of a manager's risks and the ability to assess return (and loss) potential in varying market environments.

Several factors unique to hedge fund investing put an additional premium on accurate manager evaluation. Limited liquidity can make inaccurate evaluation painful for a long time. The level of work necessary to properly perform due diligence may limit the number of investments one can make. Additionally, the personal relationship that a manager typically has with his or her investors effectively prohibits the ability of an investor to trade an investment.

In the end, the evaluation process is more art than science. Quantitative analysis is very useful, but it must give way to qualitative judgment. A disciplined, thorough approach, combined with experience in manager evaluation, offers the best potential for successful hedged equity investing.

CHAPTER 5

Arbitrage

Alfredo M. Viegas

Two thousand years ago, Roman gold and silver merchants became fabulously rich, transporting silver east to India and China, and bringing gold west to Rome. They had a tremendous arbitrage opportunity in exchange rates. In Rome, the gold-to-silver fair value ratio was 1:12, while in the East it was 1:6.

Arbitrage is a powerful way to profit from buying and selling identical things at differing prices. Profitable arbitrage situations have always existed. In the United States after the Civil War, a significant interest-rate differential existed between the North and the South, and it stayed for a few years until it was arbitraged away by a handful of savvy New York bankers.

Today, there is a market economy where arbitrage and other market activities tend to bring prices for similar goods and services into a narrow range. Some prices approach uniformity more completely than others, but markets tend to bring prices together in an efficient and relatively quick manner. A few decades ago, before the great increase in hedge funds, arbitrage of financial assets was most common on the trading floors of primary dealers and large money-center banks. The proprietary trading desks at these institutions used a variety of arbitrage trading strategies. Many of these professionals have migrated to hedge funds where they continue to practice this art.

Arbitrageurs mainly use a broad convergence-related investment theme. The bedrock principle is that the prices of 2 distinct securities will get closer over time. Managers try to eliminate market-related factors by focusing on the specific return objective of this price convergence. As of June 30, 2002, an estimated $125 billion was inverted in arbitrage-related strategies in hedge funds, or approximately 18% of the total outstanding. Figure 5.1 highlights the estimated distribution of arbitrage-related hedge fund assets. There are 3 primary arbitrage-focused hedge fund strategies: convertible

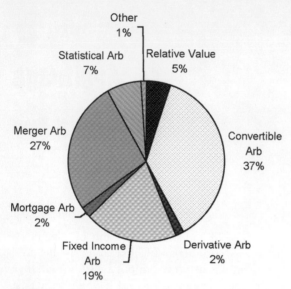

FIGURE 5.1   Arbitrage strategy asset distribution.

arbitrage, merger arbitrage, and fixed-income arbitrage. The latter strategy is much less common after the 1998 collapse of Long Term Capital Management (LTCM). In addition, there is a number of much smaller arbitrage-like specialty substrategies, such as statistical arbitrage, relative value arbitrage, derivatives arbitrage, mortgage arbitrage, options arbitrage, and closed-end fund arbitrage.

According to sources such as Altvest, Hennessee, and Tremont, the major arbitrage strategies have produced average annual returns slightly less than those of the broader hedge fund indices, but significantly better than the S&P or other comparable traditional indices. Table 5.1 illustrates this.

TABLE 5.1   Arbitrage Strategy Returns, 1993–July 2002

	CAGR %	STDev	Beta	R^2
Altvest Hedge Fund Index	16.09%	6.94%	0.32	0.46
Altvest: Merger Arbitrage Index	14.22%	4.11%	0.17	0.37
Hennessee Convertible Arbitrage	9.52%	3.88%	0.08	0.10
Hennessee Multi-Strategy Arbitrage	10.97%	5.41%	0.10	0.10
S&P 500	7.24%			
U.S. Government 10-Year Treasury	9.10%			

TABLE 5.2A Convertible Bond Trade—Example

	Cash Flow
Return When No Change in Stock Price:	
Interest payments on $1,000 convertible bond (5%)	$50
Interest earned on $500 short sale proceeds (3%)	$15
Fees paid to lender of common stock (0.75% per annum)	$ (3.75)
Net cash flow	$61.25
Annual Return	6.125%

CONVERTIBLE ARBITRAGE

Convertible arbitrage takes advantage of mispricing of the embedded option value in a convertible bond. Typically, the manager buys the underlying convertible bond and sells short the corresponding equity.

What must a good convertible arbitrage manager consider? First, he or she must understand the credit quality of the underlying bond, as most positions are inherently long the fixed-income security. This becomes the *sine qua non* of the investment position. Hence, what is the current credit rating, and is that rating likely to change over the investment-holding period? Next, the arbitrage manager must value the implicit worth of the embedded stock option. Is it theoretically cheap? What is the implied volatility of the option? What was it at issue? What does the manager project it to be over the holding period? Both securities should be reasonably liquid; otherwise an illiquidity premium should be calculated and added to the expected return to make the investment more attractive, given potential liquidity risks. Is the underlying stock borrowable and if so, what is the rebate and/or cost to effect this borrow? Finally, is there any possibility of corporate-action risk, any possible event that could trigger a revaluation of the security?

The following 3 tables (see Tables 5.2a, 5.2b, 5.2c) highlight the advantages of this strategy. The first example takes a hypothetical convertible

TABLE 5.2B Convertible Bond Trade—Example: Stock Price Goes Up 25%

	Cash Flow
Gain on convertible bond	$ 250
Loss on shorted stock (50 shares @ $2.50/share)	$(125)
Interest from convertible bond	$ 50
Interest earned on short sale proceeds	$ 15
Fees paid to lender of common stock	$ (3.75)
Net trading gains and cash flow	$ 186.25
Annual Return	18.625%

TABLE 5.2C   Convertible Bond Trade—Example: Stock Price Goes Down 25%

	Cash Flow
Loss on convertible bond	$(100)
Gain on shorted stock (50 shares @ $2.50/share)	$ 125
Interest from convertible bond	$ 50
Interest earned on short sale proceeds	$ 15
Fees paid to lender of common stock	$ (3.75)
Net cash flow	$ 86.25
Annual Return	8.625%

security trading at par, XYZ Corporation with a 5% coupon that matures in one year. This security is exchangeable into 100 shares of XYZ common stock that currently trades at $10 per share; furthermore, XYZ common does not pay dividends. The manager sets up his trade by buying the convertible at $1,000 and selling 50 shares of common stock short at $10 per share. The manager calculates that the intrinsic value of the bond is $900. This value is determined by stripping out the value of the embedded equity option of the convertible. This value should be reasonably close to the value of the company's other outstanding nonconvertible bonds adjusted for the lower coupon typical of most convertibles.

Hence, at setup the investment has the following return dynamics:

This example demonstrates the advantages of properly setting up a convertible bond arbitrage position, wherein the investor should profit not only from the bond coupons and short rebate but from changes up or down in the underlying equity price. If the stock price drops, the gain from the equity short position should exceed the corresponding loss on the long convertible bond position. Accordingly, if the stock price rises, the gain on the long convertible position should be greater than the accompanying loss on the short common stock position. Ideally, the position should generate positive cash flow, defined as bond coupon less stock dividend, less financing cost, plus short rebate. Hedging the convertible bond neutrally against the fluctuations of the underlying equity should also add incremental return whether the stock moves up or down.

Ten years ago, when interest rates were high, the average annual expected return from this strategy was around 20%. Since then, 4 developments have severely eroded the current expected annual return of this strategy to perhaps slightly below 10%. First, interest rates have fallen to historical lows, thereby reducing the current yield component of the return and also reducing the short interest rebate collected. Second, equities volatility has increased substantially in financial markets. Consequently, the embedded option feature is more expensive and requires greater forecasting insight concerning possible extreme movements in the underlying stock price. Third, corporate credit spreads have widened considerably, especially for companies rated below AAA, thereby increasing the overall credit risk of issuers without necessarily offsetting this risk with much higher current yields. Finally, this strategy's great success over the past decade in terms of providing consistent returns has attracted many new practitioners. This increased competition has potentially severely reduced the strategy's inherent arbitrage profits.

Accordingly, over the past few years, convertible arbitrage managers have turned to increased leverage and greater emphasis on short-term trading to augment returns. Over the past 9 years unleveraged convertible arbitrage has produced a compound return of nearly 10% with extremely low— 3.9%—annual standard deviation, making it one of the best hedge fund strategies. However, over the past couple of years, this strategy has experienced overcrowding issues and, with the current low interest rate environment, it will be more difficult to produce similar levels of return with similar historically low levels of risk. For investors considering these strategies, short-term trading prowess will be increasingly important. Pay careful attention to leverage. As average returns have fallen, many managers are employing greater leverage to enhance returns.

MERGER OR RISK ARBITRAGE

With this strategy, investors or managers try to take advantage of the price change of an equity security as a result of a takeover or merger. Typically, the strategy employs simultaneous long and offsetting short positions in the target and acquiring firm's securities, respectively.

Merger or risk arbitrage is a hedge fund strategy that is wholly dependent on the expected price convergence of 2 distinct securities. Typically, following the announcement of a takeover or merger of 2 companies, 1 security, usually the target company's, will rise in price while the acquirer's stock price will fall. As a result of the offer to buy the target company's shares at specific cash or exchangeable share value, their price goes up, although usually not to the full offering price. Instead, because of the risk of the deal not closing on time or at all, the target company's stock will often trade at a discount to the announced takeover price. So this strategy is mostly insulated from the systematic risks of the broader equity market.

Initial trade setup and post merger announcement risk management are the two key components of this strategy. Usually, managers do not speculate on possible or rumor-induced takeover stories. Often, many managers jump on an announced deal very soon following its disclosure. One of the very first determinants of deal performance is how the trade is initially set up and the execution prices obtained at the very outset. Next and equally critical is ongoing assessment of the risk involved in the deal closing on time, terms being revised, and possible cancellation.

In one hypothetical example, Stock A makes a cash offer to buy all the outstanding shares of Stock B at $30 per share. Before the announcement, Stock B was trading at $25 per share. Almost immediately Stock B's price jumps to nearly the offer price. When the merger arbitrageur attempts to put this trade on, he buys Stock B at a 5% discount to the offer price, or $28.50. When the offer is a cash offer, the arbitrageur merely has to buy the stock of the target company; there is no need for an offsetting sale transaction in the acquirer's stock. Why does the price of Stock B not reflect the $30 cash offer price? There is always a risk of the acquisition not closing. There could be serious financing questions—can Stock A afford the purchase? There may be regulatory issues, or large holders of Stock B that will refuse to sell their shares to Stock A. Many things may suddenly cause the offer for purchase to be rescinded and therefore cause a sharp drop in Stock B's price.

A more common transaction in this strategy employs a stock-for-stock funded acquisition,. In this type of merger or acquisition, the acquiring company will bid for the target company's stock by using its own stock as currency. Accordingly, in a stock-funded acquisition, the manager must also hedge against the possibility of the acquirer's stock falling. This is done by selling the acquirer's stock short.

In a hypothetical stock-for-stock transaction, Company A, with stock trading at $105, offers one share of its stock for each share of Company B stock, currently trading at $80. Immediately following the merger announcement, an investor could buy Company B stock at, say, $100, Company B stock having moved up sharply following the announcement. The arbitrage investor would then sell short Company A stock at $105 in an amount equal to the exchange ratio—in this case, 1-to-1. In practice, the acquirer's stock usually drops in price after making the announcement, as short selling pressure pulls down the price. But for this example it can remain at $105. As the merger date draws nearer, this $5 spread will narrow as the prices of Company B and Company A stocks converge. As this price spread narrows, return on the transaction increases. For example, if Company B stock rises to $101 and Company A falls to $104, the investor earns $1 on the long investment and $1 on the short.

Once the merger is complete and Company B stock is converted to Company A shares, the investor locks in the $5 gain regardless of the current price of Company A stock (see Table 5.3). Company B shares are converted into Company A shares, which are delivered to cover the short sale of Company A shares at $105. If, during the interim, the market has tumbled, sending Company A stock down to $80, the investor makes $25 on the short sale of Company A stock at $105, minus the loss of $20 on the

TABLE 5.3 Merger Arbitrage Trade—Example

Buy 1 share of target Company B at $100; Sell short 1 share of acquirer Company A at $105 Scenarios After Merger

	Rise in Stock A to $120	Fall in Stock A to $80
Gain (Loss) on Long	$ 20	$(20)
Gain (Loss) on Short	$(15)	$ 25
Total Gain (Loss)	$ 5	$ 5

Company B shares, for which the investor paid $100. However, if a market downturn causes Company A stock to fall significantly before the merger closes, Company B might back out of the deal. As a cover against a market downturn, some fund managers supplement their merger arbitrage investments with put options on the S&P Index, which enable them to lock in a sell price in the event the broader market falls precipitously. In this way, the investment is shielded from unforeseen market swings.

The average merger and acquisition transaction takes 4 months from the date of announcement to complete. Accordingly, a 5% profit, as demonstrated in the above example, translates into a 15% annualized gain. And with the use of leverage or borrowing, the returns can be much higher.

The greatest risk here, of course, is the risk of the merger falling through. In this case, the stock price of target Company B is likely to return to its original price of $80 or even lower if the market assumes that the deal fell through because of some inherent problems at Company B. The result would be a loss of $20 or more on the purchase of Company B stock at $100 after the deal was announced. Furthermore, if Company A stock drops after the initial announcement, its share price is likely to return to its former price of $105 after the transaction is called off, as all the short sellers cover their shorts. Any investor who shorted the stock at less than $105 then, will incur a loss on the short investment on top of the loss he could incur on the Company B shares.

The vast majority of friendly acquisition offers that are announced are completed. On average, only about 3% of good transactions break. In addition, through diversification across many such deals, fund managers are able to minimize the impact of one deal falling through. Still, as a hedge against collapsed deals, some fund managers supplement their long positions in the target company with puts on the company's stock—but only when the spread is such that the potential profit well offsets the cost of the put. Others, anticipating failed deals, short the target's stock.

Compared to the uncertainty of playing the currently volatile equity markets, arbitrage investments can give relatively consistent returns. The risk of a merger or acquisition falling through is one that a good fund manager can foresee with strong due diligence. Even hostile takeovers are fairly predictable. Careful analysis can determine the strength of a takeover target's legal or strategic defenses, the ability of the hostile bidder to finance the deal, the possibility of regulatory bodies, such as the FTC or the SEC, stopping the deal, or the likelihood of a white knight making a competing bid.

In May 2002, the Canadian gold company Placer Dome made a hostile offer to buy Australian gold producer Aurion Gold. Although Placer was able to buy over 20% of the company's shares, Aurion management made a successful case to a majority of its shareholders that the offer was too low. Placer was forced to increase its takeover price from the original 0.175 Placer shares for every Aurion Gold share to an additional $0.35 per share in cash. Despite this sweetened offer, Aurion management and shareholders continued to rebuff Placer, although it had garnered nearly 30% of the shares. Some arbitrageurs believe that Placer will have to increase its offer again and although there is very little arbitrage profit in this trade today, they continue to buy Aurion Gold shares. Placer could walk away, but investors believe it won't, now that it has acquired so much Aurion stock.

Merger arbitrage returns are largely uncorrelated to the overall movement of the stock market, with the average manager having a correlation of less than 0.40. The risks are much more manageable because they anticipate probable outcomes of specific transactions, instead of predicting far more random variables when making directional investments. The average beta measure in this strategy is a very low 0.17 versus the market.

Merger arbitrage, although it is not highly correlated to the market, is not truly market-neutral, as market downturns can sometimes disrupt the outcome of agreed deals. Merger arbitrage got bad press in the late 1980s when Ivan Boesky used inside information and bought stock in companies before mergers became public. But merger arbitrage is about capitalizing on announced transactions. It starts when a news release on a trading screen, such as Bloomberg or Reuters, announces that a bidder wishes to buy a company's stock. The release, or a same-day conference call, will typically state whether the bid is (1) friendly or hostile; (2) a definitive cash agreement (having board approval), a letter of intent, or proposal; (3) for cash or stock, or a combination of both, and whether this is subject to adjustment; (4) a tender offer (lasting 30 days) or requiring a shareholder vote (lasting 4–6 month); and (5) subject to certain conditions—due diligence, financing, anti-trust, or regulators. The portfolio manager or analyst then analyzes the terms of the proposed transaction, and assesses the likelihood that it will go through.

Merger and acquisition activity has slowed considerably from the frenetic pace of the late 1990s. Many managers have expanded their activities to include cross-border mergers and even to completely non-U.S. company mergers. Like their cousins in the world of convertible arbitrage, the competition among ever-scarcer deals has lowered returns. As returns fall, some managers use increased leverage to maintain double-digit expected annual returns. Hence, the risks of investing in this strategy are greater than at any time in the past decade due to greater competition, fewer deals, and increased use of leverage.

FIXED-INCOME ARBITRAGE

This strategy attempts to capture mispricing across and within global fixed-income markets and associated derivatives. One can often generate added return by exploiting yield curve anomalies; volatility differences; basis trading (arbitraging bond futures versus the underlying cash bonds); and tax loopholes. Typically, one needs a lot of leverage to generate meaningful investment performance. As a convergence strategy, fixed-income arbitrage managers often take positions that approximate one another in terms of rate and maturity, but are suffering from pricing inefficiencies. Risk varies with the types of trades and degree of leverage. In the U.S., this strategy is often implemented through mortgage-backed bonds and other mortgage derivative securities. This has proven to be a very profitable, but relatively unpredictable, strategy. Mortgage securities carry embedded options that are very difficult to value and even more difficult to hedge. Many managers have found attractive opportunities overseas, but are typically reticent about disclosing the specific nature of their trades. Portfolio disclosure in this strategy is hard to come by.

One of the greatest risks associated with this strategy is that the funds depend on repos to leverage their portfolio, and reverse repos to finance their short positions. In the end, they are at the mercy of the broker-dealers for liquidity. Some funds have circumvented this by raising capital via CDOs/CBOs. This locks up the capital for a specified period of time, and prevents fire sales to meet variation margin.

Mortgage-backed fixed-income arbitrage funds have relatively large spreads due to the embedded optionality and difficulty predicting prepayment speeds. A lot of these CMOs don't ever trade in the secondary market. Most managers are forced to go around the dealer community at the end of the month, to get prices so as to mark to market their portfolio. This creates two problems. First, it may be hard to get realistic prices for the securities. This makes the fund a risky investment. Also, since a lot of these CMOs are tailor-made for their original investor, the only entity that will buy them back would be the original broker-dealer that created them in the first place. So, unless the fund trades only in generic Strips, IOs, and POs, it may only get one bid for its portfolio in a time of crisis. Not exactly an enticing proposition.

Often, the best time to invest in these funds is after a market dislocation. Spreads have widened to obscene levels, and it is possible to create a great portfolio without leverage. LTCM happened to start right after the bond market meltdown of 1994, and some mortgage-backed fixed-income arbitrage funds enjoyed outstanding years after 1998 due to the narrowing of spreads after the LTCM and Russian default.

Here are examples of fixed-income arbitrage trades:

"On the Run" Versus "Off the Run" Treasury Arbitrage

Newly issued U.S. government Treasury bonds trade slightly more expensively than similar Treasury bonds that were issued in the recent past. This is because of liquidity. Newly minted bonds are referred to as "on the run," while slightly older bonds are called "off the run." The yield difference between a newly minted 10-year Treasury and a 9.5-year Treasury may be a paltry 8 or 9 basis points, but for the arbitrageur there is an opportunity to sell the newly minted bond and buy the older bond with the proceeds. If the trader can hold the bonds to maturity and use leverage, this trade can turn out to be rewarding with relatively little risk, as the two securities are basically identical except for a 6-month duration difference. The downside with this strategy is that it requires tremendous leverage because of the small price difference. Typical leverage ratios for this kind of trade range from 30:1 to 50:1.

Government Yield Curve Arbitrage

One can sell expensive 3-year and 5-year bonds and buy a cheap 4-year bond. This butterfly structure can be constructed so that it has very little exposure to absolute market levels. It can also be weighted to have minimal exposure to a change in the yield curve's slope. The purpose of the trade is simply to buy a cheap security and use expensive securities as hedges, assuming that the relationship will normalize as traditional investors shift portfolios into the cheap bonds.

Cash/Futures Basis Trading Strategies

In many of the bigger government bond markets, a bond futures contract is typically the most liquid hedging vehicle for a market-making desk. In these markets, the bond that is cheapest to deliver (the most economical bond for the trader who is short the contract to deliver to the long) will trade either rich or cheap to the fitted yield curve. As contracts expire, the cheapest to deliver may change. When this happens, the former cheapest to deliver will reprice until it is back in line with the rest of the curve. A relative value trader may anticipate this event by trading the current cheapest to deliver bond hedged with an opposing position in similar maturity bonds. As the bond falls out of the basket, and reverts to fair value, the trade can be unwound at a profit.

Relative Swap Spread Trades

In many markets, relative value traders will closely monitor bond/swap spreads or bond/euro-deposit yield spreads. The shorthand for these spreads is a TED spread, which is short for a Treasury/Euro-Dollar spread. Typically, a government bond from a G-7 country will yield less than a euro-deposit, because of the credit risk difference. A relative value trader can buy a TED spread (buy a government bond and short a strip of euro-dollar contracts) or sell a TED spread (sell a government bond and buy a euro-dollar strip). In the ebb and flow of transactions, two similar maturity bonds may have very different TED spreads. A trader simply buys the low TED spread and sells the high one. The trade is then unwound when these TED spreads revert to a fair level.

Index Replication Trades

Many of the larger government bond markets have a total-return swap market, which enables investors to pay or receive the total return of one of the industry standard government bond indices. Traditional investors often use such swaps to receive the index return instead of managing a bond port-folio. The relative value trader pays the total return of the index and seeks to replicate the total return of the index in the cash bond market. The trad-er can actually use the technicals of the bond market to his advantage by owning issues, which finance at attractive levels or owning bonds, which are cheap to the curve.

Macro Convergence Trades

Macroeconomic conditions can open up profitable arbitrage situations in many fixed-income markets. Eight years ago, before the full integration of the European Monetary Union, the government bonds of major European countries, such as Germany, Italy, France, and Spain, traded at varying spreads to one another, based upon both the credit rating of the underlying sovereign and the depth and liquidity of the local market. As European economic convergence accelerated with the passage of the Maastricht accords, traders speculated that these spreads would narrow considerably

following full convergence, so many well-known investment bank proprietary desks followed LTCM's lead in structuring very large convergence
trades. In them, the traditionally weaker and less liquid bond markets, such
as Italy and Spain, were bought, and the more developed markets, such as
Germany and France, were shorted, in anticipation that full monetary convergence would also imply similar credit risk and liquidity.

STATISTICAL ARBITRAGE

This is a quantitative strategy that finds highly correlated pairs of securities
that have deviated from their historical pricing relationship. Performance is
derived from mean reversion as the prices of the securities converge back to
their historical relationship.

The trader buys the undervalued security while he sells the overvalued
one. Statistical arbitrage managers typically use classical time series techniques (auto regression, vector error correction, cointegration) and complex
mathematical models to predict and identify recurring trading patterns of
associated securities. Some managers also use statistical decision theory and
game theory in analyzing trading pairs. Statistical arbitrage traders often
track many related pairs of securities while following index price movements, especially as the latter relate to frequent mispricing opportunities.

Statistical arbitrage managers utilize both convergence- and divergence-
related trading strategies. Mostly, these strategies expect that a previously
observed historical relationship will reassert itself after a period of deviation. Index arbitrageurs often sell short an index or index-linked future
against its constituent cash securities when there is a price misalignment.
This is a common convergence trade. Sometimes, a particular security is
halted. Sometimes, there is a large buy or sell program in the index future,
but not in the cash market. Alternatively, divergence trades look for securities' prices to move away from each other.

Although most statistical arbitrage managers primarily utilize a quantitative decision-making algorithm, there are those who utilize more subjective
selection criteria. This strategy is sometimes called relative-value arbitrage.

RELATIVE-VALUE ARBITRAGE (EQUITY MARKET NEUTRAL)

This is a hybrid strategy. Quantitatively inclined managers, who could be
statistical arbitrage managers, as well as more traditional pairs-trading
focused managers, use it. Often, securities that are highly correlated statistically may be traded in pairs using more subjective analysis criteria.
The relative-value arbitrage manager stands by his or her expressed bias
in putting on the trade. In other words, while a quantitative statistical

arbitrage manager may trade a pair of stocks based on a mean reversion expectation, a relative-value arbitrage manager will put on the same trade with more of a subjective investment expectation. The relative-value manager assumes that there is an implied hedging feature in being long and short similar securities in terms of business mix, sector exposure, and investment fundamentals.

A classic, and favorite, relative-value trade for several years was to buy Lowe's Co. stock while selling short Home Depot stock. The subjective criteria used are a belief that valuation and growth fundamentals at Lowe's were superior to Home Depot, while the quantitative criteria focused in on the correlation of the pair, owing to both historical data testing and exposure to the same economic sector. This trade worked well over the past couple of years. Home Depot has considerably underperformed Lowe's Company stock. In the past, this trade could have been in both relative value and statistical arbitrage portfolios, but the newest iteration—to expect a divergence in this trend—exists only in relative-value arbitrage portfolios.

This highlights the risk differences in these two strategies. The statistical manager will observe that the correlation of this pair of stocks has fallen greatly as Lowe's stock price has far outpaced its larger rival, having at the time of this writing, gained 52% since the beginning of 2000, while Home Depot stock has fallen 54%. The statistical arbitrage manager will see no meaningful correlation protection in reversing the trade, while the relative-value manager may put on this divergence trade to short Lowe's while buying Home Depot, despite the pair's low correlation.

OTHER ARBITRAGE STRATEGIES

There are several smaller arbitrage disciplines, which include the established strategies as well as smaller, more opportunistic trading opportunities. These smaller strategies are similarly anchored in arbitrage opportunities, which, although identifiable, quantifiable, and hedgeable, may for practical purposes not be realizable in today's capital market. Accordingly, managers may use more esoteric instruments, such as derivatives, or seek to construct a hedge that is largely a custom-designed product.

Many of these smaller strategies have a relative-value orientation or a quantitative decision-making process. Relative-value-oriented ones include capital structure arbitrage, restructuring arbitrage, and closed-end fund arbitrage. Index arbitrage, options arbitrage, volatility arbitrage, and ADR arbitrage are more mathematically driven. They are all specialist strategies and it is rare to find expertise in each substrategy in any single organization. Only a few large multistrategy arbitrage managers can support such a diverse specialist talent pool.

Capital Structure Arbitrage

You can approach this strategy in 2 ways, explicitly or implicitly. Explicit capital structure arbitrage trades buy and sell highly related securities of the same issuer or in the subsidiaries of a single issuer. For instance, many issuers have more than 1 class of share. The prices of these shares trade in ranges relative to each other, but often move out of line, or information becomes available that implies that a company will merge the 2 classes. Another example is a company near bankruptcy, which may have traded securities of a subsidiary that may survive the bankruptcy of the parent. In this example, the parent company's shares or bonds may be shorted or sold while the securities of the subsidiary may be bought. An implied capital structure arbitrage may be to determine that the sum of the traded subsidiaries of a large conglomerate trade at a premium to the market value of the parent company. In this instance, the implied trade carries a subjective expectation that the market will correct for this undervaluation of the parent company at some time in the near future.

Restructuring Arbitrage

This strategy resembles merger arbitrage in that it concerns itself with corporate dissolution or spin-offs. Typically, a company may engineer a spin-off or carve out a smaller division, often through a dividend, merger or, outright new share sale. The arbitrage manager has opportunities similar to those in classic merger arbitrage; an announced ratio or valuation is placed on the restructuring, but the market does not fully reflect this value in the current price of the security. Sometimes, companies engage in complex refunding plays, such as issuing of rights, or other highly dilutive strategies to meet pressing financial obligations. The market often takes such announcements negatively. This creates opportunities for the astute manager who correctly values the new securities' impact or successful placement. Another typical arbitrage opportunity in restructuring trades involves correctly valuing the debt profile of a troubled company. Correctly buying and selling debts and bonds of such an enterprise can result in significant gains from anticipating haircuts or forced debt revaluations that bankruptcy courts or debtor committees may decree.

Index Arbitrage

This is a statistical arbitrage strategy that primarily focuses on price differences between stock index futures and the underlying stocks. The markets for the most liquid indices are quite efficient. This arbitrage is fairly simple to evaluate and execute. To compete in this strategy, a manager must maintain a very low cost structure and have access to state-of-the-art program-trading hardware.

Options Arbitrage and Volatility Arbitrage

These strategies, often interrelated, are designed to take advantage of mis-pricing between derivatives and their theoretical values. Volatility arbitrage is a directionless strategy that sells short-term call and put options to prof-it from option premium decay and volatility mean-reverting tendencies. The trade is then hedged by buying longer term call and put options to limit downside risk. Volatility differentials can also be exploited in more tradi-tional options arbitrage, which normally scans for pricing irregularities in markets of similar options across time and strike prices. In either case, pur-chasing an undervalued option, whether directly or synthetically, and hedg-ing the position with the underlying security or a more expensive option of the same issuer can express these strategies.

Closed-End Fund Arbitrage

This is a specialist relative-value strategy that exploits implied pricing dif-ferences in the estimated $15 billion closed-end fund universe. Closed-end funds are aging, and they face rapid extinction due to inefficient pricing and poor liquidity. The arbitrageur can exploit the estimated $3 to $5 billion of discounted value in this category via a strategy of activist shareholder tac-tics and clever hedging alternatives. The basic theory underlying this strat-egy is that most closed-end funds trade at 20% to 35% discounts to their net asset value, because of illiquidity and poor sponsorship by market deal-ers. Consequently, an arbitrage manager can buy the discounted fund, short the equivalent portfolio either in the cash or derivative marketplace, and lock in the spread of the current discount.

Unlocking that spread contraction is a challenge. Sometimes, the market will correct it somewhat through mean-reversion, and at other times the manager must become involved in proxy or shareholder activist activities to pressure the closed-end fund company to narrow the gap. A recent example this year was the NYSE-listed Mexico Fund, which was a closed-end fund that invested in Mexican stocks traded on the Mexico City stock exchange. Some closed-end fund arbitrage managers bought a position in this fund, then hedged it via sales of the fund's most recent reported holdings. In the next few quarters, they pressured the manage-ment company to offer to redeem shareholders in cash or in the fund's holdings at net asset value. This specialist strategy can be successful, but it is a niche strategy because of low liquidity and requisite shareholder activism.

ADR Arbitrage

This specialist strategy is among the oldest and least well known of active arbitrage strategies. There is a high barrier to entry, because you need to act fast and have low costs to be competitive. As a result, it is mostly practiced for the proprietary accounts of large dealers and investment banks, and most hedge funds find it difficult to compete. Nevertheless, it is a highly profitable and low risk strategy that essentially relies upon the minute pricing irregularities of similar issues traded simultaneously on different markets in different exchanges and countries. Price difference, currency movements, and the specific impact of local market flows often distort the price of one of the traded securities, and a fast arbitrageur can lock in the difference. As most ADRs and ordinaries are fungible, this allows for trade settlement in the same security. This, in turn, allows for essentially riskless profit, if the manager is fast enough to arbitrage the difference, or has sensitive market information regarding upcoming flows that may temporarily distort the price of one of the securities.

For example, a dealer might know of a large block of Deutsche Telecom stock that is about to be sold on the New York Stock Exchange. The sale drives the price in New York down to 25 cents. The arbitrageur has already sold Deutsche Telecom stock in Frankfurt at higher prices, and now can buy the ADR traded in New York, and instruct the custodian bank to deconstruct the ADR and deliver ordinary Deutsche Telecom shares in Frankfurt against the sale, netting the arbitrageur the benefit of the difference. Although this strategy seems simple, it is highly dependent on low cost and highly automated trading infrastructure.

MULTISTRATEGY ARBITRAGE

Over the past few years, a number of the larger managers who use convergence and arbitrage-related strategies have been offering products that combine various arbitrage strategies under a single umbrella. The larger organizations can shift assets where they see the best opportunities. This dynamic asset allocation helps them take advantage of changing market conditions. Only the largest and most well-funded hedge fund managers can assemble the talent pools this requires.

CONCLUSION

Arbitrage strategies are valuable assets in any alternative investments portfolio. The low correlation and high principal protection are particularly important in a weak equity market environment. Their low relative correlation and low volatility give them great fixed-income characteristics without sacrificing equity-like returns. The recent overcrowding in merger arbitrage and convertible arbitrage strengthens the hand of the largest and most successful managers, who can offer well-staffed and knowledgeable multistrategy offerings.

New strategies and relatively unpopular or small market niches can provide higher relative returns without the concomitant risks associated with the more competitive and larger strategies. Nevertheless, the constant search for market inefficiencies will continue to provide ample opportunity for astute arbitrage managers to make handsome returns for their investors, who, in turn, will be able to sleep well at night, knowing their investments are insulated from the vagaries of market fluctuations.

CHAPTER 6

Global Macro Funds

Gary Hirst

Aqualified investor looking for large capital gains should consider global macro funds. If one had invested $100,000 with the model global macro fund manager George Soros when he started in 1969, it would have grown at an annualized rate of 35%, increasing to $215 million in 1995, assuming reinvestment of all returns.

This fact alone explains why global macro funds are the most talked-about hedge funds. They stand out for 4 reasons. They are often very large. Their positions are sometimes prophetically timely. Their positions are often in currencies, which are the core of all finance. Finally, some global macro fund managers have been assigned near-mythic reputations by the financial press.

WHAT ARE GLOBAL MACRO FUNDS?

Global macro funds may use almost any investment technique to take long and short positions in securities, futures, forwards, options, physical commodities, or any other assets that may even include real estate and venture capital. Their managers' decisions to buy and sell are based on top-down, economic analyses of current macroeconomic conditions, rather than narrower fundamental or technical views of securities' prevailing prices. If speculation means taking positions in assets by forecasting that their values will change, global macro fund managers are pure speculators.

Global macro funds are sometimes confused with the large, long/short equity funds invented by the *Fortune* writer Alfred Winslow Jones in 1949. The name "hedge fund" arose because other financial writers assumed that if a fund were long some equities, and short others, it was "hedged." Now, the term hedge fund usually means any fund that avoids the restrictions imposed on mutual funds, such as limitations on taking short positions, no matter what investment style it follows.

The term "global macro" is also somewhat incorrectly applied to large equity funds like the multibillion-dollar funds managed by Zweig-DiMenna Associates, because they combine macroeconomic market timing with stock picking.

It is sometimes confused with technically driven multibillion-dollar futures funds like those managed by Campbell & Company and John W. Henry & Company Inc., which use completely different investment methodologies.

GROWTH OF GLOBAL MACRO FUNDS

George Soros' Quantum Fund was the first global macro fund, and the only one extant in 1980. Zurich Capital Markets extensive hedge fund database had 2 global macro funds in 1985, 13 in 1990, and 58 in 1999. Table 6.1 shows that the growth of global macro funds has been small compared to the growth of all hedge funds.

Though small in number, global macro funds tend to be large in size. In 1990, the average asset size of a global macro fund was $361.5 million, 8.3 times the average size of all hedge funds, which was $43.4 million. Global macro funds comprised 55% of the hedge fund universe then.

Figure 6.1 shows the size of global macro funds versus all hedge funds over time.

The average size of these funds grew steadily until they peaked in 1997 when there were 61 macro funds, each averaging $1.308 billion in assets

TABLE 6.1 Growth of Global Macro Funds Versus the Total Hedge Fund Universe

Date	Total No. GM Funds	Total No. All Funds	Total GM Assets $mm	Total HF Assets $mm	Average size of GM fund	Average size of any hedge fund	GM fund size times any hedge fund
1980	0	1	0	193	0.0	193.0	0.0
1985	2	22	0	814	0.0	37.0	0.0
1990	13	197	4,700	8,532	361.5	43.3	8.3
1995	40	698	18,807	53,392	470.2	76.9	6.1
1996	50	904	25,510	76,325	510.0	85.1	6.0
1997	61	1,115	79,759	109,576	1,307.5	98.3	13.3
1998	57	1,011	38,152	112,158	699.0	110.9	6.3
1999	58	1,170	24,943	132,128	403.5	112.0	3.6
2000	37	800	10,100	113,500	273.0	141.9	1.9
2001	45	981	6,200	123,600	137.8	126.0	1.1

Figures do not include futures funds.
Source: Zurich Capital Markets.

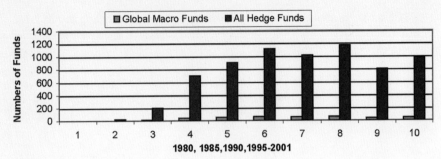

FIGURE 6.1   Global macro versus all hedge funds.

compared with a total of 1,054 other hedge funds with an average size of $28.3 million. In 1997, global macro funds made up 73% of the hedge fund universe.

Figure 6.2 shows the average size of global macro funds versus all hedge funds over time.

By the late 1990s, some global macro fund managers had retired. Others returned assets to shrink their funds because they believed that market opportunities for them had reached capacity. The number of global macro funds, and their size as a percentage of the hedge fund universe, declined. The number has begun to rise again, but global macro funds' total assets, as a percentage of the total hedge fund universe, continue to decline.

Figure 6.3 shows the asset growth of global macro funds versus all hedge funds over time.

In 2000, there were just 37 global macro funds out of the total universe of 800 hedge funds, and their average size was twice that of all hedge fund. By the end of 2001, there were 45 global macro funds in a total universe of 981, but their average size was only $137.8 million in assets versus the average size of all hedge funds, which was $126.9 million.

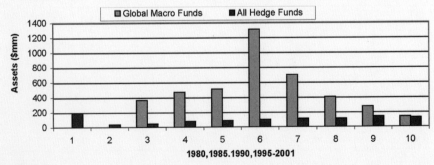

FIGURE 6.2   Average size of global macro versus all hedge funds.

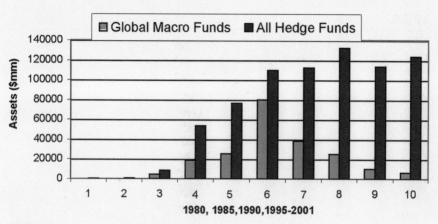

FIGURE 6.3 Asset growth of global macro versus all hedge funds.

Some say that the day of the giant global macro fund is over. Others say that all the managers who handled mega-funds have retired, and there are no good global macro fund managers left in the world. However, investors should remember that almost no one had heard of George Soros in 1980, but by 1986, he was very well known, and after 1992, he was a household name. Good macro fund managers are out there now. One day, the general public will consider some of them great. It's up to investors to work hard to identify them, and have the discipline to stick with them for the long term.

GLOBAL MACRO FUND RETURNS

Global macro fund managers tend to target annual returns of 15% to 20% net of fees. From 1990 to the present, the average annual return from all global macro funds was 15.36% versus 14.67% from the hedge fund universe as a whole. Compared to total hedge fund returns, global macro funds are more volatile. Table 6.2 illustrates this. In the high return years, their performance more than justified investing in them. In 1990, for example, global macro funds produced a median 20.15% return, 2.5 times more than the median return produced by all hedge funds, which averaged an 8.22% return.

In 1991, global macro funds earned 40.69% versus 25.15% for the entire hedge fund universe. This outperformance of the hedge fund universe continued until 1994 when global macro funds lost 4.37% versus a small positive return of 3.85% for all hedge funds. Since then, they have tended to keep up with or underperform all hedge funds.

Figure 6.4 shows the returns of global macro funds versus all hedge funds over time.

TABLE 6.2   Returns of Global Macro Funds Versus the Total Hedge Fund Universe

Date	Total GM Returns %	Total HF Returns %	GM to HF Return ratios
1990	20.15	8.22	2.45
1991	40.69	25.17	1.62
1992	16.94	13.60	1.25
1993	33.80	21.85	1.55
1994	(4.37)	3.85	—*
1995	17.54	18.09	0.97
1996	11.82	17.88	0.66
1997	18.24	18.29	1.0
1998	3.74	7.07	0.53
1999	11.56	23.85	0.48
2000	7.50	11.69	0.64
2001	6.76	6.44	1.1
Average Annual Return	15.36	14.67	Average GM to HF return ratio 1.05

*Ratio not calculable.
Source: Zurich Capital Markets.

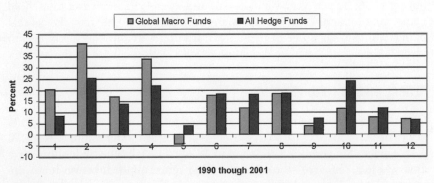

FIGURE 6.4   Returns of global macro funds versus all hedge funds.

Given the current worldwide economic changes, and the way global macro fund managers take positions, this strategy still has the potential to outperform the hedge fund universe.

HOW GLOBAL MACRO FUND MANAGERS TRADE

Global macro fund managers are unique because of their broad knowledge of all markets. They are top-down analysts of world economic conditions who are able to translate their views into timely market decisions by investing in any asset class, anywhere in the world.

George Soros, the progenitor of global macro hedge funds, is the best example. Soros has become a very attractive model for current global hedge fund managers simply because, on balance, he has earned an immense amount of money for himself, and for investors who had the discipline to stay with him for a long time. He described his ideas and his career in 2 books, *The Alchemy of Finance* and *Soros on Soros*. His public image, as a heroic loner against a hostile world in which he does great deals against all odds, is universally appealing. He is a mythic figure.

Soros became rich by recognizing large-scale financial imbalances or the beginnings of large-scale trends that even experienced traders had not yet detected. Ironically, now that he is in his early 70s, Soros is not terribly rich, nor does he want to be.

He concluded in 1980 that $25 million is enough for anyone to live on. Since then, he has literally given away most of the money he has made, to rebuild and strengthen the economic institutions of Eastern Europe in general, and his native Hungary in particular, which were destroyed by the imposition of Soviet communism in Eastern Europe after the Second World War. His background, ideas, and actions can offer some useful rules about how to choose global macro funds, and who their clients should be.

THE ARCHETYPAL MANAGER

George Soros was born in Budapest in 1930. His father, born in 1896, served on the Russian front in the First World War. He was captured and sent to Siberia, from which he escaped. He became a lawyer. Conditions in postwar Hungary, the rise of National Socialism in Germany, rising anti-Semitism in Hungary (the Soros family was Jewish), hiding under false identities during the Second World War, and the Communist takeover honed his survival skills. Soros says that it was this particular survival talent of his father that led him to take up speculation as a profession.

Soros left Hungary in 1947, and earned a degree at the London School of Economics where the Austrian-born British philosopher Karl Popper tutored him. Popper was a critic of logical positivism. He believed that social and political progress can only be made one step at a time. Popper later became a friend. They forged an important intellectual relationship that led to Soros's theory of how markets work.

Though he began his professional career as a toy salesman, Soros quickly turned to merchant banking in 1953. In 1956, he went to New York to work as an international stock arbitrageur. He caught the

European stock investment boom that swept Wall Street in the late 1950s, first as a securities analyst and trader, and later as an institutional salesman writing reports on European securities. The foreign stock boom lasted until President Kennedy introduced the interest equalization tax that imposed a 15% surcharge on foreign investments in 1961. This destroyed the foreign stock investment business overnight.

From 1961 to 1963, Soros spent time on a philosophical dissertation while he worked on Wall Street. He also set up a model portfolio to generate institutional business, which he explained was very valuable. "Testing your views is essential in operating in the financial markets," he said.

He started a long/short equity hedge fund with $4 million in 1969 for Arnhold & S. Bleichroeder. When he left in 1973, he had $12 million under management. He renamed his fund the Soros Fund, and his leading analyst Jim Rogers followed him as a junior partner.

In 1978, he changed the name to The Quantum Fund, invested in technology, and did well until 1980. From September 1981 until 1984, he ran The Quantum Fund as a fund of funds. However, these were lackluster years, the worst being 1981. The fund was down 26% in September, and ended that year down 22%.

CREATING A PHILOSOPHY OF FUND MANAGEMENT

Soros decided to become an active manager again. Arguably, he should be given credit for creating the global macro management style. He began to position his assets to take advantage of larger trends he called macro trends. Within these larger trends, he picked stocks and stock groups. In 1985, he added currencies to take advantage of his analysis of a major shift in currency values brought about by the Plaza Accord.

In 1985, he also began working on *The Alchemy of Finance,* which would be published in 1987. It describes his investment method. He wrote with the idea that the management of his fund would be a real-time experiment that would stimulate his thinking.

On September 22, 1985, the Group of Five decided, in a meeting at the Plaza Hotel in New York, that the dollar, which had been very strong during the early 1980s, was too high. They entered an agreement to depreciate the U.S. dollar.

Soros analyzed the situation, went long the yen, and later wrote that the real-time experiment in September 1985 contributed to his successful currency position. He wrote that the strategy "paid off handsomely." The fund returned 114% in a 15-month period, in part because of leverage. "I already had a position," he said in *Soros on Soros,* "and could afford to increase it and go for the jugular."

REFLEXIVITY

The core of Soros' philosophy of investing, rooted in his personal experience, is that people's understanding of the world is inherently imperfect. He notes that people seek to understand situations in which they participate, but facts and their perception of those facts usually differ. Thus, it is their perceptions of facts that make up reality. It is an interpretation inspired by physicist Werner Heisenberg's Uncertainty Principle, stated in 1927, which says, "The more precisely the position is determined, the less precisely the momentum is known in this instant, and vice versa."

Soros saw similar behavior in markets, so he theorized that there is an innate divergence between the expectations of the people taking part in events and the actual outcomes of those events. Sometimes, this divergence is so small that it can be disregarded. Other times, it is so large that the divergence itself becomes an important factor in determining the course of events.

On the one hand, there is what Soros called the cognitive function. Reality is reflected in people's thinking. On the other hand, there is what he called the participating function. People make decisions that change reality, something that occurs quite often in markets.

The 2 functions work in opposite directions, so they can interfere with each other. The interaction between them takes the form of a 2-way reflexive feedback mechanism, what Soros called "reflexivity," which is the core of his analysis for trading.

People cannot obtain perfect knowledge of the market because their thinking is always affecting the market, and the market is, in turn, reacting to their thinking. This makes analysis of market behavior much harder than it would be if the assumptions of perfect knowledge in classical economics were valid. Soros believes that because of this, there is an element of uncertainty in economic processes, which has been largely ignored.

Reflexivity is a radically different view of the role that people's reactions play in shaping events. A chain of events is not made up facts, as classical economics assumes. The links are facts to the participants' thinking that connect to other participants' thinking to the next set of facts. This means that one cannot confine one's thinking to facts. One must take into account the thinking of all participants including one's self. In *The Alchemy of Finance*, Soros illustrated this thesis with the conglomerate boom of the 1960s, the REITS in the early 1970s, and the international boom of the late 1970s that culminated in the Mexican crisis of 1982.

In financial markets, prevailing trends reinforce each other until the gaps between them become so wide that they bring about catastrophic collapses. There are also static disequilibriums, rarely found in financial markets that are characterized by very rigid dogmatic modes of thinking that can prevail for a very long time until change occurs. The Soviet Union is an example.

Soros insisted on formulating a thesis before taking a position. His famous British pound trade is the best example of how global macro managers think and act, and it also illustrates why currencies are often their most profitable arena.

THE IMBALANCE OF THE BRITISH POUND

When *The Alchemy of Finance* came out, people talked about it, but not many understood it. One reason was that Soros had failed to position his fund properly for the Crash of '87. All this changed in 1992, when, according to the popular press, Soros was the man who broke the Bank of England, a misrepresentation engendered perhaps by the archetypal myth of the hero triumphant against titanic financial forces. Nevertheless, the reporting of this event established global macro managers in the public mind as the best and the brightest of all asset managers.

In fact, what Soros did was to identify a massive imbalance or disequilibrium. It began when he recognized sometime in 1992 that for macroeconomic reasons, the British pound was overvalued against the Deutschemark and the U.S. dollar.

In April 1992, sterling was at $1.75. It rose until early September reaching a high of $2.00, then fell dramatically to $1.52 by the end of the year. Soros set positions to take advantage of this, and earned more than $2 billion on a leveraged $10 billion that he ultimately committed to this idea. The foreign currency markets were so large then that his positions did not move the market when they were set. No other markets could have yielded so much in so short a period of time, which is one reason why global macro fund managers use currency markets. Currencies are the world's largest and most liquid markets.

This situation illustrates how global macro managers, in general, think. The imbalance that Soros saw was a series of mistakes being made by the UK government. His theory of reflexivity described exactly the British government's imperfect understanding of their situation.

The Bank of England created an unworkable arrangement when it agreed, in the Maastricht Treaty, to maintain a sterling exchange rate within a narrow band against the Deutschemark. Obsessed with the possibility of inflation because of the unanticipated expense of unification with East Germany, Germany kept a lid on inflation by increasing interest rates. Meanwhile, Britain was in a recession, but had agreed to the European Exchange Rate Mechanism. High interest rates would only exacerbate its situation. Something had to give.

Unwilling or unable to see the conflict, the British were stuck in a high interest-rate policy, and even raised interest rates twice in a single day. To make matters worse, on September 15 and 16, the Bank of England used a total of $24 billion of their U.S. dollar reserves to buy sterling, cutting their then current reserves of $44 billion to less than half.

Realizing that they would have to abandon this policy, the British announced they were withdrawing from the Exchange Rate Mechanism. Soros had analyzed the situation correctly, and established and maintained currency positions that effectively shorted the British pound. He earned instant international fame for himself in particular, and for global macro hedge fund managers in general.

CHOOSING A GLOBAL MACRO FUND MANAGER

As George Soros' story should suggest, the manager is more important to the success of a global macro fund than to the success of other hedge funds. He or she must understand how the entire financial world works. Global macro managers must understand how central banks and monetary authorities function. They must understand the *de jure* and *de facto* political constraints under which they operate. They must also understand the cultural milieu in which they function.

For example, German central bankers, some of whom still recall stories of the runaway inflation of the Weimar Republic, make inflation fighting their first priority. They must understand that the U.S. Federal Reserve has three responsibilities: to fight inflation, to maintain a healthy economy, and to uphold orderly financial markets. The new European Central Bank is charged only to fight inflation.

Knowledge of how currencies behave is critically important because from 1986 to the present, some 50% of returns from non-U.S. equities, and as much as 70% of returns from non-U.S. fixed-income securities, have come from currency fluctuations.

General experience is another criterion for choosing a global macro manager. He must have inquisitiveness, intellect, and experience to grapple with the most diverse and complex global investment challenges of the day.

Can the manager give you a cogent justification of his performance? What exactly is his investing style? Soros noted that he tried to change his style of investment to fit current economic conditions, and that over the years, The Quantum Fund had "changed its character many times." Has the manager changed his investment style during the lifetime of the fund? If so, why?

CHOOSING A WELL-MANAGED GLOBAL MACRO FUND

It is most important to understand a manager's investment philosophy and how disciplined he or she is. One must ask how much capital can be managed efficiently with the strategy a particular fund is using. Global macro funds tend to be larger than others.

Who makes the important decisions? Are decisions delegated to oth-ers? If so, to what degree, and what is their experience? For the first few years of his fund, Soros made all the decisions. He delegated authority in 1981, and resumed full authority in 1984. By 1987, he had delegated all of the decision-making responsibility to a very small number of managers for whom he acted as an overseer, guide, and coach.

In 1966, George Soros made up a $100,000 model portfolio as a sales tool to develop business with institutional investors. This was the forerun-ner of his Quantum Fund. He found very quickly that his prospects and clients accepted his good ideas. They rejected the bad ones. He concluded that testing one's views is essential to operating in financial markets. Prospective managers should explain how they test their ideas, and with whom they discuss them.

Decision-making for the global macro funds run by Martin Zweig and Joe DiMenna, which are patterned on Soros' original concept for The Quantum Fund, is divided. Martin Zweig analyzes macroeconomic condi-tions, while Joseph DiMenna picks the stocks that the funds will be long or short. It is very important to understand how decisions are made, who makes them, and who has the final say.

LEVERAGE

Hedge funds seek absolute returns. They usually use leverage. Leverage is not easy to quantify because there are different ways of creating it. The notional amount of leverage itself is not important *per se*. What is impor-tant is how a manager is using the leverage. Volatility is an indicator of how leverage is being used. It can be quantified by risk statistics including Sharpe Ratios and similar measures.

ATTITUDES TO CLIENTS' ASSETS

In 1934, John Templeton, a student at Yale, walked by a New Haven bank where he had $100 in a checking account. Seeing a long line, he realized there was a run on the bank, and that his money was as good as gone. He went into the bank and asked to open a savings account. The astounded clerk deposited his checking account holdings into a new savings account even though he was completely at a loss as to why this young man was put-ting money into a bank that was surely going out of business.

Templeton did what he did because he had learned in a money and banking course at Yale that the U.S. had just insured bank savings accounts for 2% of their total value, but that checking accounts still had no insurance. Templeton's value-based reasoning was that the $2 saved was better than nothing. He was repaid $2 by the U.S. government some 2 years later. Will the manager whom you hire think this way about saving clients' assets? Good asset managers are dedicated to preserving their clients' capital.

APPROPRIATE INVESTORS

The only appropriate investor for a global macro fund is one who understands a manager's philosophy of asset management. If a prospective investor were doing his or her own trading or investing, would he or she be comfortable using the same strategy as the manager of this fund? It is a dangerously simple question because investors are often seduced by high returns.

As has been shown, global macro funds tend to be at the higher end of the volatility spectrum. Investors who become concerned during periods of disappointing returns may not be suitable investors for global macro funds.

Does the investor have a strategic investment plan? Is he or she psychologically able to stick to this plan? The greatest danger for investors lies in abandoning their well-thought-out investment plans during periods of underperformance. Investors must plan for these contingencies. They must also have the discipline to follow their strategic investment plans in times of temporary tactical setbacks. If the normal variation of returns of global macro funds would cause an investor to abandon his or her investment plan, this type of fund is not a suitable investment.

HOW MUCH TO INVEST

An investment in a global macro fund should not be too large a percentage of an investor's total net worth. For conservative investors, it should certainly be no more than 10%. For aggressive investors, perhaps up to 20% might be suitable. These are arbitrary figures that can only serve as guidelines.

For any investment, consistent performance is the most important criterion, simply because the way to wealth is compounding positive returns every year. When they make money, global macro funds should add significant incremental returns to a well-diversified portfolio. When they don't, their underperformance should not have a negative impact on total portfolio returns.

CONCLUSION

Used properly, good global macro funds are worth the effort it takes to find them. They can offer a proven means of capturing a significant source of returns over the long term that few other asset management styles can provide. With proper money management, global macro funds can play an important role in well-managed portfolios.

CHAPTER 7

Managed Futures

Frank Pusateri

Futures trading is risky business, according to conventional wisdom. Anyone who uses 10 or 20 times the value of something as leverage is taking a risk. Most individual investors who trade futures are thought to lose money. They tend to be undercapitalized, carry overly large positions, and lack a systematic approach to trading the markets. Moreover, most investors have not developed the risk control and money management necessary to survive a string of losing trades. They trade futures part-time and compete with professionals who trade for a living.

Managed futures provide those investors who are aware of the benefits of futures trading an alternative way to enjoy the advantages of trading futures.

INTRODUCTION

A U.S. Commodity Trading Advisor (CTA) is a money manager who trades mainly futures. The Commodity Futures Trading Commission (CFTC) and the National Futures Association (NFA) regulate U.S. CTAs. Investors can invest with an individual CTA through an individual account or a commodity pool. Investors can also invest with a group of CTAs selected by a commodity pool operator (CPO) or a sponsor in a commodity pool. Many investors are invested in futures or with CTAs through vehicles in which a percentage of the assets are allocated to futures trading. The required minimum investment for a CTA or a commodity pool can be as little as $2,000 or more than $1,000,000. Investors in managed futures include individuals and institutions, such as pension funds and endowments.

Many investors avoid managed futures because they have an unfamiliar structure and terminology. Futures are forward contracts. A trader buys or sells something that settles at some time in the future. The trader does not pay for what was bought, or borrow money to finance the purchase.

Instead, he or she makes a good faith deposit. If the price goes too far against the trader, the trader must put up additional funds to hold the position. Words like initial and maintenance margin, leverage, and notional funds come up in this context. The terms "commodities" and "futures" seem to be used interchangeably, but seem to mean different things.

Brokerage firms that handle futures transactions must have separate registrations as Futures Commission Merchants or Introducing Brokers. Industry professionals are generally required to obtain a Series Three registration. Potential investors who want to have an account managed by a CTA have to open a separate commodity account using a completely different set of account forms. Many firms and industry professionals avoid managed futures because of these complications.

Information about managed futures may not be readily available. Daily closing prices are not published in most local newspapers. The financial press does not publish many articles on managed futures, and rankings of CTAs and CPOs are hard to come by in the mass media. A key word search on the Internet under "futures" yields over 800,000 entries, about 7,000 for managed futures and just over 2,400 for commodity trading advisors. Few of these seem useful in selecting a CTA or CPO.

The taxation of futures profits and losses requires the filing of a Form 6781. This is totally different from forms for stocks, bonds, or mutual funds. Positions are marked to market annually and taxed as if they have been closed out at every year-end. They are arbitrarily allocated 40% short-term capital gains and 60% long-term capital gains.

So why consider managed futures?

Trading futures can add diversification to an investment portfolio. Futures can be the investment vehicle one uses to take advantage of economic uncertainty. Profitable futures trading opportunities require only that prices move. An uncorrelated investment in futures may improve a portfolio's overall return for a given level of risk.

Physical commodities like corn, crude oil, and coffee have futures contracts. Financial futures allow the trading of stock indices, foreign currencies, and interest rates. Global exchanges allow easy access to foreign stock index and interest-rate futures. In futures, it is just as easy to go long as short, and the cost and financial requirements are the same.

Last but not least, there are exceptional futures traders. Some of them have achieved significant absolute returns for investors for more than 20 years. Outstanding traders in any investment vehicle are hard to find. Arbitrarily limiting one's universe of traders based on what they trade is not an intelligent investment decision.

FUTURES EXCHANGES

Most U.S. commodity exchanges were founded in the middle to late 1800s. Many earlier examples of commodity trading show that forward contracts are not new. The first known commodity contracts were agricultural and included grains, butter, eggs, and cotton. They were designed to be settled by delivery of the physical commodity. Later contracts included precious metals like gold and silver. In the 1970s, foreign currency and interest rate futures were introduced. In 1982, stock index futures began trading. Futures contracts since then have proliferated in number and type. Futures contracts are global with major exchanges in London, Paris, Germany, Japan, and Singapore. Futures contracts are denominated in most of the world's major currencies, including the U.S. dollar, the Japanese yen, and the British pound. Their trading volume just over 40 years ago was under 5 million contracts annually. According to *Futures Industry*, the magazine of the Futures Industry Association, the Chicago Mercantile Exchange (CME) alone did over 120 million contracts in the first quarter of 2002. The 3-Month Eurodollar futures, which trades on the CME, did over 50 million contracts. The Euro-Bund futures, traded on Eurex, did over 47 million contracts.

The futures exchanges provide an organized marketplace for trading standard contracts of a specific commodity with a specified quantity and quality (grade), with settlement or delivery at a predetermined time. Different commodities may have contracts that vary in size and margin requirements. For example, the New York Mercantile Exchange gold contract has a size of 100 ounces, a current price of approximately $300/ounce, a total value of about $30,000, and an initial margin requirement of about $1,350. The Chicago Mercantile Exchange S&P Index futures contract has a current quote of around 1032, a total value of about $260,000 and an initial margin requirement of about $20,000. Futures contracts can be offset at any time during market hours prior to expiration, thereby closing out an open position and establishing the position's profit or loss. The profit or loss on the open position on almost all futures exchanges is settled when the position is offset.

Futures exchanges usually provide a continuous market during market hours, through either pit or electronic trading. The trader has both liquidity and price discovery. In times of extreme price uncertainty, a trader may be unable either to execute a trade or to execute it at the price on a quote machine. Prices are set by bids and offers. If everyone wants to buy and no one wants to sell a futures contract, there is no liquid market. Some exchanges have price limits. The futures contract cannot trade beyond a certain price range for a given time period. Quote machines show prices, not volume, for each trade. One contract traded creates a price. This does not mean that any significant volume has been traded at a specific price.

U.S. futures exchanges have clearinghouses, which are the counterparty for each trade. The clearinghouse guarantees the settlement and payment of financial obligations. The clearinghouse's assets, and the guarantees and deposits of its member firms back this guarantee. This eliminates the counterparty risk associated with the over-the-counter markets.

Futures contracts are traded on leverage. Initial margins typically range from 5% to 10% of a contract's total value. Stock Index futures tend to have the highest initial margin requirements. A relatively small margin deposit can control a commodity position of up to 20 times its value. A small price move, like from $300/ounce to $310/ounce in the price of gold, results in a profit or loss of $1,000 on an initial margin requirement of about $1,350. Funds on deposit in a commodity account often earn interest even when used to margin trades.

Detailed information on most futures exchanges, and their contract specifications, are generally available on the Internet. The exchange web sites are listed in most of the Internet's financial directories.

MANAGED FUTURES HISTORY

The Managed Futures Association's "Major Events in the History of the Managed Futures Industry" states that the first commodity fund was started in 1949 and the first known managed account to be traded by a CTA was opened in 1965 with $2,000. The mid-1970s saw the offering of the first public commodity funds. The first public multiadvisor fund began in 1976, and 1980 saw the first CTA managing over $100 million. By 1981, CTAs were managing around $1 billion. Today, Campbell & Co., Inc. manages over $2 billion and the Managed Account Reports database lists CTAs that currently manage around $30 billion.

COMMODITY TRADING ADVISORS

CTAs come in all shapes and sizes. Some are one-person shops and others have dozens of employees. Some trade their own money and others don't. Some are managing as little as $100,000 and others over $1 billion. Some trade futures as a hobby, but most are full-time professionals. Some have glossy brochures and professional marketing staff, and others believe performance speaks for itself. Many of the best CTAs find that size is an advantage in trading and have minimum account sizes of $1,000,000 or more. Most CTAs with large minimum account sizes have a commodity pool for smaller investors.

Most CTAs offer market and business experience, a systematic trading approach and a history of redundant success to the potential investor. Not every CTA does this. Some have little or no track record. Some even admit to losing money and think they have a better plan for the future.

CTAs are allowed to present simulated performance, also called hypothetical performance, showing how their trading would have done had they traded. This is usually done where the CTA is using a trading system that can be back-tested. Unprofitable simulated track records don't seem to exist. Often, a CTA will show great returns in simulated trading, and fall apart in actual trading. There are better and worse ways to back-test a system. Unfortunately, every CTA presenting a simulated track record believes he or she has back-tested the system the right way. It is extremely difficult to tell otherwise.

CTAs generally trade using either technical or fundamental analysis of the markets, or a combination of both. CTAs who pick and choose from some combination of technical analysis for indicators and/or fundamental analysis are generally called discretionary. They still have systematic approaches to trading the markets. They just haven't programmed their trading approaches into a computer. Long-term successful CTAs almost always use a disciplined trading approach.

Most CTAs are technical traders and trend followers. A technical system is testable on historical data and leaves no room for discretion. It eliminates subjective factors. Technical analysis of the markets is generally based on the study of historical daily, weekly, or monthly commodity prices, volume, and/or open interest. Technical traders tend to utilize charts of prices and/or computers to identify historical patterns that they can model mathematically, to determine if they were profitable in the past. They use the profitable models to trade, with the assumption that these historical patterns will recur. If these market price patterns recur, the CTA's investor accounts will make money. To cope with the possibility of changing markets, many technical CTAs periodically reevaluate their models based on the most recent price data.

The successful technical CTA uses the computer as a tool just like paper and pencils, and understands the limitations of the computer. The smart trader is aware of how easy it is to fool oneself. It is easy to curve-fit a model to the past and show that one would have bought the market lows and sold the market highs. Models that fail tend to be overly complicated. It seems the more variables a model has, the less likely it is to be profitable in the future. CTAs use different timelines to develop their models. Some use as little as 3 years and others use over 20 years. Those CTAs who use the most years feel safer assuming that future markets will behave like past markets. The CTA also must decide whether to trade the same parameters for every commodity or to customize the parameters to each individual commodity. Again, CTAs using the same parameters believe the additional data points gained by testing across multiple commodities make for safer assumptions.

After having identified one or more profitable trading models, the technical CTA must develop a trading program, including what to trade and how much of it. Is it the model that makes the most money or the model with the best return-to-risk characteristics? How does one define risk, volatility, drawdowns, or risk of principal? Should the CTA trade one model or multiple models? What does the CTA do if the model is very profitable in financial futures and unprofitable in physical commodities? Does one want to trade a model that is parameter-sensitive or one that isn't? The computer can process enormous amounts of data on hundreds of markets, but in the end the CTA has to decide which commodities and models to trade.

Fundamental analysis is based on the study of the external factors that affect the supply and demand of a particular commodity, and forecast price moves and prices. Such factors might include weather, government policies, and domestic and foreign political and economic events. Fundamental CTAs must still manage risk. It is possible to be right on one's forecast—a correct drought prediction, for instance—and yet be wrong on the market. Markets prices do not have to react as the CTA has forecast. The markets may already reflect the expectation of a drought. They may not care if there is a drought. Fundamental CTAs usually have a methodology for liquidating a losing position. Once in a while, a fundamental CTA shows up whose answer to losing money is to add additional positions. No significant CTA in the industry does this.

Savvy CTAs, in addition to developing a systematic trading approach, also manage their position and portfolio risk. They attempt to keep their losing trades small so they can continue trading. CTAs often try to limit their risk on any one position to 1–2% of account equity. They try to mix and match the commodities they select so that their positions cannot all lose at the same time. Some manage overall long and short exposure, not wanting to be long or short too high a percentage of their portfolio. Others limit their total long or short position in individual market sectors. For example, if they trade 6 currencies against the dollar, they may limit their net long or short position to no more than 4.

Successful CTAs attempt to preserve capital during losing periods. At a loss of 1% of account equity per trade, a CTA would have to lose on 50 trades in a row for the investor to hit a 50% stop loss without ever having made a profitable trade. At a loss of 10% of account equity per trade, the stop loss is hit after 5 trades. Obviously, the latter is much likelier.

Over the last 20 years, a few significant events have severely tested CTAs' risk control and money management. Many investors and CTAs don't consider event risk because it is quite infrequent. The U.S. grain embargo, the OPEC oil embargo, the Gulf War, and President Carter's dollar defense plan all significantly changed futures values. Futures contracts that were thought to have uncorrelated price movements did not diversify.

Long crude oil and long gold positions during the Gulf War reacted similarly to war news. Event risk is real and the CTA who is a survivor plans for it.

Many CTAs recommend that investors close their accounts if they lose a certain amount (stop loss). This amount usually ranges from 20% to 50%. Some CTAs will automatically liquidate an investor's account at the stop loss. Most wait for instructions from the investor and treat the stop loss strictly as a recommendation. A stop loss is not a guarantee. The actual prices at which an account is liquidated will determine the actual loss.

CTAs trade different portfolios of futures contracts. Some trade only one contract; others trade over 100. The CTA trading everything ensures participation in any major price move. For those trading large numbers of commodities, a major price move in any one commodity might have little or no impact. They may need major price moves in 10 or 12 markets to show a profit. In a concentrated portfolio, a small move may cause major profits or losses. Some CTAs use less initial margin to control risk and others use more, so that they can control their risk by spreading their market exposure across numerous commodities. Some CTAs position size based on volatility and others have fixed position sizes. Portfolios with more contracts tend to have larger minimum account sizes, but less volatility. Larger account sizes allow for more sophisticated risk control and money management. The CTA's choice in a $50,000 account boils down to whether or not to trade a futures contract. In a large account, the CTA can decide to trade a contract of any size up to the maximum position.

While a CTA is allowed to use the entire equity in a client's account for initial margin, the typical CTA will use between 5% and 50%. This leaves funds available to meet maintenance margin calls, should the prices go against their open positions. CTAs size their accounts to have a cash reserve so they can absorb the worst drawdown they expect, and still keep trading. The CTA in fact uses less leverage than is available. Some CTAs, whose initial margin requirements are less than 10%, are using little or no leverage.

Many CTAs size their accounts to provide not only initial margin and a reserve for their expected worst drawdown, but also an additional reserve they do not intend to use. Sophisticated investors have determined that a $200,000 account of a CTA who has a maximum initial margin requirement of $20,000 and who recommends the account be closed at down $40,000, can be funded with $60,000. The CTA does not really need the extra $140,000, for which the investor may have a better use. For track-record proposes, the $140,000 is called notional funds. CTAs who accept notional funding include disclaimers about the risks in their disclosure. The investor should be aware of the fact that the 10% loss in a $200,000 account shown in the CTA's track record is a 33.3% loss on funding of only $60,000.

Specialized programs trading specific futures or market sectors do exist. Common types widely offered in the last 10 years trade financial, energy, and grain portfolios. In the past, specialized programs have capitalized on current public interest. When gold and silver prices were skyrocketing, metal portfolios were common. Today, after years of quiet precious metal markets, specialized metal portfolios have generally disappeared. Instead, there is an abundance of specialized portfolios trading stock indices. Investors like to short the stock market. A few CTAs trade spreads. They may be long a commodity like soybeans and short the products of processing soybeans—soybean meal and soybean oil.

All futures traders don't solicit investors under the label of managed futures. In the early 1980s, a commodity pool was established to trade interest rates using cash and futures. Today, such a fund would most likely be marketed as a hedge fund and not refer to managed futures, even though it traded futures and was registered as a commodity pool. If they started over again today, many of the futures industry's most successful CTAs would probably operate as hedge funds. Many global macro hedge funds trade mainly futures. One should select and evaluate these traders just as one would select and evaluate a CTA.

An investor opening an individual account to be managed by a CTA gives the CTA a limited power of attorney. This allows the CTA to execute trades for the investor's account. The CTA has no access or control over the funds in the account. The funds reside in an account in the investor's name at a brokerage firm. There are generally no restrictions on the investor's closing of the account. The investor is responsible for all the expenses associated with trading. These may include brokerage commissions, exchange fees, NFA fees, and give-up fees. The investor usually authorizes the brokerage firm to pay the CTA's fees from the account.

CTAs are generally paid a management fee and an incentive fee. Most investors accept this statement as fact and assume that there is a standard way of calculating fees. There isn't. Management fees seem to run from 0–2% annually, and are charged monthly or quarterly, either in advance or arrears. Incentive fees are generally 20–25% of profits and are generally billed quarterly. Some CTAs do not charge incentive fees on the interest earned in an investor's account and others do. Some CTAs charge management fees on the profits the investor leaves in an account, even if they do not trade them. Profits can be defined as trading profits or the change in account equity adjusted for deposits and withdrawals. Using the change in account equity should reduce profits for previously paid fees. CTAs sometimes negotiate fees. It never hurts to ask.

Most CTAs will trade between 1,000 and 5,000 contracts per $1,000,000 in investor equity. They consider 6 months a long-term trade and some will hold a trade for as little as one day. The trend toward lower commission rates has allowed CTAs to profitably trade shorter term positions. CTAs do not intend to take delivery on contracts and will usually liquidate the investor's positions before delivery. The investor will receive a Confirm or Purchase and Sale Statement from the brokerage firm, documenting the daily transactions in his account. The investor also receives a month-end statement that recaps the month's activity. The investor with an individual commodity account will get lots of mail. With all this information, it is tempting to review one's investment on a daily basis. This is a bad idea. Those who are worried about what is happening on a daily basis should not be investing with a CTA. They will have losing trades. It is okay to have losing trades; losing trades are part of making money.

Most Commodity Trading Advisors registered in the United States with the CFTC are required to provide a disclosure document to potential investors. This document provides the investor with the same standard information for each CTA—among other things, the CTA's principals and their backgrounds, any administrative, civil or criminal actions, their trading approach, what they trade, how they are paid, and their track record. The standardized track record format does not leave much room for creative accounting, so it is fairly easy to compare CTA performance. Footnotes to the track record disclose the definitions by which the record was prepared.

One area of the track record that deserves additional attention is interest. Some CTAs show little or no interest, and others go as far as including proforma interest. In a high short-term interest rate environment, a CTA showing proforma interest could show performance 5% or more higher than a CTA showing little or no interest, strictly as a result of the interest calculation. The same CTA could show a 10% annual return on a 10% drawdown or a 15% annual return on a 10% drawdown. While CTAs are allowed to limit their history to the last 5 years, it is fairly common practice for CTAs to give their history and track record since inception. Any CTA who does present limited information should be asked why. CTAs who solicit only sophisticated investors—called Qualified Eligible Persons—who meet criteria for income and net worth are not required to supply the same standardized information, and some choose not to.

Registered CTAs who are soliciting or trading investor accounts are also required to be members of the NFA. The NFA is the futures industry's self-regulatory organization. The NFA has adopted standards for training and experience. It screens all individuals and firms who wish to become members. The NFA audits members for compliance with its rules and regulations. A CTA's audit will include a review of the CTA's promotional literature, disclosure document, track record, and record-keeping. Both registered CTAs and CPOs are subject to an audit review by the NFA. They generally expect to be audited every 2 to 3 years. The NFA web site, www.nfa.futures.org, shows if a CTA or CPO is involved in any regulatory actions, NFA arbitration awards, or CFTC reparations cases.

Not every commodities trader has to register. Small traders and small commodity pool operators may be exempt if they do not solicit. Foreign currency traders who trade the interbank market are exempt. Brokers trading with a power of attorney may not have to register. Therefore, they don't have the same disclosure requirements.

COMMODITY POOLS

A commodity pool is a vehicle by which investors combine their capital to speculate in futures. This usually allows the investor to invest with CTAs who would otherwise be unavailable and can provide better cost structures, administrative convenience, and limited liability. Commodity pools are offered as both public and private funds. Units in a commodity pool are sold to investors through a security offering, with a prospectus.

There is no typical structure for a commodity pool. Pools have been done in the U.S. as both Limited Partnerships and Limited Liability Companies. Both protect the investor against the loss of more than the investor's initial investment. General Partnerships, which are rare, do not. Profits or losses are passed through to the investor for tax purposes. Brokers selling a commodity pool may receive compensation from a front-end load, which is charged to the investor or deducted from the investor's investment. CPOs and CTAs are compensated with various combinations of management fees, incentive fees, interest, and commissions. Some pools have one trading advisor and others have two or more. Some are designed to replicate overall CTA performance and are called index funds. Others guarantee the return of the investor's initial investment after 5–7 years. Some guarantees are achieved through the purchase of bonds and others are based on the credit rating of a guarantor. Some guaranteed pools increase the amount of the guarantee annually if they are profitable. Investing in a guaranteed fund does not ensure good results. In fact, some guaranteed pools reduce the funds committed to trading in order to provide the guarantee. Most pools do not pay out profits. Investors who leave their profits in a commodity pool are increasing their trading size.

Commodity pools do not generally allow the investor to see the specific positions they hold. They also generally limit the investor's liquidity by restricting redemptions to a monthly, quarterly, or yearly basis with some notice. Most commodity pools have a liquidation clause so that if the initial value of a fund unit declines 50% the pool will be liquidated and the proceeds will be distributed to the investors. This is not a guarantee. It is possible to lose more than 50%.

In a multiadvisor commodity pool, the operator is responsible for selecting the CTAs, and the allocation and reallocation of capital across them. The CPO usually has the resources to review hundreds of CTAs, and the clout to conduct a detailed level of due diligence. For example, CPOs usually visit the office of each CTA they are seriously considering, and they periodically visit ones they hire. The CPO can usually get copies of a representative account to verify the CTA's track record and to analyze the actual trades. The CPO of a multiadvisor pool tries to combine CTAs who have different trading styles, creating a portfolio of CTAs who profit in different types of markets, to reduce risk and have a smoother equity curve.

Many CPOs for large institutional investors will run a separate portfolio of individual accounts or a separate pool for the investor. Often, the investor will participate in the selection of the CTAs. This way, the investor gets the advantage of a commodity pool without some of the disadvantages.

HOW TO CHOOSE A COMMODITY TRADING ADVISOR

The investor who decides to include managed futures in her portfolio has to choose a CTA or a CPO. Many investors ask an industry expert to guide them. Some follow the expert's advice and others use the expert to narrow the potential pool of CTAs to a reasonable number that they can review in depth. Most experienced professionals have more information than the average investor could find. For example, watching the day by day performance of other client accounts managed by a CTA can give substantial insight into any risk that has been masked by monthly data. When obtaining professional help, it is good to find out how the expert gets paid. It is not unusual for an account executive to be paid part of the CTA fees. This should be disclosed. Account executives paid by CTAs are incentivized to promote only those who will pay them.

The investor who decides to go it alone is faced with the problem of how to select 1 CTA from the hundreds available. Picking next year's best-performing advisor or even 1 ranked in the top 10 is really just about luck. No one can predict the future. No one can point out next year's best-performing stock or mutual fund. Unless one can predict the types of markets that will occur—trending, choppy, etc.—and which markets will have major trends—energies, currencies, etc.—the best one can do is pick an advisor who will be successful if there are profitable trading opportunities and who will protect one's principal if there are not. The longer one lasts with a CTA, the greater the likelihood of profitable trading markets.

Everyone has some idea of how the stock market did last year. The financial press is continually publishing ratings of mutual funds by category. One knows if plus 20% or minus 10% was good or bad compared to the universe. With commodity trading advisors one also needs to develop a perspective. Was plus 30% average, above average, or below average? Was the 30% average made on no drawdown based on month-end performance, or a 50% drawdown? How did similar traders perform? It is possible to obtain the performance of other similar CTAs and create one's own benchmark? There are also services that publish indices of CTA performance, broken down by trading approach and portfolio.

Many investors would do better if they had realistic expectations. For example, high returns are always accompanied by high risk. No matter what the track record says, there are no risk-free returns. CTAs have profitable periods and losing periods. Some investors inevitably open at the start of a losing period. Closing their account because of initial losses just guarantees that they lose. With a little effort and some redundant planning, investors are more likely to find a CTA they are comfortable staying with, should they start in a losing period.

One of the worst mistakes an investor can make is to open a managed account with a CTA who does not satisfy the investor's investment needs. The investor should start by defining his objectives. What is he hoping to accomplish by investing in managed futures? How much is he going to invest? For example, the investor who is worried about inflation is probably better off with a CTA whose portfolio is heavily weighted to physical commodities.

A $1,000,000 investment has access to more CTAs than a $5,000 investment. The investor should decide whether or not he is willing to invest in a commodity pool. He should decide how experienced the CTA should be both in length of track record and equity under management, and in other realms. He should define his profit objective, his tolerance for risk, and whether or not he would be more comfortable with the trading of particular markets or a particular trading style. This information can be used to quickly eliminate CTAs who do not fit the investor's goals.

Because it is fast and efficient, it is easiest to narrow the potential universe of CTAs by the use of statistics. It is comforting to select a CTA from a universe that has done well in the past. Again, one must keep in mind that there are no risk-free programs managed by CTAs. Investors will find 1-, 2-, or 3- year track records that, based on month-end performance, show high returns with little or no risk. It is best to be skeptical. The risk is there and it always appears, sometimes as a very unpleasant surprise.

There is no correct method for picking a CTA. The final selection should really be a qualitative one. The investor is not hiring a computer; he is hiring an individual or group of individuals. He is seeking future performance, not past performance. He is dependent on the CTA's ability to analyze the markets, even if they are 100% systematic. Someone had to pick the markets and the system, or systems, the CTA trades.

Quantitative Analysis

Selecting CTAs based only on statistics involves some dangerous assumptions. The most dangerous is that past performance has some bearing on future performance.

CTAs are required to use a disclaimer—"Past Performance Is Not Necessarily Indicative Of Future Results." The predictive ability of past performance is the subject of continuous debate, not only in managed futures but also in more traditional investments, like mutual funds. One should use past performance to rank traders by a return-to-risk criteria, or to evaluate a CTA's performance against an index of similar CTAs to get to a small number of CTAs to review in detail.

Statistics assume that a limited number of month-end data points (there are only 60 in the required 5-year track record for a CTA) are statistically significant, and that these points tell one everything one wants to know. This, at the very least, assumes that a CTA's worst drawdown coincides with month-ends. A drawdown is more likely to start during a month and end during some other month. This means the month-end numbers will understate the drawdown. At no time will the month-end numbers overstate the CTA's drawdown. Statistical analysis also assumes that the CTA has made no changes to the trading program or the commodities traded.

Most of the available statistical data is based on the performance published in the CTA's disclosure document. While CTAs are required to provide performance tables for the program they are offering, these tables may not tell the investor enough. If the CTA has multiple account sizes, the table's returns may not reflect the account size the investor wants to open. Larger accounts often trade more commodities and have less risk. Other clients who opened their accounts earlier with the CTA may have fee schedules that are lower. Large accounts may have lower commission rates.

Some people believe that a 100% gain followed by a 50% loss means a profit of 50%. This is only true if the investor took out the profits or did not double the position sizes when she was up 100%. It is possible to have a performance table that shows positive percentage returns while the sum of the dollar profits is negative. Data can be misleading if one does not take the time to understand them.

Performance analysis should not be limited to checking the numbers. Absolute returns do not tell the entire story. Some CTAs take more risk than others, so for any given time period they may be more profitable. Some use more margin. Risk is a very hard variable to quantify. Some people use the

Sharpe Ratio even though it uses volatility as a surrogate for risk. Volatility is not necessarily risk. A CTA who makes a positive return of between 0% and 10% monthly may be very volatile, but not very risky. Volatility calculated over time periods—daily, monthly, or annually—often yields different rankings when comparing CTAs.

There are many ways of ranking CTAs, and new, "better" ways are being devised all the time. They can be ranked by absolute return, return to some measure of risk, or by return to money used, either initial margin or initial margin plus the dollar risk. The issue of ranking is further complicated by the question of time period. Most professionals try to choose a time period that includes different types of trading markets, some trending and some not, or a period covering times when the average CTA has been both profitable and unprofitable. There is no perfect answer. Most professionals use multiple types of rankings to ensure that the CTA they are interested in is highly ranked on a variety of measures.

Investors tend to use dollars lost as risk. Some use losses on initial principal and others losses from peak month-end equity. There is a difference. Is an account that went from $100,000 to $150,000 to $120,000 risky? Depends. The account never lost any money, but did fail to keep all its profits. It had either a 20% or 30% drawdown, depending on the denominator.

Long-term trend followers tend to exit a position after the trend has reversed. Some in the 1980s might have bought gold at $400/ounce, ridden it to $800/ounce and got out when the price dropped to $650/ounce. At 100 ounces/contract, the trend follower's track record might show monthly profits totaling $40,000 on one contract followed by monthly losses of $15,000 without ever making a second trade. Is there risk in this trade? Yes. Did the investor ever have a loss? No.

There are data vendors in the futures industry who provide information, statistics, and rankings of CTAs. Some of them provide information not found in the CTA's disclosure document, such as average margin requirements and round turns per $1,000,000 invested. Most of them are on the Internet. The Managed Funds Association, at www.mfa.org, maintains links to many. Some provide data on the Internet and others are publishers. Some are free and others fairly expensive. The oldest vendor is called Managed Account Reports. A partial list of other information sources would currently include Autumn Gold Investments, IASG, Barclay Trading Group, Traderview, and International Traders Research. They have rankings, and investors can prepare their own after buying databases. Every CTA is not in every database, so it is advisable to look at 2 or 3. There are also a lot of statistical packages available, for more or less money.

Does a new account always have the same risk and/or performance as established accounts? Would it have suffered the same drawdown as a fully invested account? Many CTAs manage the positions they open for new accounts to avoid major drawdowns. Many will only buy or sell new positions. Others put on a combination of new positions and low-risk existing positions. These CTAs manage the risk to one's initial investment. The risk to this in the first months of trading may be substantially different from the risk when one is fully invested. Newcomers' account performances may differ from the performance of established accounts.

CTAs do have limits on the number of contracts they can trade. This may be an exchange set limit or it may be a market limit set by what they can execute. These limits tend to impose a maximum on the amount of money a CTA can trade. As a result, many CTAs with long successful track records are not taking new investors. A CTA may get too big. Their slippage in order-execution prices from what they expect may increase so that the cost of executing a trade increases. They may not be able to trade additional contracts for new investors because of exchange limits. The CTA is often tempted to trade other futures contracts to be able to take additional investors. Does this change make any evaluation using the past track record invalid?

When combining CTAs in a portfolio, many investors and professionals use correlations to find CTAs that complement each other. This involves few data points. Also, investors should not be concerned if the CTAs make money in the same month. They should be concerned if they lose money in the same month. If one only uses losing months, the number of data points is much too small.

A track record, even if one does not believe in statistics, can provide some important information when combined with some questions. Long track records show success in surviving. They may even indicate the CTA has adapted to different market environments. Comparative performance shows how the CTA did compared to a peer group. Improved performance compared to a peer group might indicate the CTA has learned from past mistakes and has become a better trader today. Deteriorating performance raises questions.

Qualitative Analysis

It is possible for a CTA to have a great track record and very few profitable trades. In the late 1970s, it seemed like a good idea to select CTAs using statistics. The author identified a CTA with great numbers. He was not alone. It turned out that the CTA had been long coffee for something like 3 years and the profits from this 1 trade were so large, they masked the losses on the other trades. Investors need to know where and how the money was made so that they can assess whether or not this can be repeated.

A review of a CTA's individual trades, if possible, reveals the source of the CTA's profits, and whether or not the CTA does cut losses short. Such a review should include percentage winners/losers, average gain/average loss, profit or loss by futures contract, largest winning trades, and largest losing trades. The best CTA is the one who made money when expected and controlled losses when there was no money to be made. The CTA should not depend on any one market for profits, but should cut losses and follow the trading approach described in the disclosure document. Investors can look for changes in the trading approach over time. They can compare this information with similar CTAs' records. If the average trend-follower shows profits on 40% of the trades and one shows profits on 80%, it is time to ask what the performance would have been if the percent of profitable trades were average.

Many professional asset allocators have developed questionnaires that they use to help evaluate CTAs. The questions usually explore in more detail information the CTA has already provided on a general basis. They might request specifics of the advisor's trading strategy, such as a listing of the markets the CTA has made a profit in and what length trend is necessary for a profitable trade. Risk control and money management are usually explored to determine if the CTA's answers show a different risk than the track record. Many CTAs name a risk percentage higher than their track record shows. The evolution of the trading strategy and any historical changes, along with current research and planned changes, help to evaluate the relevance of past performance. Unfortunately, most CTAs seem to know what the correct expected answers are.

Many professionals prefer CTAs who are students of the markets, who have a passion for trading. They feel these CTAs are always watching, always questioning, and always wondering if there is a better trading methodology somewhere. Others worry about organizational skills, the ability to handle losses, and increased equity under management. Skeptics believe it does not matter how you enter a trade. They believe that money management and risk control make a successful CTA. With the proliferation of computing power and the availability of commercial packages for technical market analysis, it is important to determine a CTA's competitive edge.

One can find a competent CTA who should profit if the markets provide profitable trading opportunities. One might even select the best CTA or one in the top 10. It's possible to improve the odds. Any 10 experts in managed futures will probably have 10 different ways to select a CTA. But there will be some common ground. The CTA needs to survive long enough for the trading approach to have a fair chance at working. Trading approaches end up designed to be profitable in certain types of markets. Some require long trending markets, others choppy markets. Few CTAs will be profitable in all kinds of markets. Some CTAs use multiple systems to profit from different types of markets. Many have unsuccessfully looked for indicators that would forecast the market environment so they would know which system to trade. Successful CTAs have the resources to ride out the swings in the markets.

INVESTMENT STRATEGY

Investors in managed futures should seek the rewards necessary to justify the risk of futures trading, and the time and effort they put into researching CTAs. Why take the trouble to invest in futures to make 10% to 15% per year, when the stock market has compounded at over 10% annually?

Systems do seem to stop working. CTAs who have been successful for years suddenly have no winning trades. It may be because there are too many people trading the same system, attracted by the CTA's success. It may be that the markets do change. It may be the CTA is too big and the added execution costs are too high a burden.

There is much debate over whether any value is added by proactive investment management as compared to passive investment management. While one can prove statistically that the investor will profit from buying dips in performance, few, if any, investors have the patience necessary to use such a strategy. Rebalancing among several CTAs can be a good strategy.

Someone who invests in managed futures with the expectation of making 20%, and immediately makes 40%, has achieved her objective, and should consider taking profits. If one makes money, one should keep some of it. No one knows how high is up, but everyone sooner or later suffers a drawdown. Salespersons find it easiest to promote CTAs after periods of high performance. New accounts should not be opened after unusually profitable periods.

Investors need to find the best possible cost structure without sacrificing expertise. Too many investors are too cost conscious. They end up with the CTA who works the cheapest. They end up getting what they paid for. CTAs who charge only incentive fees inevitably have back-to-back losing quarters and no cash flow. After all, they are running a business. A business with no cash flow and ongoing expenses is not a successful business.

It is important to establish one's stop loss before trading. No selection procedure is perfect. Even the best of asset allocators makes mistakes. The best time to establish one's parameters is before starting. It is the time the most rational decisions are made and the time in which the investor should set objectives. Analysis of the CTA's historical track record and outright asking the CTA will help establish a stop loss. It is amazing how many intelligent investors will decide to stay one more day again and again after they have hit their loss limit.

There are better and worse ways to close an account. Because of the prevalence of incentive fee compensation in the managed futures industry, the investor has an incentive to stay with a losing CTA. Many people will dis-agree with this philosophy, but one should never turn a substantial profit into a loss. It's best to put some money in one's pocket if money has been made.

Investors should diversify their investments if they can. If one CTA makes money in long trending markets, and a second makes money in whipsaw markets, in all likelihood the combination will provide a smoother equity curve. One problem with this is that each CTA is usually paid a sep-arate incentive fee, so it is possible to be paying one CTA incentive fees while you are losing money overall. Some CTAs have multiple trading strategies in the same account. They might trade a long-term trend-follow-ing program and a short-term momentum program to smooth their ac-counts equity and to limit risk.

PERFORMANCE MONITORING

The selection of a commodity trading advisor should be accompanied by a method of monitoring ongoing performance. Does the CTA fit the investor's objectives? Is the trading program working as she expected? If she hired a CTA who trades physical commodities to protect against inflation, and the CTA stops trading physical commodities, the CTA should be terminated. If she expected low volatility and the daily numbers show high volatility, it is time to reconsider. If the CTA hits the stop loss, it is time to close the account.

Monitoring should be designed to identify potential problems as soon as possible to limit losses. Sometimes, advisor performance deteriorates. This can be due to changing markets, size, or system obsolescence. An investor should continually compare an advisor's current performance to past performance, and to the performance of similar advisors.

CHAPTER 8

Manager Searches and Performance Measurement

Meredith A. Jones
Milton Baehr

The amount of money directed into hedge funds in 2002 was staggering for an asset class that in 1998 was called on the carpet for nearly bringing down the entire market. At that time, Long Term Capital Management (LTCM) and its consortium of financial wizards was rescued by an unprecedented bailout organized by the Federal Reserve, causing a furor in the financial press and prompting inquiries by the House Committee on Banking and Finance. Despite dire predictions about the future of hedge funds and rumors of potential increased regulation, the hedge fund industry today enjoys steady growth and has generally benefited from the demystification spurred by LTCM.

In fact, with the proliferation of hedge fund databases, consultants, conferences, and literature, it is perhaps easier to jump into the hedge fund arena now than it has ever been. And with mutual funds and the markets flagging, the incentive to invest in hedge funds is perhaps stronger than ever. However, the lessons of LTCM, and other unfortunate hedge fund experiences should not be shunted aside in a race for capital preservation and higher returns. Careful selection and screening of managers remains the key to bolstering portfolio returns.

SOURCES OF HEDGE FUND MANAGER DATA

Databases

Since the mid-1990s, hedge fund databases have been a favorite hunting ground for investors seeking a hedge fund manager. Antoine Bernheim started the trend in 1990, when he published the first *U.S. Offshore Funds*

Directory. This book, which gave investors one of the first glimpses into the "secret" world of offshore hedge funds, reported annual returns, assets under management, strategy, and contact information on 78 funds. Managed Account Reports (MAR), Tass Management, and Hedge Fund Research (HFR) followed suit, publishing directories of U.S. and offshore funds, beginning in 1994.

However, perhaps the most significant battle of the hedge fund revolution was won on May 29, 1997, when the SEC released a no-action letter to Lamp Technologies, Inc. This letter gave Lamp, and the other data vendors that would later rely on the letter, the ability to disseminate information on its password-protected website about private investment companies exempt from registration under Section 3(c)1 and 3(c)7 of the Investment Company Act of 1940. In the original Lamp offering, funds were charged a fee for posting their results on the site and were restricted from offering any services or products for sale. Furthermore, all visitors to the site had to be accredited and agree to a 30-day "cooling off" period.

Shortly thereafter, the database race was on. Upstart Alex Shogren of Tuna Capital, LLC was one of the first out of the gate. In late 1997, he launched HedgeFund.net, a free online database of hedge fund information for investors and hedge fund managers. In 1999, with the backing of Tremont Advisors, Hedgeworld.com entered the fray. Altvest, which started as a consortium of family offices and was later purchased by Investor-Force, was the next to start a hedge fund site. Soon, accredited investors needed to look no further than their search engine to find thousands of hedge fund listings. (see Table 8.1)

TABLE 8.1 Hedge Fund Data Vendors

Company	Availability
HedgeFund.net	Free
Barclay Global Hedge Source	Commercial
Eurekahedge Asian Hedge Fund Database	Commercial
Hedge Fund Intelligence (AsiaHedge, InvestHedge and EuroHedge databases)	Commercial
Morgan Stanley Capital International	Commercial
Tass/Tremont	Commercial
Hedge Fund Research (HFR)	Commercial
U.S. Offshore Funds Directory	Commercial
MARHedge	Commercial
Altvest	Commercial
Hennessee Group	Proprietary
Van Hedge Fund Advisors	Proprietary

Today, the only real decision seems to be how much one should spend to get access to hedge fund information. While the quality and quantity of information available in free databases is often maligned, how much difference truly exists between fee and free databases?

A quick comparison of 3 leading data vendors—HedgeFund.net, a free online alternative investment database that contains approximately 2,400 funds, Hedge Fund Research (HFR), and Tass, subscription-only databases that contain approximately 1,850 funds and 2,000 funds, respectively—yields some perhaps surprising similarities. Mid-2002 releases of each database show that performance data appears to be updated consistently by each provider. Approximately 30 days after month-end, 82% of the funds in HedgeFund.net had reported performance, while 83% of HFR funds and 85% of Tass funds had also reported. After 60 days, 90% of the HFR funds had reported, while 91% of the Tass funds and 93% of HedgeFund.net funds had reported through the same period. "Funds" are defined by the databases as limited partnerships or separately managed accounts. Figures may include U.S. and offshore funds, funds of funds, Commodity Trading Advisors (CTAs), and long-only managers, as well as multiple share classes of a fund. It is also important to note that HedgeFund.net is currently the only database that retains defunct or non-reporting funds. These funds were removed prior to making the above calculations.

In terms of qualitative information, all 3 databases list basic contact information and strategy descriptions for the managers they cover. Some information that can be used in the screening process, however, is missing from the HedgeFund.net database, which relies on managers to input their own data. It does not always indicate whether or not a fund uses leverage, which is of utmost importance to those concerned about unrelated business taxable income (UBTI). This is income from leverage that is taxable, even if the investing entity is normally tax-exempt. As a result of UBTI, most tax-exempt institutions prefer to invest in funds that use no leverage or are domiciled offshore. The HedgeFund.net database also doesn't generally show whether a fund is listed on an exchange (useful to those setting up funds of funds in Europe), whether there is an offshore vehicle, or whether it employs geographic specializations.

Finally, in a spot review of data, most monthly returns were entered exactly the same. The largest discrepancy for an annual number was less than 50 basis points, hardly enough to influence an investment decision. However, when qualitative data was examined, it was often different between 2 or more of the databases. It is probably a good idea, therefore, for investors to double-check this information.

The real difference between the three databases appears to be simply the universe covered. The list below shows the number of hedge funds that are "exclusive" to each database, indicating that often funds will choose to report to only 1 database.

Database	Number of Funds	Number of Exclusive Funds
HedgeFund.net	2,400*	1,100*
Tass	2,000	700
HFR	1,850	500

*Including defunct or nonreporting funds.

Many of the funds included in the pay databases but excluded from HedgeFund.net are larger, more recognizable funds. In fact, it seems that HedgeFund.net often attracts emerging managers with less than $25 million under management, while Tass and HFR have a greater number of funds with more than $500 million under management.

	<$25 million	<$200 million	>$500 million
HedgeFund.net	900	200	60
Tass	720	260	85
HFR	800	230	80

Generally speaking, larger funds, being less hungry for assets, do not feel the need to cast a wide net, preferring the relative obscurity of a fee-only or proprietary database to an easily accessible listing on the Internet. For those interested solely in larger funds, one of the subscription or proprietary databases could provide the best selection of hedge fund managers. For those investors looking for a complete sample of hedge funds, access to multiple databases, whether fee or free, is a necessity.

Investors looking for funds off the beaten path can also access proprietary databases. These databases often contain information on larger funds, closed funds, and funds with ultraconservative legal counsel that will not permit them to freely disclose their information. Van Hedge Fund Advisors International, Inc. and The Hennessee Group both maintain proprietary databases for their consulting clients, as well as for their internal use. While these databases do contain gems not easily discovered, except by simple word of mouth, accessing them usually involves subscribing to a comprehensive consulting package. Therefore, before contacting a company that maintains a proprietary database, one must first make a decision about the level of service one needs to venture into the hedge fund arena. Consulting services are generally available for a fee between 25 basis points and 1%.

Industry Publications and Websites

Additional resources for hedge fund investors are industry publications and websites. MAR was one of the first to produce a monthly hedge fund publication. In recent years, the number of periodicals devoted to alternative investments has grown substantially. *Hedge Fund Alert*, Infovest21, *EuroHedge, Alternative Investment News, Private Equity Week*, HedgeWorld.com, Albourne Village, and others all provide information on hedge fund openings, closings, frauds, blowups, and strategic partnerships. Some publishers, including *EuroHedge* and *MARHedge*, list funds and performance in their monthly publications. In some cases, investment professionals leaving other firms to start their own hedge funds relay information to hedge fund publications as a way of raising awareness of their new fund, and encouraging seed capital. Others, like Infovest21, have gone so far as to schedule regular miniconferences to introduce managers to prospective investors.

Prime Brokers, Administrators, and Word of Mouth

Prime brokers are also a good source of hedge fund manager data, especially for emerging and smaller funds. Large institutional clearing firms like Bear Stearns, Bank of America, Morgan Stanley, and Goldman Sachs provide the lion's share of prime brokerage services to hedge funds. In fact, of the funds that named their prime brokers in HFR, HedgeFund.net, and Tass, over half of the managers in each database reported using one of these firms as their prime broker. Even more reported clearing some portion of their trades through one or more of them.

Many of the large brokerage houses also run hedge fund incubators, where managers entering the hedge fund fray can devote time to trading while the prime broker deals with such issues as location, back office, and execution. Developing contacts at the various prime brokers can help identify top talent early.

Other service providers have also become involved with raising assets for hedge funds and can serve as good sources of hedge fund data. Offshore administrator Citco got into the advisory business in 1996 and continues to introduce several funds (which it also administers) to clients. Royal Bank of Canada also introduces hedge funds to clients, and has provided leverage for those clients who wish to maximize their hedge fund returns. Bank of Bermuda, another offshore administrator, started an Australian incubator called the Kangaroo Fund in 2001. Even the funds themselves are getting into the game. In November 2001, Mesirow Advanced Strategies, a multimanager hedge fund, teamed up with Adam Brass and Jeffrey Izenman to form a new hedge fund incubator, raising $375 million in seed capital from hedge fund-savvy investors, such as Bear Stearns.

Indeed, despite the SEC embargo on hedge fund advertising, it is hard to avoid information on hedge funds these days. But perhaps the oldest method of discovering hidden gems remains one of the best: word of mouth. Networking with other hedge fund investors is a tried and true method for picking up the name of a new manager or two. Alternative investment conferences have proliferated over the past several years, with organizations such as the Institute for International Research, Information Management Network, Financial Research Associates, and others offering a menu of conference topics and locales from which to choose. These conferences offer great opportunities to network with hedge fund investors and managers alike.

Analytic Software

As hedge fund databases proliferated and more investors became interested in adding hedge funds to their portfolios, the need for analytical software grew. Although firms such as Ibbotson, Möbius, and Micropal had developed software, it was primarily focused on traditional, long-only managers and did not adequately address the issues involved with analyzing alternative investments. These existing products concentrated on benchmark analysis and paid little attention to absolute returns, which are a hallmark of hedge fund investments.

Data suppliers like MAR (in conjunction with Burlington Asset Management) and Tass developed software so they could better market their databases to alternative investors. Recognizing a need for a comprehensive alternative investment software solution, Strategic Financial Solutions, LLC developed the PerTrac Asset Allocation and Performance Measurement System. First released in 1996, PerTrac was the first product to combine both qualitative and quantitative information, and address both benchmark and absolute returns analysis. PerTrac also featured an open-ended data structure that allowed users to perform asset allocation across multiple databases, be they traditional or alternative. Several firms have followed PerTrac's lead, developing software to help their clients search for hedge fund investments. Altvest, for example, has developed a product that generates statistical reports on those managers in the Altvest database using web-based software. With the demand for hedge fund analytics increasing, even software providers from the traditional investment world, like Ibbotson and Zephyr, are trying to ease into the alternative market.

With the variety of investment analysis options, it is up to the investor to determine his or her needs before making a software purchase. It is important to remember, however, that hedge funds require different investment tools from traditional investments. The ability to search for qualitative information is an important function that any analysis package should contain. Also, as noted above, it can be helpful to have access to multiple databases to get the most complete hedge fund universe from which to select investments. Therefore, the ability to import and review information from multiple data vendors is essential. Other functionalities, such as custom-report generation and stress testing, may be desirable, based on one's specific investment needs.

MANAGER SEARCHES

Developing an Investment Mandate

Perhaps the most critical stage in any manager selection process involves the investor asking and answering some hard questions. Clarifying the investment mandate is crucial before manager screening can begin. Investors have to clarify their risk/reward objectives, look at their overall portfolio, and do some soul-searching before getting swept away by returns.

Take, for example, a hypothetical investor who, in 1999, was attracted to a manager simply because he posted consistent 2 percent gains each month, regardless of market conditions. Drawn in by stability and high returns, the investor subscribed to the fund. Shortly thereafter, the manager began to post losses and three months later, redemptions were suspended. The investor, needless to say, was unhappy, but was locked in the fund while it unwound positions.

What did he miss? While the fund did meet our ficticious investor's risk/reward profile (low risk, consistent high returns), it also had several underlying characteristics that the investor did not fully appreciate and that were incompatible with his investment style. The fund invested in Regulation D private placements, which, since they are private placements in a public company, are not particularly liquid instruments. Furthermore, the portfolio companies tended to be small biotech and technology ventures, with market caps between $75 million and $300 million, further constraining liquidity during periods of market stress. Finally, because no ready market exists for the securities, the portfolio was marked monthly with a theoretical pricing model. What had been steady 2% gains became losses as the securities in the portfolio were actually liquidated and therefore *de facto* marked to market. Had the investor asked himself some thoughtful questions before making the investment, he might have saved himself some grief.

In developing an investment mandate, one should consider the following: What is my risk/reward profile? What does "risk" mean to me? Is it the risk of not achieving a certain return or the risk of losing money? If a fund delivers high returns, can I handle double-digit drawdowns? What is the minimum return necessary for this investment to positively impact my portfolio? What kinds of investments (small/mid/large caps, private equity, real estate, cash management) do I have and what kind of diversity do I require? Do I have a bias against certain types of instruments (asset-backed securities, technology or biotech stocks, public or private convertibles, micro cap stocks)? What are my liquidity requirements? Will I need to redeem capital each year for taxes, expenses, etc.? What reservations, if any, do I have about portfolios that are not marked to market?

Quantitative Screens

Selecting Meaningful Comparative Statistics
Once the investor has determined his or her investing goals, the next order of business is to quantitatively screen the hedge fund database. Unfortunately, many investors approach this phase of manager selection with preconceived statistical prejudices based on a misunderstanding of the proper use of statistics. Each investor also has a different, pre-conceived notion of risk. To some, "risk" is the uncertainty of achieving an expected return. To others, it is not making a minimum acceptable return. Still others define risk as losing money.

Standard deviation is a perfect example of this general lack of statistical understanding. Investors sometimes begin a quantitative screen by stating they want a manager with a low risk, and, equating high standard deviation with high risk, prepare to use standard deviation as a comparative statistic. However, in truth, standard deviation is merely a measure of predictability. A high standard deviation simply means that the manager is volatile, not that the manager is risky or will lose money, while a low standard deviation means a manager is generally consistent. For example in Figure 8.1, we see a manager whose return pattern exhibits overall consistency, which results in a low annualized standard deviation of 3.8%. On the surface, this investment would appear very attractive.

However, when actual returns are plotted on the x-axis in Figure 8.2, a much different picture emerges. This fund, while maintaining a low standard deviation, has a compound annual return of less than 1%, and the fund has lost money almost as often as it has generated profits.

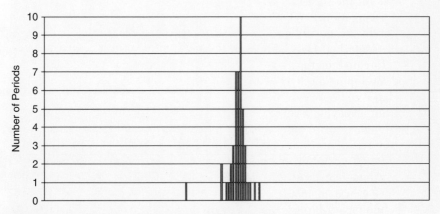

FIGURE 8.1 Distribution of monthly returns.

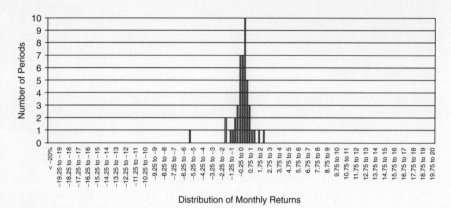

FIGURE 8.2 Distribution of monthly returns.

Looking for managers based on standard deviation also tends to unjustly penalize those managers with high upside volatility. The manager in Figure 8.3 has a standard deviation of 22.5%, which is generally considered high. However, his monthly returns are skewed to the upside as the result of several months of 15%-plus returns.

One of the main differences between traditional and alternative investment analysis is the acceptance of the fact that volatility is acceptable, as long as it is on the upside. Therefore, investors should consider downside deviation as a more appropriate measure of an investment's risk. Downside deviation also introduces the concept of minimal acceptable return (MAR) as a risk factor. Consider a retirement plan with annual liabilities of 8%. The real risk to this plan is failure to earn 8%, not high or low standard deviation.

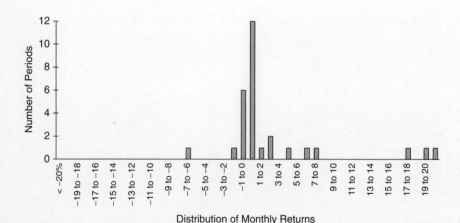

FIGURE 8.3 Distribution of monthly returns.

Downside deviation considers only the returns that fall beneath the MAR, ignoring upside volatility. If the MAR is set at 10%, as in Figure 8.4, downside deviation only measures the variation of returns below this value.

So, with standard deviation out of the equation, so to speak, what statistics can be used to compare funds? Certainly, returns may seem useful, but returns do not take into consideration the risk of a particular investment. Therefore, investors should always use risk-adjusted statistics, such as the Sharpe, Sortino, Sterling, or Calmar ratios. A good reference for statistical formulas is available on the Strategic Financial Solutions website. Links to Strategic Financial Solutions, LLC, and other organizations mentioned in this chapter are available in Appendix B.

The Sharpe ratio, introduced in 1966 by Dr. William F. Sharpe, is perhaps the best-known risk-adjusted statistic. The formula subtracts an assumed risk-free rate of return from the investment's average return and divides by the standard deviation for the same period.

$$\text{Sharpe Ratio} = \frac{\text{Mean} - \text{Risk Free Rate}}{\text{Standard Deviation}}$$

$$\text{Sharpe Ratio} = \frac{\sum_{i=1}^{n} \left(r(i) - r_{rf} \right)}{\sigma}$$

This generates a number that investors can use to compare investments. It should be noted that one must always compare apples to apples. All comparative statistics should be calculated over the same time period.

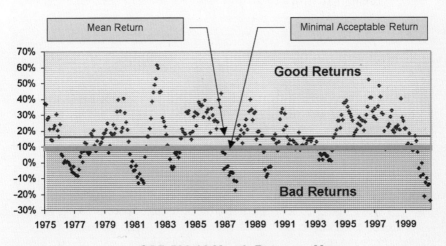

FIGURE 8.4 Downside deviation.

Here is a comparison of 2 very different investments. Fund A has a return of 10% and standard deviation of 8% while Fund B has a return of 20% and standard deviation of 16%. Assuming a risk-free rate of 4%, Fund A has a reward-to-risk ratio of .75, while the ratio for Fund B is 1.0.

$$Sharpe(A) = .75 = \frac{10 - 4}{8}$$

$$Sharpe(B) = 1 = \frac{20 - 4}{16}$$

Comparing the Sharpe ratios, Fund B would be the better investment. According to Sharpe, a higher standard deviation is not bad, as long as it is accompanied by a proportionally higher return. It is important to understand that such comparative statistics are not intended as absolute numbers and should only be used to evaluate a manager's relative relationship to his or her peers.

Because upside volatility may decrease the Sharpe ratio of some investments, Dr. Frank A. Sortino introduced the Sortino ratio as an alternative. The Sortino ratio is calculated much like the Sharpe, but uses the concept of downside deviation in place of standard deviation in the formula. In other words, the Sortino ratio equals the return, minus the minimum acceptable return, divided by the downside deviation.

$$Sortino\ Ratio = \frac{Mean - Minimal\ Acceptable\ Return}{Downside\ Deviation}$$

$$Downside\ Deviation = \sqrt{\frac{\sum_{i=1}^{n} d(i)^2}{n}}$$

Where $d(i) = 0$ if $(r(i) - MAR) >= 0$, or $d(i) = (r(i) - MAR)$ if $(r(i) - MAR) < 0$

Frank Sortino prefers that another method be used for calculating the Sortino ratio. Details on Sortino's preferred method can be found at www.sortino.com.

One can see the difference in Table 8.2 between Sharpe and Sortino by comparing two indices, the S&P 500 and the Lehman Aggregate Bond-Index.

Stocks and bonds both have approximately the same Sharpe ratio here. However, if the objective is to achieve a MAR of 10%, the Sortino ratio heavily favors stocks. For lower desired returns, the Sortino favors bonds.

Drawdown analysis is another excellent way to screen hedge funds. A drawdown is the maximum amount of loss from the equity high until a new equity high is reached. In Figure 8.5, the blue line represents an investment peak for the S&P 500.

TABLE 8.2 Comparing Sharpe and Sortino ratios

Period January, 1976 to August 2001	Lehman Bonds	S&P 500	Winner
Sharpe(5.00% risk-free rate)	0.69	0.64	Lehman Bonds
Sortino(MAR=10.00%)	(0.14)	0.37	S&P 500
Sortino(MAR=5.00%)	1.15	0.88	Lehman Bonds
Sortino(MAR=0%)	3.01	1.48	Lehman Bonds

The red dot indicates the lowest point or valley of the drawdown. The distance between the green lines is the depth, peak to valley, of the drawdown. The length of the drawdown and the time to recovery are also notable.

For a risk-adjusted view of drawdown analysis, the Sterling and Calmar ratios can provide additional comparative information. Commodity fund operator Dean Jones, of Reno, Nevada, created the Sterling ratio. The Sterling ratio is the annualized return for the last 3 years divided by the average of the maximum drawdown in each of the preceding 3 years, plus an arbitrary 10%. Jones added the extra 10% to the drawdown since he believed that all maximum drawdowns would be exceeded.

$$\text{Sterling Ratio} = \frac{AverageROR(\text{last 3 years})}{abs(AverageDrawdown - 10\%)}$$

Where D1 = Maximum Drawdown for first 12 months
Where D2 = Maximum Drawdown for next 12 months
Where D3 = Maximum Drawdown for latest 12 months
Average Drawdown = (D1 + D2 + D3) ÷ 3

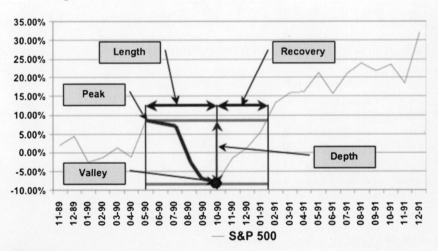

FIGURE 8.5 Drawdown analysis.

The Calmar Ratio was created by a fund of funds operator, Terry Young of Santa Ynez, California. The Calmar ratio is the annualized return for the last 3 years divided by the maximum drawdown during those years.

$$\text{Calmar Ratio} = \frac{AnnualizedROR(\text{last 3 years})}{MaximumDrawdown(\text{last 3 years})}$$

Drawdowns can be caused by any number of things, including market stress, giving back part of unrealized profits after a large run up in equity, or just poor trading. From a quantitative perspective, however, it is important to analyze the depth of all of the manager's drawdowns, the number of drawdowns, and the length of time to recovery.

Using Hedge Fund Indices to Screen Funds   Hedge fund indices can be helpful in deciding which strategies offer the best hopes for finding a fund that fits the investment mandate. Figure 8.6 shows the primary categories from the HFRI Hedge Fund Index.

Each strategy has a distinct risk/reward profile. The points that fall above the diagonal line have superior Sharpe ratios. Those interested primarily in wealth preservation may want to consider funds in the convertible universe, denoted by the red cross above. Investors with higher risk tolerances, who are looking for aggressive funds and high returns, might choose to search for an energy sector manager, the blue triangle on the graph. Although funds for almost every appetite can be found in all

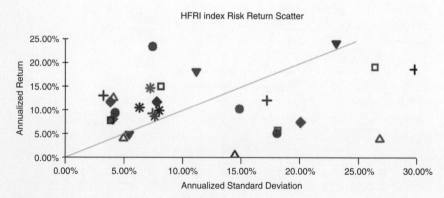

FIGURE 8.6   HFRI Risk-Return Scatterplot.

categories, certain strategies lend themselves to particular risk/reward profiles more than others. Market-neutral, arbitrage, or equity hedge categories are often stocked with managers who can deliver more consistent, though generally not spectacular, returns. Macro, emerging markets, and technology and biotech funds tend to exhibit more volatility, but sometimes with meaningfully higher returns.

Setting Up Quantitative Criteria   Once the investment mandate is set and the investor has determined which comparative statistical criteria he wishes to use, it is time to actually begin screening the hedge fund data for potential investments. As previously mentioned, prepackaged data and software programs make the quantitative screening and eventual portfolio construction very easy. We used PerTrac 2000 SE$^{(TM)}$, a product of Strategic Financial Solutions, LLC.

All too often, investors let arbitrary wish lists govern their statistical screens. Simply deciding that one wants a manager with a 3-year track record, no losing months, an annualized return greater than 15%, and a Sharpe ratio greater than 2 does not guarantee that such managers exist, or that, if they do exist, they will be open to new investment.

To ensure that one selects the best funds from a quantitative standpoint, it is better to think in terms of percentiles rather than absolutes, looking for superior fund managers comparatively, rather than searching for an investment fantasy. For example, let's assume the investor has defined his investment mandate and knows that she is looking for a fund of funds with a minimum acceptable return of 10%. She can use analytical software to separate funds of funds, and then continue to screen those funds by statistical measures.

The first step is to narrow the investment universe to include only funds of funds. Using the Hedge Fund Research database, the investor searches for funds of funds, narrowing her fund universe from approximately 1,700 funds to 254 funds. To make sure she is comparing apples to apples, she screens for funds with a minimum-length track record. Because the markets experienced a significant stress point in 1998, the investor decides to search for only those funds that have been trading for 5 years or more, narrowing the sample to 124 funds. Next, she searches for all funds with an annualized return greater than 10%, since this is her MAR. This reduces her universe to 91 funds. Rather than search each record for her wish-list criteria, she begins ranking the funds by percentile to determine reasonable search characteristics. Since the investor has decided that 10% is the MAR, there is no need to rank on annualized return, so she moves along to the Sharpe ratio.

Figure 8.7 shows that a fund must have a Sharpe greater than 1.28 to be in the top quartile of these funds. In Figure 8.8, it's clear that to be in the

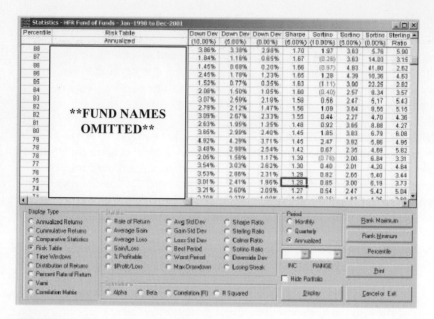

FIGURE 8.7   HFR fund of funds–Sharpe 1.26.

Percentile	Risk Table Annualized	Annualized ROR	Maximum Drawdown	Losing Streak	Standard Deviation	Gain Deviation	Loss Deviation	Down Dev (10.00%)	D
88		17.60%	(3.22%)	0.00%	8.10%	7.20%	3.82%	3.65%	
87		11.62%	(3.31%)	0.00%	3.50%	2.33%	4.13%	2.58%	
86		9.11%	(3.44%)	0.00%	2.43%	1.53%		2.08%	
86		28.46%	(3.52%)	0.00%	8.42%	7.37%		3.12%	
85		8.30%	(3.53%)	0.00%	2.27%	1.29%		2.05%	
84	**FUND NAMES OMITTED**	7.37%	(3.58%)	(0.59%)	4.16%	2.46%		3.50%	
83		38.26%	(3.70%)	0.00%	9.65%	8.50%		2.66%	
82		13.72%	(3.76%)	(0.72%)	7.83%	7.04%	4.39%	3.86%	
82		13.36%	(4.17%)	(0.27%)	5.02%	3.94%	0.28%	2.79%	
81		25.80%	(4.26%)	(0.60%)	9.07%	7.28%	2.68%	4.14%	
80		11.51%	(4.30%)	(0.03%)	3.96%	2.38%	8.73%	3.09%	
79		6.96%	(4.40%)	0.00%	3.02%	2.05%	8.88%	2.68%	
78		13.45%	(4.61%)	0.00%	4.12%	2.45%	6.48%	3.06%	
78		8.93%	(4.71%)	0.00%	3.16%	1.97%		2.70%	
77		12.57%	(4.71%)	0.00%	4.03%	2.55%		3.00%	
76		14.42%	(4.84%)	0.00%	3.75%	2.76%		2.39%	
75		18.60%	(5.50%)	0.00%	7.38%	6.00%	4.91%	3.86%	
74		10.32%	(5.65%)	0.00%	8.99%	7.59%	5.80%	5.35%	
74		12.81%	(5.73%)	(4.65%)	5.79%	5.17%		3.01%	

Display Type: Annualized Returns, Cumulative Returns, Comparative Statistics, Risk Table, Time Windows, Distribution of Returns, Percent Rate of Return, Vami, Correlation Matrix

Statistic: Rate of Return, Average Gain, Average Loss, Gain/Loss, % Profitable, $Profit/Loss, Avg Std Dev, Gain Std Dev, Loss Std Dev, Best Period, Worst Period, Max Drawdown, Sharpe Ratio, Sterling Ratio, Calmar Ratio, Sortino Ratio, Downside Dev, Losing Streak

Correlations: Alpha, Beta, Correlation (R), R Squared

Period: Monthly, Quarterly, Annualized; INC RANGE; Hide Portfolio

Rank Maximum, Rank Minimum, Percentile, Print, Display, Cancel or Exit

FIGURE 8.8   HFR fund of funds–maximum drawdown 5.5%.

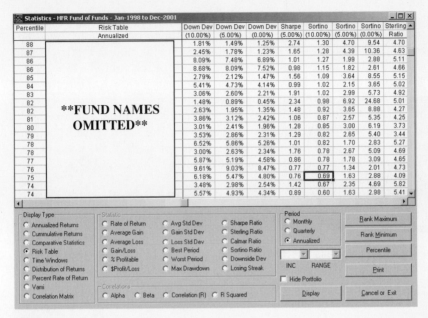

Statistics - HFR Fund of Funds - Jan-1998 to Dec-2001

Percentile	Risk Table Annualized	Down Dev (10.00%)	Down Dev (5.00%)	Down Dev (0.00%)	Sharpe (5.00%)	Sortino (10.00%)	Sortino (5.00%)	Sortino (0.00%)	Sterling Ratio
88		1.81%	1.49%	1.25%	2.74	1.30	4.70	9.54	4.70
87		2.45%	1.78%	1.23%	1.65	1.28	4.39	10.36	4.63
86		8.09%	7.48%	6.89%	1.01	1.27	1.99	2.88	5.11
86		8.68%	8.09%	7.52%	0.98	1.15	1.82	2.61	4.66
85		2.79%	2.12%	1.47%	1.56	1.09	3.64	8.55	5.15
84		5.41%	4.73%	4.14%	0.99	1.02	2.15	3.65	5.02
83		3.06%	2.60%	2.21%	1.91	1.02	2.99	5.73	4.92
82	****FUND NAMES OMITTED****	1.48%	0.89%	0.45%	2.34	0.98	6.92	24.68	5.01
82		2.63%	1.95%	1.35%	1.48	0.92	3.65	8.88	4.27
81		3.86%	3.12%	2.42%	1.06	0.87	2.57	5.35	4.25
80		3.01%	2.41%	1.96%	1.28	0.85	3.00	6.19	3.73
79		3.53%	2.86%	2.31%	1.29	0.82	2.65	5.40	3.44
78		6.52%	5.86%	5.26%	1.01	0.82	1.70	2.83	5.27
78		3.00%	2.63%	2.34%	1.76	0.78	2.67	5.09	4.69
77		5.87%	5.19%	4.58%	0.86	0.78	1.78	3.09	4.65
76		9.61%	9.03%	8.47%	0.77	0.77	1.34	2.01	4.73
75		6.18%	5.47%	4.80%	0.76	0.69	1.63	2.88	4.09
74		3.48%	2.98%	2.54%	1.42	0.67	2.35	4.69	5.82
74		5.57%	4.93%	4.34%	0.89	0.60	1.63	2.98	5.41

Display Type
- Annualized Returns
- Cummulative Returns
- Comparative Statistics
- Risk Table
- Time Windows
- Distribution of Returns
- Percent Rate of Return
- Vami
- Correlation Matrix

Statistic
- Rate of Return
- Average Gain
- Average Loss
- Gain/Loss
- % Profitable
- $Profit/Loss

- Avg Std Dev
- Gain Std Dev
- Loss Std Dev
- Best Period
- Worst Period
- Max Drawdown

- Sharpe Ratio
- Sterling Ratio
- Calmar Ratio
- Sortino Ratio
- Downside Dev
- Losing Streak

Correlations
- Alpha
- Beta
- Correlation (R)
- R Squared

Period
- Monthly
- Quarterly
- Annualized

INC   RANGE
- Hide Portfolio

Rank Maximum
Rank Minimum
Percentile
Print
Display   Cancel or Exit

FIGURE 8.9   HFR fund of funds–Sortino .69.

top quartile for drawdown, funds must have lost less than -5.5% during their maximum drawdown.

To be in the top quartile for the Sortino ratio (using an MAR of 10%), funds must have a Sortino greater than 0.69 (see Figure 8.9).

Using this series of quartile rankings the investor is methodically building her realistic search criteria. Now, she can search her funds of funds universe for only those funds with a Sharpe ratio higher than 1.26, less than a 5.50% maximum drawdown and a Sortino ratio greater than 0.69. In other words, she is trying to find funds with top quartile performance in all criteria categories. As a result, the investor finds 23 funds out of 124 that, based on her criteria and compared with the peers of those funds, are quantitatively the cream of the crop.

Another reason that investors consider hedge funds is to diversify from their long-only portfolios. So, a final step in her quantitative search might be to find funds with a negative correlation to the S&P. This reduces her list of 23 to 4.

This same search process can be completed on virtually any universe of funds, including hedge funds, CTAs, separate account managers, and mutual funds. The important thing is to take the extra steps necessary to establish reasonable search parameters and avoid setting the bar too high for any fund to hurdle.

This also holds true for basic searchable qualitative criteria, such as lockup, redemption notice, number of annual redemptions, etc. For example, if an investor is only interested in Regulation D funds with no lockup, 30 days notice, and monthly exits, he or she could be looking for a long time. Because Regulation D private placements do not offer that kind of liquidity to the fund managers, the fund cannot prudently offer it to its investors without having a liquidity mismatch that could result in the suspension of redemptions. However, for a long/short equity manager, this type of liquidity may be more common. If the investor sees what is normal for the peer group, he or she will have more fruitful manager searches.

Qualitative Screens

After the investor has selected the funds to target based on quantitative statistics, she must evaluate each one qualitatively. Some basic qualitative screens include the following:

- Is the fund open to new investment? Before an investor starts the sometimes arduous process of qualitative screening, it is important to know whether the fund is accepting new investments and, if so, how long the fund intends to remain open. If a fund is near to closing, it makes sense to determine if the investor can complete her review before the fund stops accepting new investors.
- How much leverage (if any) does the fund use? This is especially important to those subject to unrelated business taxable income (UBTI).
- What is the liquidity of the fund? How many times each year can an investor make withdrawals? Are investors subject to an initial lockup? Can one get out earlier with a redemption penalty? How much notice does one have to give?
- Does the manager have a substantial investment in the fund?
- Is the fund listed on an exchange?
- Because hedge funds are set up both onshore and offshore, it is important to note if the fund is open to U.S. investors.

This type of information is usually provided by the major data vendors, and can be quickly screened. Where the rubber meets the road, however, is during the course of a full qualitative screen, often referred to as due diligence. Qualitative issues specific to each hedge fund strategy is covered elsewhere in this book. However, some general issues should be covered with every fund, regardless of investment style.

Learning from Hedge Fund Closures and Missteps of the Last 5 Years

Long Term Capital Management, Tiger, Quantum, Maricopa, and Manhattan are perhaps some of the most famous and infamous names in the hedge fund industry. Each has received its share of press coverage during the past 5 years. Some has been generally positive, as in the case of Tiger and Quantum. Most coverage, however, served only to underscore worst-case scenarios for hedge fund investors.

LTCM had perhaps the most infamous hedge fund debacle in history. For nearly a year after the initial bailout, hedge fund investors, Congress, the financial press, and regulators could talk of little else. The near-collapse of this monolithic hedge fund caused ripples throughout the financial world and even drew talk of increased hedge fund regulation. When the smoke cleared, several things were painfully clear. LTCM was highly overleveraged (most estimated leverage to be greater than 50:1), and the fund provided little or no transparency to investors or the counterparties that extended leverage to it. Therefore, leverage and transparency are key factors to examine in any qualitative review of a hedge fund.

While leverage can boost returns, it should be used judiciously for the strategy and reactively to prevailing market conditions. Each investment strategy can withstand different amounts of leverage. For example, typical long/short strategies, where long positions and their offsetting hedged positions are normally not highly correlated to one another, generally use lower leverage, in most cases Reg T or less. Regulation T leverage is generally defined as leverage less than 2:1. There is more information on Reg T borrowing at http://www.bankinfo.com/Regs-aag/reg12220.html.

An arbitrage strategy, which normally has more strongly correlated positions and plays for smaller returns between those positions, is often more leveraged. It is not uncommon to find a convertible or mortgage-backed securities arbitrageur leveraged at 5:1 or more. All managers, regardless of strategy, should reevaluate their leverage ratios as market conditions change. The leverage that is prudent for a long-biased hedge fund during a roaring bull market may not be during sharp or protracted market downturns. Likewise, during periods of credit dislocation, convertible, fixed income, and mortgage-backed arbitrageurs may choose to ratchet down their leverage to avoid drawdowns and margin calls.

If a fund will not provide a certain degree of transparency to potential or current investors, it is perhaps best to walk away. Had LTCM provided more transparency to its investors or counterparties about their degree of leverage, the situation might not have become so critical. There is, however, some debate over the level of transparency required from hedge funds. Some investors demand complete transparency on a daily basis. Others feel this level of transparency is unnecessary given the liquidity constraints on hedge fund investors. They argue that knowing about risky positions does them little good, since they may be locked into the fund for another month, quarter, or year. It is important to negotiate an acceptable level of transparency before making a hedge fund investment, and even the most hands-off investor should have access to basic information, such as amount of leverage used (including notional leverage generated by the use of derivatives), number of positions, concentration of equity in top positions, market outlook and positioning, audited financial statements, custodial relationship, references, and full work and educational history.

Michael Berger's Manhattan Investment Fund's history illustrates this issue. The SEC charged Berger in January 2000 with inflating his fund's assets and returns while losing nearly $400 million shorting Internet stocks. Berger allegedly sent falsified account statements for 39 consecutive months to his administrator, a division of Ernst & Young, which then prepared and disseminated net asset values and individual account balances based on this faulty information. Even the financial statements, based on Berger's fictitious returns and audited by Deloitte & Touche Bermuda, did not disclose the actual performance of the fund. Berger's own newsletter detailed his consistently bearish view during the greatest bull market in history. He might have been caught earlier if someone had reviewed the underlying portfolio positions. However, what would have made the most difference in this case is transparency at the custodial level. Direct access to the fund's prime brokers/custodians for quarterly account balance reviews might have revealed the problem sooner. Direct access to every custodian used by the fund is of utmost importance when evaluating a hedge fund manager. This independent third-party verification of a fund's stated assets could make the difference between success and failure of an investment. In the words of Ronald Reagan, we must "trust, but verify."

David Mobley, Sr., refused to have Maricopa Investment Corporation's financial statements audited, saying that an audit might give away his proprietary trading system. In hindsight, this was a warning bell. In February 2000, Mobley was indicted for defrauding investors of $59 million through losing investments and high-priced personal expenditures.

An audit is as fundamental to due diligence as oxygen is to breathing. Audits give yet another third-party verification of account balances, profits, and losses. Starting with the year that ended December 31, 2001, the AICPA requires the disclosure of financial highlights in audits. Audits can reveal weaknesses in a manager's trading strategy by showing where gains and losses were concentrated (long side, short side, industry sector, etc.). They can also alert investors to trouble due to large withdrawals. Even more importantly, they give existing and potential investors the ability to see how profits and losses are determined. Whatever system the hedge fund manager uses to mark his or her portfolio is disclosed in the financial statements, allowing the investor to judge whether or not it is prudent.

When subjective pricing is involved, it is even more critical to examine audited financial statements to see if the pricing system makes sense. In Regulation D investing, for example, a manager may hold illiquid private placements for more than 12 to 18 months. Rather than post flat returns with periodic "pops" as gains are realized, many managers have developed models to mark their portfolios. One manager may take a percentage of the anticipated gain up front and the remainder when gains are actually realized. Another might amortize expected gains over the projected length of the investment. Both are logical ways to mark the portfolio. However, the first is probably more conservative and allows for less slippage if unrealized gains are given back as positions are actually unwound. The investor must get comfortable with any portfolio-marking method or be prepared for a potential rude awakening down the line. Appendix A, written by Todd Goldman of Rothstein Kass & Co, provides a full discussion on return calculations.

George Soros and Julian Robertson were hugely successful for more than 2 decades. However, both managers, considered pillars of the hedge fund community, started experiencing difficulties in 1998 as assets ballooned. Explaining his failure to continue posting above-average returns, Robertson reported that assets had grown too large to be effectively deployed.

Asset size is a very important performance factor in evaluating and monitoring hedge funds. Many managers tend to post their best returns when their funds are small and nimble. As assets increase, managers may be forced to change their initially successful strategies. To keep capital in play, they may resort to one of the following tactics:

1. Looking outside their area of expertise for additional investment opportunities. Some outgrowths are logical and can prove profitable— merger arbitrage managers looking at other event-driven opportunities, convertible managers looking into Reg D, etc. However, there is always a risk when a manager deviates from his or her tried-and-true strategy.
2. Concentrating more money in top-tier investment ideas, thus increasing the risk that one particular investment could seriously affect the entire fund.
3. Moving from top investment ideas to second-, third-, or fourth-tier opportunities, thus compromising the fund's performance.
4. Keeping a large amount of the fund in cash, thereby lowering returns.
5. Farming out portions of the investment management process to other subadvisors who may not have the manager's level of experience, credentials, or back-office infrastructure.

6. Spending more time managing the organization and less time managing the fund, leaving the day-to-day investment decisions to more junior personnel.

These lessons from the past provide pointers for making any hedge fund investment.

Kicking the Tires: The On-Site Visit

The on-site visit is one of the most important parts of the due diligence process. This is the best chance to assess the primary traders and decision-makers, ask due diligence questions, check out systems and fund infrastructure, discuss actual portfolio positions and trades, inquire about competitors, etc. The investor can use this opportunity to ask about past performance difficulties or triumphs. He can use the manager's statistical profile to thoroughly review the track record, asking about drawdowns, volatility, and periods of market stress. After all, a manager's performance can only result from market weakness/strength, luck, or trader skill. The on-site visit is the best chance to check which of these has most impacted the manager's track record. A thorough on-site visit should last at least a few hours, and the investor should attempt to talk to as many people in the organization as possible.

Additional Resources

Simply put, due diligence is no more than trying to discover all the ways that one could lose money in a fund, and determining if those risks versus the potential returns justify an investment. If one combines this with a thorough examination of the manager's background (education, regulatory history, and past employment) and strategy, and gets independent third-party verifications when possible, one is well on the way to completing a qualitative review. The Alternative Investment Management Association and Hedge-Fund.net. have sample due diligence checklists that investors can use as additional resources. In addition, many managers have completed due diligence checklists for institutional clients and will share this information. Hedge fund consultants can help with this part of the screening process as well.

PERFORMANCE MEASUREMENT AND MONITORING

Hedge fund investments must be constantly monitored to make sure that the manager applies his or her strategy consistently, and that performance stays within acceptable parameters. This involves both quantitative and qualitative reviews on a periodic basis. The quantitative side of performance measurement and ongoing monitoring involves evaluating the manager against his past performance, as well as market and peer benchmarks. Qualitative monitoring consists of many of the same questions and reviews performed during the initial due diligence process. Together, they can help evaluate when and if to increase allocations, partially redeem from a manager, or fire a manager.

Quantitative Monitoring

There are many ways to monitor a hedge fund investment quantitatively. The easiest is for the investor to simply watch the monthly returns and determine if the return patterns have changed. In other words, is the investor achieving his or her MAR? The investor should also benchmark the manager against various market and hedge fund indices, both of which are important measures of a manager's success.

For example, one long/short manager may invest primarily in technology stocks. Benchmarking that manager exclusively to a predefined long/short or technology index only gives part of the picture. The manager should be compared to a market benchmark to determine how well the fund is performing against the stocks in that sector. Then, if possible, the manager should be benchmarked against a long-only investment in that sector to quantify the trader's skill (for which the investor is generally paying a 1% management fee and a 20% incentive allocation). Finally, the investor should benchmark the hedge fund manager against his peers to determine if he or she is still comparatively the best hedge fund manager for the investment mandate.

Table 8.3 compares the performance of a long/short technology manager with the HFR Technology Index and the NASDAQ.

This hedge fund manager has been underperforming the market benchmark for the past 3 months, but over the long term he has significantly outperformed the market. What has happened in the last few months? Why have returns, once historically so strong against the benchmark, dwindled in the last year? The up capture measures the investment's compound return when the benchmark was up, divided by the benchmark's compound return when the benchmark was up. The greater the value, the better. The down capture measures the investment's compound return when the benchmark was down, divided by the benchmark's compound return when the benchmark was down. The smaller the number, the better. Here, the manager's recent performance indicates that a disturbing trend is developing.

Compared with actively managed technology mutual funds, the historical performance of the fund is sound. For the last rolling 1-, 3- and 5-year periods, this long/short manager handily outperformed his mutual fund

TABLE 8.3 Performance Comparison

(All returns longer than 1 year are annualized)

Performance Analysis	1 Month	3 month	6 month	YTD	1 Year	2 Year	3 Year	5 Year	7 Year	10 Year
Product										
HFR Technology Index	(4.93)%	(1.99)%	(7.37)%	(29.78)%	(29.78)%	(25.55)%	12.16%	26.13%		
NASDAQ	1.15%	12.76%	(6.30)%	(14.54)%	(14.54)%	(13.96)%	16.64%	20.60%		
	1.03%	30.13%	(9.73)%	(21.05)%	(21.05)%	(30.77)%	(3.83)%	8.60%		
+/− HFR Technology Index	(6.08)%	(14.75)%	(1.07)%	(15.23)%	(15.23)%	(11.59)%	(4.48)%	5.53%		
+/− NASDAQ	(5.96)%	(32.12)%	2.36%	(8.72)%	(8.72)%	5.21%	15.99%	17.53%		

Annualized Statistical Analysis	ROR	Standard Deviation	Sharpe	Alpha	Beta	Correlation R	R2	Tracking Error	Active Premium	Info. Ratio
Product	20.89%	29.15%	0.62							
HFR Technology Index	19.89%	26.56%	0.63	5.45%	0.82	0.75	0.56	19.99%	0.99%	0.05
NASDAQ	9.48%	34.91%	0.30	16.57%	0.50	0.60	0.36	29.14%	11.40%	0.39

	Up Capture	Down Capture	Up Months	Down Months	Proficiency Up	Ratios Down	Overall	Profitable Months	Treynor Ratio	Jensen Alpha
HFR Technology Index	60.77%	83.32%	81.08%	86.21%	45.95%	51.72%	48.48%	91.89%	19.40%	0.37%
NASDAQ	43.54%	74.08%	75.68%	79.31%	43.24%	68.97%	54.55%	91.89%	31.63%	1.08%

counterparts, with the average specialty-technology mutual fund (not shown in chart) returning −38.2%, −1.2% and 9.41%, respectively, in those periods. Historically at least, this hedge fund manager has certainly earned his higher fees. However, in the last quarter technology-specialty, long-only mutual funds strongly outperformed this manager, which again, raises some questions for the manager.

Finally, the fund is checked against its hedge fund benchmark, in this case the HFR Technology Sector Index. Again, this manager underperforms in all but the 5-year rolling return category. The up capture has increased to 60.77%, but the down capture has peaked at over 83%. It is clear that the long/short manager, while historically quite strong, has missed a good deal of the market upside in recent years, and has not been particularly effective at hedging out risk during market downturns. Based on this information, one can then look for qualitative reasons why this manager is underperforming his peers, and perhaps begin screening for a replacement fund.

While it was relatively simple to gauge the performance of this long/short technology manager against his peers, some categories, such as long/short (no sector or specialty), funds of funds, convertible arbitrage, opportunistic, event driven, etc., don't lend themselves as easily to benchmark comparisons. The same style analysis that works with mutual funds does not yield much useful information on investments that are often unique. For example, a study of convertible arbitrage hedge funds with 5-year records shows that those managers are generally correlated neither to their peers, nor to the index. In fact, almost 73% of those funds had a correlation of 0.6 or less to the HFR Convertible Arbitrage Index, and a 0.5 correlation is no better than flipping a coin. This means that no meaningful conclusions can be drawn when comparing the performance of a convertible arbitrage fund to its index.

For these managers, it is best to develop a peer group that has a high correlation to the hedge fund in question. The investor could do this by performing a statistics search with analytical software and locate all funds in the hedge fund universe that have a correlation greater than 0.7 with this manager. Then he could construct an index with this resultant peer group. By monitoring the R squared (Coefficient of Determination) between the manager and this custom index he would notice deviations in style. He could also use this peer group analysis to monitor relative performance.

Value at Risk and Stress Testing

Value at Risk is an increasingly popular quantitative monitoring tool. VaR attempts to estimate the level of loss that a portfolio might produce given extreme probabilities. Boiled down to a single number, this holdings-based tool can help determine some of the risk involved in a hedge fund portfolio. However, while VaR is useful, it is also somewhat dangerous to read too much into one number. Value at Risk does not, for example, take into consideration the risk of a market crash. It does not make allowances for the liquidity of various instruments. It also requires a fairly static portfolio (or very frequent position updates) and a manager who is willing to divulge all positions regularly and often.

For managers less inclined to divulge information about their portfolio holdings, return-based Monte Carlo stress testing can help determine the overall risk of the investment. By running thousands of scenarios, this process can determine the range and probability of possible future returns for a given investment. Figure 8.10 shows an example of Monte Carlo stress testing on a single hedge fund investment.

The 1st percentile (sometimes referred to as Value at Risk) shows that the worst-case scenario is a return of 0.83% and the 99th percentile (approximately 3 standard deviations from the mean return) indicates the expected return could be as high as 34.17%. The 99th and 1st percentiles for the expected Sharpe ratio are of 3.247 and −0.3, respectively.

These numbers point out that historical statistics may not necessarily be indicative of future results. They also tell one what to expect in a best- and

Portfolio Simulation Reports

File   Print   Workbook Designer

All Portfolio Statistics   Select Statistic

	A	B	C	D	E	F	G	H	I	J
1	All Portfolio Statistics	Annualized Return	Annualized Standard Deviation	Annualized Sharpe (RF)	Annualized Semi Deviation	Average Gain Deviation	Average Loss Deviation	Annualized Downside Deviation (MAR)	Annualized Downside Deviation (RF)	Annualized Downside Deviation (0%)
2	Number Simulations	1,000	1,000	1,000	1,000	1,000	983	1,000	1,000	1,000
3	Mean	16.85%	9.88%	1.219	11.90%	6.04%	9.47%	6.80%	6.34%	5.89%
4	Median	16.77%	9.98%	1.160	11.52%	6.03%	5.00%	6.88%	6.43%	5.98%
5	Standard Deviation	7.07%	1.95%	0.752	3.92%	1.47%	3.27%	2.25%	2.21%	2.15%
6	Maximum	43.28%	16.13%	3.897	26.45%	11.23%	19.89%	13.11%	12.49%	11.84%
7	Minimum	(6.48%)	4.03%	(0.849)	4.09%	2.50%	0.00%	0.77%	0.51%	0.28%
8	99th Percentile	34.17%	14.01%	3.247	22.70%	9.46%	15.62%	11.74%	11.10%	10.45%
9	95th Percentile	28.91%	12.97%	2.583	19.10%	8.51%	13.64%	10.31%	9.74%	9.16%
10	90th Percentile	25.68%	12.42%	2.204	17.22%	8.02%	12.88%	9.61%	9.08%	8.66%
11	80th Percentile	22.42%	11.52%	1.796	15.15%	7.26%	11.88%	8.79%	8.27%	7.74%
12	75th Percentile	21.24%	11.23%	1.666	14.26%	7.03%	11.49%	8.40%	7.88%	7.36%
13	70th Percentile	20.21%	10.96%	1.558	13.53%	6.86%	11.16%	8.08%	7.62%	7.12%
14	60th Percentile	18.47%	10.41%	1.361	12.51%	6.48%	10.62%	7.47%	7.01%	6.54%
15	50th Percentile	16.77%	9.98%	1.160	11.52%	6.03%	10.00%	6.88%	6.43%	5.98%
16	40th Percentile	15.19%	9.38%	0.985	10.60%	5.51%	9.50%	6.22%	5.79%	5.40%
17	30th Percentile	13.51%	8.86%	0.815	9.61%	5.07%	8.63%	5.65%	5.26%	4.88%
18	25th Percentile	12.40%	8.56%	0.711	9.20%	4.88%	7.90%	5.43%	5.04%	4.66%
19	20th Percentile	11.02%	8.23%	0.570	8.58%	4.67%	7.23%	5.00%	4.50%	4.08%
20	10th Percentile	7.73%	7.28%	0.281	7.11%	4.15%	5.28%	3.90%	3.43%	3.05%
21	5th Percentile	5.71%	6.56%	0.118	6.04%	3.76%	1.82%	2.58%	2.17%	1.74%
22	1st Percentile	0.83%	5.46%	(0.300)	4.65%	3.27%	0.16%	1.70%	1.33%	1.00%
23										
24	Simulation Method:	Bootstrap		Benchmark:	Barra S&P 500					
25	Simulation Data Start:	Oct-1996		Portfolio:	Hedge fund Manager			100.00%		
26	Simulation Data End:	Dec-2001								
27	Number of Periods:	63								
28	Simulation Period:	Monthly								
29	Number of Years:	3								
30	Number of Simulations:	1000								
31	Re-balancing:	(None)								
32	Risk Free Return:	5.00%								
33	Minimal Acceptable Return:	10.00%								
34	Fixed Random Sequence:	Yes								

FIGURE 8.10   Monte Carlo simulation.

worst-case scenario. It is up to the investor to determine if the potential upside returns outweigh the potential downside risk. Stress tests also can be done on entire portfolios of hedge funds, and for best results should be rerun regularly and after periods of market stress.

Qualitative Monitoring

Managers must constantly be monitored for unacceptable strategy drift, leverage, liquidity, or concentration that deviates from historical norms, decreasing transparency, personnel changes, and unusual capital inflows and outflows. A thorough review of the annual audit is critical, as are periodic calls to verify account balances with custodians and rechecks of regulatory standings. Continuing on-site visits should be scheduled, as well as conference calls to discuss market conditions and portfolio positioning. Perhaps the best way to view qualitative monitoring is as a mini-due diligence that covers the key issues that were discovered in the original due diligence, as well as the fundamental aspects mentioned above.

When to Fire a Manager

While it is important to know the potential risks and downside of any investment through screening and monitoring, putting that knowledge to work can be an entirely different ball game. Investments are made into hedge funds in large part due to the managers' expertise and ability to adjust their strategy as they believe market situations warrant. Calling the manager or redeeming every time one does not agree with a trade, or every time the manager ventures slightly out of his historical parameters can actually do more harm than good. Hedge fund managers have been known to fire investors for this kind of "backseat driving."

The key to ongoing monitoring is to constantly evaluate whether the manager still meets the original investment mandate. If the investor is uncomfortable with illiquid investments and the manager moves into distressed debt, mortgage-backed securities, or Reg D private placements, the investor will probably want to reconsider the investment. The same holds true if he hired an aggressive manager who historically targeted 20% returns, but has recently become far more conservative. While the investor should always hold conversations with the manager about changes to the investment strategy, it is ultimately up to the investor to decide if the investment remains a good fit for his overall portfolio.

Several scenarios should trigger an almost automatic redemption, however. If the manager suddenly declines to participate in ongoing reviews, or if he opts to stop having his financial statements audited, the investor should probably immediately reconsider his investment. However, the investor should realize that even if he or she disagrees with a manager's portfolio or current level of risk, most hedge funds have liquidity constraints, and as a result, the investor may not be able to redeem from the fund before the portfolio changes or a drawdown occurs.

CONCLUSIONS

The hedge fund industry is constantly evolving. What was a highly secretive asset class reserved for millionaires is moving more into the mainstream with each passing day, and there are initiatives underway that will continue to push hedge funds forward. For example, the Managed Funds Association has petitioned the SEC to allow hedge fund advertising. Institutions in the U.S. and abroad are pushing for more liquidity and transparency. However, as more investors and managers jump into the fray, there are bound to be new tales both of victims and victors. Each investor's story will depend in large part on careful manager searches and intelligent performance-monitoring.

END NOTE

Please see Appendix A for guidance on calculating rates of return for hedge funds, and Appendix C for a discussion of Value at Risk, an important risk measure in both traditional and non-traditional investing.

CHAPTER 9

Risk Management for Hedge Funds and Funds of Funds

Leslie Rahl

WHAT IS RISK?

Risk is the possibility of bad outcome. It is a real-world concept, not just a mathematical one. There are many different types of risks (see Figure 9.1).

Risk is not new; it has always existed. What is new is how people measure and manage risk, and the language they use to talk about it.

How did people manage risk before Value at Risk (VaR), tracking error, etc.? One of the ways was by simplistically limiting the investments that could be included in a portfolio. Rules such as "all securities must be AAA and less than 3 years in maturity" were common. Ninety-five percent of Orange County's portfolio met these criteria. Although 3 years was the final maturity criterion, it had securities with durations of more than 15 years. Credit ratings are just that—credit ratings. They may attempt to rate the ability of the counterparty to pay its obligations, not the willingness of the counterparty to pay its obligations, or the volatility of the price of the security if sold prior to maturity. Limiting the types of investments does not limit the leverage of the portfolio, as Orange County learned. Techniques used to control risk usually relied on guidelines that were often vague and subject to different interpretations, especially after something went wrong. Examples of judgmental guidelines include "low" interest-rate risk; "high" liquidity; "highly" correlated; and "hedging is allowed."

Other techniques need to control risk are seemingly obvious guidelines that are open to interpretation upon further inspection. For example, "government securities" could include or exclude U.S. government securities; foreign government securities; aging structured notes; and barbell strategies, such as long the 10-year, short bills and long bonds. Further, "no commodities" could include or exclude commodity-linked notes.

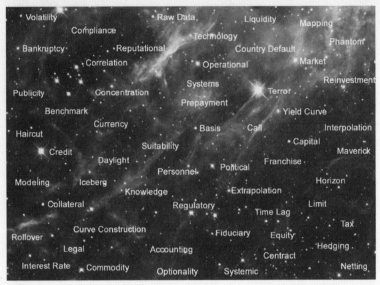

(Partial listing)

FIGURE 9.1 Galaxy of risks. *Source:* © CMRA.

The author has been in the financial markets for 30 years, but she has yet to figure out how to make money without taking risks. Risk management is not about eliminating risk. It is about making sure one understands the risks one takes, and keeping the risk/reward equation in proportion.

The goals of risk management should be to minimize uncompensated and unanticipated risks. A fund manager needs to understand its risk, understand how its portfolio would behave under adverse conditions, and identify triggers and techniques to be employed if risks rise too much.

A robust risk management framework has many facets (see Figure 9.2).

♦ Overall, only 13% of respondents made adjustments of
  some kind to the "market" prices they receive from their
  valuation sources. The most frequently made adjustments
  are for liquidity and time zone.

Types of Adjustment	% Making Adjustments
Liquidity	6.8
Time Zone	4.2
Size	5.8
Holding Period	0.1
Other Adjustments	1.3

FIGURE 9.2 Adjustments to "market" prices. *Source:* CMRA NAV/Fair Value survey.

Only about a third of the components of a robust risk management program are quantitative. It is a mistake to get mesmerized by the numbers. They are important, but only part of the risk management exercise. There is no substitute for qualitative judgments in investing decisions. The goal of risk management is to provide risk insight. Often quantitative reports provide data but not information. This makes for ineffective risk management. It is a waste of time to crunch a lot of risk numbers and not use them. The key is to integrate risk management and risk thinking into one's dialogue and decisions. The goal should be a risk-aware organization.

Risk management must connect this dialogue and decision. This requires a common risk language.

People need to prioritize their risks. It is not practical, and rarely necessary, to manage all risk categories with the same intensity of effort. Some portfolios, for instance, are highly sensitive to volatility levels and the shape of the volatility curve, and require robust attention to volatility, while other strategies, such as equity long/short, are largely insensitive. Leveraged portfolios are sensitive to financing arrangements and require significant attention to the risk of haircut changes, etc., while nonleveraged portfolios need not focus on this star in the galaxy.

In addition, the way one approaches risk management needs to be consistent with one's management style. There is no point in having an extremely formal and rigid risk management program in an informal organization (see Figure 9.3).

Compliance is an important component of risk management (see Figure 9.4). One must follow rules, and correct aberrations in a timely manner. However, this is only a small part of risk management.

Compliance and risk management do overlap, but each function has very different agendas. Compliance focuses primarily on following rules and

Where are you on this scale?

Informal ←————————————————————→ **Formal**

Informal	**Formal**
• Operate on trust "Do the right thing	• "If it is not written here, don't do it"
• Rely on culture to control risk	• Slows innovation and frustrates managers
• Often leaves room for "adverse innovation"	• Often removes reward available at acceptable risk

FIGURE 9.3 Policy issues. *Source:* © CMRA.

FIGURE 9.4 Compliance doesn't equal risk management. *Source:* © CMRA.

regulations. Risk management focuses on understanding risks and making proactive decisions about them.

TRANSPARENCY

Risk transparency is one of the key issues facing the hedge fund world today. Managers are frequently unwilling to provide position transparency, and investors usually do not have the resources to interpret it. Risk transparency is a standard set of risk factors that can provide investors with a meaningful snapshot of a hedge fund's risk (see Figure 9.5).

Standardization is key, so that one can aggregate risks across an investor's portfolio of funds.

FIGURE 9.5 Transparency tug-of-war between managers and investors. *Source:* © CMRA.

TABLE 9.1 Different Perspectives

Institutional Investor	Hedge Fund
Adheres to "best practice" in risk management.	The manager has broad discretion and should be judged on results.
Institutional investors need to fully understand the risks in each fund in which they invest.	Many strategies are highly proprietary and hedge fund performance is compromised by disclosure.
Institutional quality funds must have infrastructure, stability, and a well-defined process that is not dependent on any single individual.	Risk management, compliance, and regulatory oversight are a drag on performance.

Source: © CMRA.

A survey released by Capital Market Risk Advisors (CMRA) and the Alternative Investment Management Association (AIMA) found that:

1. Only 7% of funds of funds and 4% of individual hedge funds indicated that they have had potential investors decline to invest based on lack of transparency, but 64% of investors claim they have declined to invest.
2. 86% of investors indicate that transparency is an issue in selecting hedge funds and funds of funds.
3. 69% of investors are satisfied with the information they receive from their hedge funds and funds of funds, but 29% of investors have had requests for information turned down by the hedge funds and funds of funds in which they invest.
4. Only 14% of hedge funds indicated that investors request more information than they receive.
5. 66% of funds of funds would find a standard set of risk factors very valuable or extremely valuable for portfolio construction, and 55% for marketing/client reporting.

TABLE 9.2 Perceived Impact on Hedge Funds of Position Level Disclosure

	Funds of Funds	Hedge Funds
Depends on Strategy	34%	25%
Not at All / Minimal Impact	41%	39%
Significant Impact / Material Impact	24%	36%

Source: CMRA/AIMA.

TABLE 9.3   Regularly Received Information

Concentration	45%
Exposures vs. Limit	45%
Position-Level Detail	36%
VaR	18%
Sensitivity	10%
Stress Test Results	9%

Source: CMRA/AIMA.

6. Disclosing detailed position-level information is considered "significantly" or "materially" compromising to the performance of a hedge
   fund by only 24% of funds of funds and 36% of hedge funds.
7. Investors regularly receive the following information from funds in
   which they invest (see Table 9.3).
8. 60% of the investors who get full position level detail have their own
   tools to analyze the remainder. They skim the information.
9. When funds of funds have detailed position information for the funds
   in which they invest, they use it in a variety of ways (see Table 9.4).

VALUE AT RISK

VaR is one, but only one, risk-measuring technique (see Figure 9.6).

VaR is a critical component of risk management in the twenty-first cen-
tury. While VaR is more meaningful for some hedge fund styles than others,
it needs to be supplemented, not ignored.

VaR alone, however, gives only a 1- or 2-dimensional insight into a
multidimensional set of risks. One of the lessons learned or relearned by
banks and investment banks as well as hedge funds is that VaR alone is not
enough to measure and manage risk (see Figure 9.7).

VaR does not, for instance, effectively measure spread risk, correlation
risk (see Figure 9.8, page 146) etc. Nor does it effectively capture the additional risks of leverage. It would be a mistake, however, to ignore the value
and insight it does provide, just because it is not the be-all and end-all.

STRESS TESTING

Once-in-a-lifetime events seem to occur every few years.

TABLE 9.4   Uses

Review to make sure that the instruments comply with guidelines	54%
Input into a risk management system and monitor the risks	26%

Source: CMRA/AIMA.

- Aging
- Alpha
- Bank Tracking
- Benchmark Equivalents
- Beta
- Bucketed Sensitivity
- Concentration
- Convexity
- Correlation
- Country Exposure
- Coverage Ratios
- Credit Rating
- Current Risk Exposure
- Delta
- Devaluation Risk

- Dollar Face
- Duration
- DV01
- Effective Duration
- Extension Risk
- Factor Analysis
- Gamma
- Gap Analysis
- Likelihood of Default
- Loan to Valuation Ration
- Mark to Market
- Mark to Model
- Option-Adjusted Spread
- Position Reports
- Potential Risk Exposure

- Prepayment Sensitivity
- Relative Value
- Rho
- Risk Rating
- Scenario Analysis
- Sensitivity
- Sharpe/Treynor Measures
- Shortfall Probability
- Simulation
- Spread Analysis
- Standard Deviation
- Stress Testing
- Theta
- VaR
- Vega

(Partial listing)

FIGURE 9.6 Common risk measures. *Source:* © CMRA.

There has been at least a 10 standard deviation event in at least 1 market every year for the past decade. Although no one can accurately predict the next surprise, any approach to risk management needs to assume that there will be surprises. Stress testing needs to consider the unthinkable. Closed markets, shell-shocked employees functioning at half-speed, and offices that disappeared permanently need to be considered. If an investor chose to liquidate positions held under duress, would the manager have access to the list of positions and legal paperwork required?

Stress testing is an essential tool in the risk arsenal (see Figure 9.9).

Benefits

- Portfolio measure of risk

- Uniform measure of risk across all risk types

- Aggregates risk based on correlations or market observed relationships

- Value at risk or potential loss is an easily understood, intuitive concept

- Widely adopted by practitioners and regulators

Cautions

- Not worst case scenario

- Not a cumulative loss measure

- Not market scenario driven, based on assumptions using history of market moves

- Not sufficient as only risk measure; requires risk management process

FIGURE 9.7 Benefits and cautions of VaR. *Source:* © CMRA.

FIGURE 9.8   Caution. *Source:* © CMRA.

There are many different types of stress tests (see Figure 9.10).

Correlations tend to go out the window in times of stress. Everyone knows that in a crisis, correlations go to +1 or −1, but they tend to forget this between crises. Robust risk management must consider a portfolio's performance under stressed as well as in normal correlations.

Some of the stress tests to consider include:

- What would be the impact on the portfolio if the bid/offer spread widens?
- What would be the impact of all correlations going to 1?
- What would be the impact if the prime broker increased the haircuts on repos?

RISK BUDGETING

Investors have begun to focus on risk dollars spent to achieve return. One of the important lessons of the 1998 Long Term Capital Management crisis

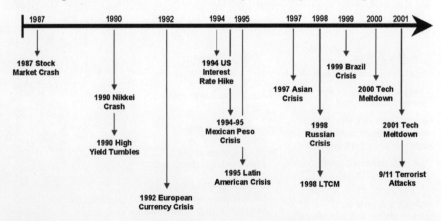

FIGURE 9.9   Unexpected financial shocks. *Source:* © CMRA.

FIGURE 9.10 Stress testing approaches. *Source:* © CMRA.

was the significance of "iceberg risk." Even if the visible tip of an iceberg is large, what lies beneath the surface can be many times larger and may also take on unpredictable shapes.

Historically, institutional investors have used asset allocation as their core process to determine their investment strategy. The asset allocation process classically starts with the choice of asset classes and follows the direction of Figure 9.11.

Allocating investment dollars is an important tool, but it doesn't address the need to efficiently allocate risk appetite and to reflect the changing dynamics of risk. Asset allocation emphasizes return, outperformance, and P&L flows. Risk budgeting adds another dimension—it is also a function of volatility and correlation, as well as a function of dollars. Constant assets in a risk-budgeting framework can result in widely fluctuating risk.

Risk-budgeting is not an optimization exercise. All else being equal, an investor who maximizes risk-adjusted performance will perform better than one who does not.

While risk-budgeting and risk-adjusted return management need not necessarily go hand in hand, they usually do. Risk-budgeting enables a plan sponsor to evaluate the portfolio contribution of various exposures to risk. The first step is to determine current risk exposures. Once a plan sponsor has developed the ability to measure the risk of each of its managers and strategies, using the risk measure as the denominator of the risk-adjusted return equation is a simple and powerful next step. The ultimate goal is to have risk as the basis of strategic risk management.

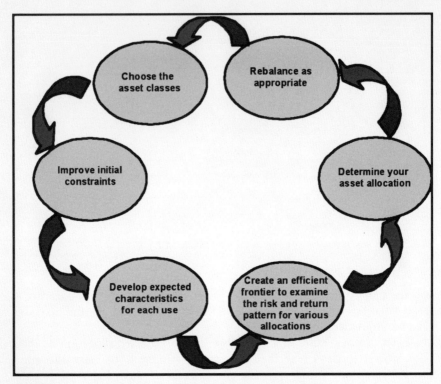

FIGURE 9.11   Asset Allocation Process Cycle. *Source:* © CMRA.

The effective use of risk-budgeting requires a sophisticated understanding that not all VaR calculations are the same, and that market risk VaR does not cover the galaxy of risks that a portfolio faces. All portfolios being budgeted with a risk amount should adopt a consistent risk-measuring methodology.

While risk-budgeting is an innovative and important concept, risk needs to be more broadly defined than VaR and/or traditional risk measures. Stress test results and sensitivities need to be integrated into the denominator of the risk-adjusted reward equation. Stress test results need to include sensitivities not only to market moves, but also to the assumptions underlying VaR as well as mark-to-market net asset value (NAV).

Risk-budgeting alone—or any single approach for that matter—is not the answer. An organization needs a disciplined approach to risk, one that includes the quantitative aspect but does not rely exclusively on it. The

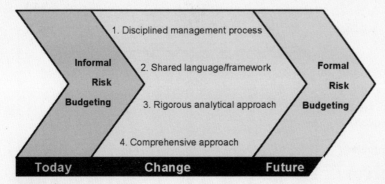

FIGURE 9.12 Risk budgeting transition. *Source:* © CMRA.

author believes strongly that only about one-third of the components of a good risk management approach are quantitative (see Figure 9.12).

REPORTING

Data ≠ Information.

To maximize the value of risk reports they need to be understandable; comparable; and aggregatable.

Analyzing risk reports for a fund over time can provide valuable insights. Comparing the *ex ante* risk for an individual fund with its target provides the investor and the investment manager with an assessment of whether risks are in line with expectations. They should discuss significant deviations. It can also be useful to analyze a stray portfolio that, over time, pushed a manager's guidelines to the limit. By trending risk sensitivities, investors can proactively diagnose "style drift," and avoid surprise shifts in risks/returns.

Risk-attribution reports can highlight the extent of diversification within a fund and highlight any concentrated positions or exposures that should be discussed with the hedge fund manager.

Risk reporting should be multidimensional, so it can effectively reflect the multidimensional nature of risk (see Figure 9.13).

Hedge fund managers have 2 primary audiences for risk reporting— themselves and their investors.

Hedge fund managers' internal risk reporting needs are different from those of their investors. Although the push for improved risk transparency is primarily driven by investors, many hedge fund mangers are grudgingly finding that risk tools can actually help them manage their portfolios better. Their own risk management needs are not very different from those of

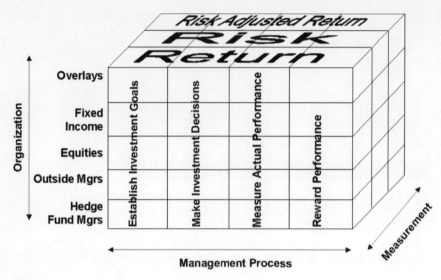

FIGURE 9.13 Internal dimensions. *Source:* © CMRA.

the proprietary trading desks of the 1980s, from which many hedge fund managers hail. Their attitudes are also similar to bank traders' attitudes when risk management tools and techniques are first introduced.

Investors' needs, however, are quite different. Investors need risk information from the funds in which they invest for 3 primary reasons:

1. To help them meet their fiduciary responsibilities and ensure that the funds in which they invest are well managed, risk-wise
2. To help them assess the overall risks of their portfolios of hedge fund investments, as well as their overall portfolios (traditional plus alternative investments)
3. To determine whether or not they are achieving the diversification benefits they wanted from their alternative investments

One should be able to "slice and dice" risk reports. They also need to track more subtle risks over time, such as price transparency characteristics; liquidity; bid/offer spreads; prices overridden; changes in correlations; and stress test results.

For some examples of useful reports, see Figures 9.14–9.17 (pages 151–152): But the best risk reports communicate comparatively. Risk measures are valuable when looked at over time (see Figures 9.18–9.20, page 153). Peer-group comparisons, when possible, are incredibly valuable (see Figures 9.21–9.23, page 154).

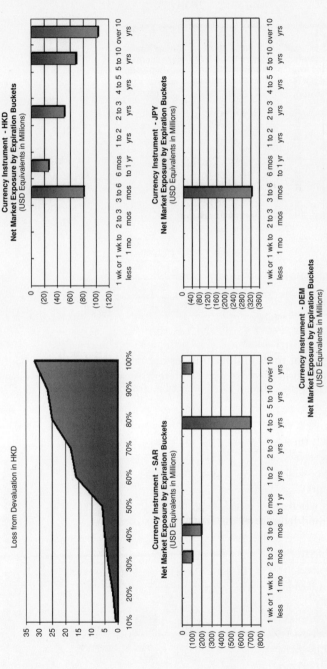

FIGURE 9.14 Risk at a glance, currency exposure. *Source:* © CMRA.

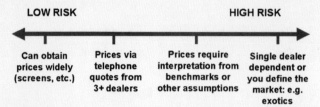

FIGURE 9.15   How does your mark to model exposure breakdown by price type. *Source:* © CMRA.

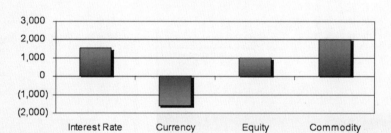

FIGURE 9.16   Risks at a glance, broad asset allocation. *Source:* © CMRA.

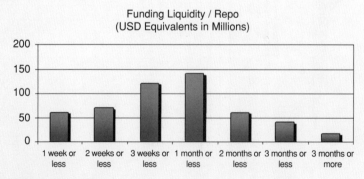

FIGURE 9.17   Risks at a glance, liquidity. *Source:* © CMRA.

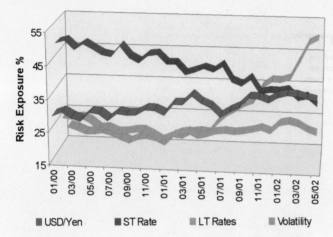

FIGURE 9.18 Trending var sensitivities. *Source:* © CMRA.

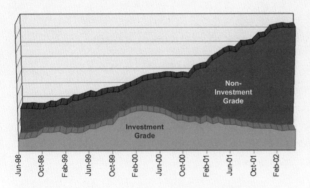

FIGURE 9.19 Net asset value. *Source:* © CMRA.

FIGURE 9.20 Portfolio credit characteristics. *Source:* © CMRA.

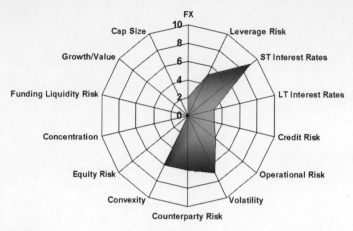

FIGURE 9.21 Comparative benchmarking, portfolio A. *Source:* © CMRA.

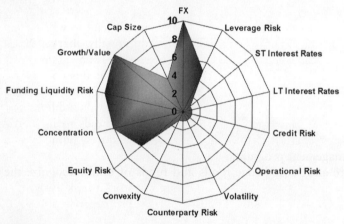

FIGURE 9.22 Comparative benchmarking, portfolio B. *Source:* © CMRA.

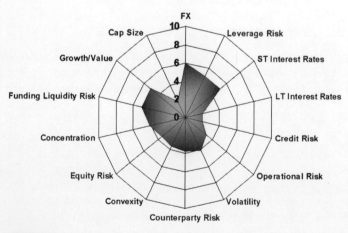

FIGURE 9.23 Comparative benchmarking, portfolios A and B. *Source:* © CMRA.

LIQUIDITY

Liquidity, or the lack of it, is probably the one risk that has traditionally received the least focus and yet has inflicted the greatest damage. Understanding a portfolio's liquidity is a critical component of effective risk management.

The Russian/LTCM crisis showed that valuing positions at midmarket, when positions are large and liquidity is poor, can be very misleading.

Experience shows that a crisis can dramatically dry up liquidity. While it is a natural human reflex, liquidating the most liquid instruments in a portfolio to meet margin demands can be, and was, in many cases, a death knell. The remaining portfolio is skewed to illiquid instruments and, therefore, even less able to meet the liquidity demands of a fast-moving market than the original portfolio.

During periods of market stress, bid /offer spreads tend to widen, further exacerbating the liquidity risk and cost. Additionally, market crises tend to send historical correlation out the window. All instruments move to a correlation of $+1$ or -1. While everyone knows about this correlation truism at some level, it is rarely factored into the risk equation. Strategies such as convergence trades, basis trades, etc., are most vulnerable to this correlation phenomenon. It is critical for such funds' needs to include a measure of this crisis effect. It is critical to explicitly address liquidity in a robust risk management program.

While more and more hedge funds and funds of funds recognize the value of branding themselves with institutional investors as risk aware and well risk-managed, some have overdone it and promote their risk process as greater than it is. This is a new type of risk.

DUE DILIGENCE

Even when a risk management review is included in due diligence, it often includes a look at risk management in isolation, rather than as an integral part of a fund's management. It is important to identify whether a fund's risk management process is consistent with the complexity of its strategies, as well as its management style ("If it's not written, don't do it" versus "Use your judgment").

In addition to standard risk questions, investors in traditional as well as alternative strategies should look how alpha is generated; inherent risks and relevant risk measures; risk-mitigation strategies; level of transparency; and performance. Expanding on performance, investors should look into realized performance (absolute, and where applicable, benchmark relative);

risk-adjusted performance; prospective performance; realized volatility; and prospective volatility.

Other investor considerations are portfolio-construction implications of allocation; prospective warning signs; and potential blow-up scenarios.

RISK-ADJUSTED PERFORMANCE

While performance measurement is a well-developed science, risk-adjusted performance measurement it is still a work in progress. When considering candidates for the risk-adjusted performance denominator, market risk is often a starting point. Various techniques for measuring market risk are evolving, but best practice generally includes some combination of VaR, stress test results, and scenario analysis results. While VaR alone is a reasonable measure of market risk for some portfolios, risks of many arbitrage-type strategies are better represented by stress tests and scenario analysis.

AN APPROPRIATE MEASURE OF RISK

One increasingly popular definition is:

> Market risk = highest of VAR (stress test 1, stress test 2, ...
> scenario analysis 1, scenario analysis 2, ...)

Stress tests should be based on the nature of the portfolio, and might include large market shocks, and changes in correlations, liquidity, shape of yield curve, "sector" definitions, volatility level, and shape of volatility curve.

Scenario analyses are generally created by applying stressful historical periods of market behavior (e.g., the crash of 1987, the Fed tightening in 1994, the Tequila crisis, the Asian meltdown, Russian/LTCM, the tech bust, 9/11) to current portfolios, to assess the impact if history were to repeat itself.

The next challenge is choosing the time horizon. One approach might be to match the horizon chosen for return, though longer horizons are generally more useful.

But what about other risks above and beyond "market risk"? While very important, operational risk, reputational risk, etc. are even harder to quantify than market risk. It is better to start simple and use a risk-adjusted return measure that captures market risk, and get used to a risk-adjusted world while fine-tuning one's definition and quantification of risk.

IMPACT OF LEVERAGE

In hedge fund absolute-return space, how should leverage affect risk-adjusted returns?

The primary challenge is to define leverage. The most common measure is gross balance sheet assets to equity, whether or not it is adjusted for off-balance-sheet transactions. However, there are many variations, including VAR to equity, margin ratio, etc.

Once one selects a measure of leverage and clearly communicates it to everyone who might need to interpret the de-leveraged, risk-adjusted returns, the actual calculation is simple.

NET ASSET VALUE (NAV) OF LESS LIQUID INVESTMENTS

All risk management measures assume knowledge of today's value of the portfolio and attempt to measure how much that value can change, based on changing circumstances. Some funds, however, are invested in securities with limited liquidity, large bid/offer spreads, or other characteristics that make valuation an exercise in estimation.

The author examined a mortgage-backed hedge fund, reviewed the dealer prices provided on December 31, and found differences that ranged from 6% to 44% among the prices provided by 5 dealers. With such price differences, the different methodologies for incorporating dealer quotes can yield significantly different results. For example, using the average of the dealer quotes created up to a 4-point difference in valuation versus using the "drop the high and low, then average" method. The precipitous devaluation of the Lipper convertible portfolio and the Heartland municipal portfolio is an example of this phenomenon. The risk measures of these types of investments need to be grossed up to reflect the uncertainty on the base evaluation. An illiquid, micro-cap stock, private placement, or structured note with a VaR of 2 is "riskier" than a portfolio of IBM stock with a VaR of 2 (see Figure 9.2 at beginning of chapter).

Valuation overrides by managers need to be carefully monitored. There are good reasons why a valuation from a commercial feed and/or from dealers is not as accurate as one made by a manager who is familiar with the nuances of the market. This is especially the case for instruments that are matrix- or model-priced. Overriding can, however, be an opportunity for manipulation. It should be carefully controlled and monitored by all parties. While most respondents to the recent survey on valuation practices indicated that adjustments represented less than 2% of net asset value (NAV), some indicated that the adjustment in aggregate represented up to 30% of NAV.

REPUTATIONAL RISK

People who lose money like to blame someone else.

The best in a peer group can still lose a lot of money. Beating the S&P is not as exciting in a down year as in a bull market. Picking the right peer group can be critical.

Not having the guidance of written policies and procedures is bad practice—having them and not following them can be disastrous. Litigation is rarely affected because someone didn't have policies and procedures, but it can be affected when they existed, but were not followed. Merrill Lynch Investment Management (MLIM) learned this the hard way.

No one should agree to guidelines he or she can't implement and track. Meaningful limits need to be trackable and tracked. Guidelines should be as specific as possible, to avoid multiple interpretations. No matter how well one does business, one should expect problems when things go wrong.

Preventive measures should not only prevent misfortunes, but should also protect the manager from the harsh scrutiny that follows when misfortunes do occur.

Poorly defined statements and assumptions in marketing materials can be problematic. All written and verbal communications are opportunities for reputational risk. Unilever and MLIM are good examples of this. Even informal communication (e.g., e-mail, taped telephone conversations, letters) can create reputational risk.

Receiving risk information and doing nothing with it increases fiduciary risk. While institutional investors need information to fulfill their fiduciary responsibilities, having access to information that they don't understand can create liability and/or reduce their ability to maintain that they "didn't know."

CHAPTER 10

Structured Products—
Then and Now

John Kelly
Kirk Strawn, CFA, CIMA

Structured products target specific risk/reward levels and provide a potential layer of protection to the investor. Principal-protection structures have been especially important for investors who are relatively new to alternative investment strategies, or who have a specific principal floor value they do not wish to fall below. Although new terminology is emerging all the time, many of the concepts that are being applied to structured products have existed for some time—almost 2 decades in some instances.

This chapter explores some of the important concepts that are central to an understanding of structured products, as well as some of the newer concepts that orbit the subject. This is not an exhaustive piece on the subject, and many investment professionals may have a different perspective on the items discussed, but it may offer some clarity on the subject and provide some informative insights to the investment community.

This discussion aims to answer several questions. What are structured products? How did they emerge? How have they developed? Which principles have guided the design and management of structured products? Which challenges do providers of structured products face, and how have they dealt with them? And finally, what makes structured products appealing to institutional and private investors alike?

THE STRUCTURED PRODUCT CONCEPT

Structured products are highly engineered investments that offer exposure to a variety of investment strategies in an attractive form. They are designed to fulfill certain objectives, such as to provide increased exposure to investment strategies through the use of leverage, to meet certain regulatory requirements, or to provide tax-efficient exposure to investments in certain offshore jurisdictions. However, a primary interest of investors is the ability of structured products to provide exposure to alternative investment strategies while they guarantee to return a minimum of the investors' initial investment capital, or principal, when the product reaches its maturity date. The so-called principal-protection structure is one of the most common and popular forms of structured product. This chapter will focus primarily on principal-protected products.

Many of today's structured products invest across a range of investment strategies, styles, and managers with the objective of achieving specific risk/return outcomes. The strategies can be actively or passively managed. Additionally, the overall approach may be to follow a traditional long-only investment style, or, more typically, hedge fund strategies, including managed futures, arbitrage, equity long/short, distressed securities, and funds of hedge funds.

THE EARLY PRINCIPAL-PROTECTION STRUCTURE

To illustrate principal-protected products and structuring flexibility, it is worth going back to the 1980s, when some of the first capital-guaranteed, or principal-protected, products were launched. This type of product provided investors access to a managed-futures alternative investment approach while assuring them that, at a minimum, their principal would be returned to them when the product reached maturity.

Figure 10.1 illustrates how this early structured product worked. In this example, the product is legally structured as a special purpose vehicle with limited liability. The investor's principal of $100, shown in the box on the far left of the diagram, is used in 2 ways. First, approximately $60 is used to purchase fixed-income securities, such as U.S. Treasury zero-coupon bonds to secure the principal. These securities increase in value over the life of the product to a level that matches the initial investment value and thus underpins the principal protection promised to investors. To enhance the security of the principal, these securities are pledged to a bank, in exchange for which the bank issues a guarantee of principal. Second, the balance of the capital, $40 or 40% of net asset value (NAV), is used for exposure to the alternative investment approach on a leveraged or unleveraged basis, with the objective of generating the targeted risk/reward outcome set by the investment manager.

PRESERVING PERFORMANCE POTENTIAL

In addition to the high caliber risk-adjusted performance achieved by many alternative investment approaches, the concept of the principal-protection

The diagram below shows the general principles of a basic guaranteed structure.

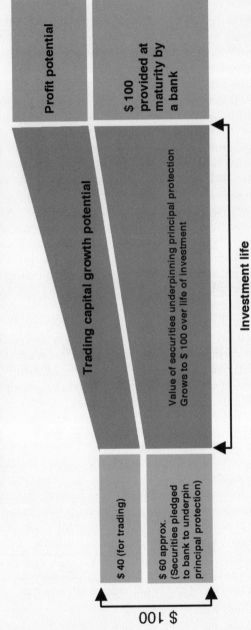

Profit potential

$ 100 provided at maturity by a bank

Trading capital growth potential

Value of securities underpinning principal protection Grows to $ 100 over life of investment

Investment life

$ 40 (for trading)

$ 60 approx. (Securities pledged to bank to underpin principal protection)

$ 100

Schematic illustration. [1]The exact proportion invested in US Treasury zero coupon instruments may vary. There is no guarantee that a fund will experience a profit as depicted above.

FIGURE 10.1 Example of an early structured product.

structure has been a major driver of investor interest in structured products over the past 20 years. The guarantee to return the principal at maturity has obviously proven attractive. Worth noting are the way this has been achieved and the structuring principles that have driven the design and management of these products.

A sound principle that was established during some of the more successful early initiatives in product structuring was ensuring that any principal-protection arrangement does not materially affect the performance potential of the underlying investment approach. Principal protection would be less appealing if the use of net asset value to secure the arrangement were to diminish the return potential of the underlying investment program within a product. Thus, the real attraction of principal-protected products has hinged on the ability of their managers to structure and manage the product so that there is a very high probability that they will deliver returns similar to those of nonguaranteed products pursuing the same investment approach. As with a nonguaranteed product, the manager should determine the level of trading capital required to ensure that the product is solidly positioned to fulfill its risk and return objectives. The manager must also monitor the level of available trading capital and adjust leverage or gearing just as he or she would for nonguaranteed products.

Figure 10.2 demonstrates the similarity in performance of 2 products launched simultaneously by Man Investment Products, one guaranteed and the other nonguaranteed, which invest in the same program.

From the mid-1980s to the mid-1990s, managed futures investment programs provided the investment platform for many principal-protected structures. Because managed futures funds trade on margin, they offer inherent leverage that is beneficial to principal-protected product structures. This is best explained using Figure 10.3 (see page 164), which illustrates cash usage for managed futures products.

The column on the left shows the cash usage of a nonprincipal-protected managed futures product based on a proprietary strategy, which has a track record dating back to 1983. The diagram shows that to be in a position to generate the target annualized return, only 15–20% of net asset value is used as futures margin to gain the desired market exposure. A greater portion would obviously generate a potentially higher return, but would also push the volatility above what the manager considered a viable level for a conservative investor looking to incorporate this investment into an existing portfolio. The balance of the capital, 80–85% of net asset value, is held in cash on short-term deposit.

The right-hand column of the diagram indicates the cash usage for a principal-protected structure. Approximately 60% of net asset value is invested in zero-coupon bonds and pledged to a bank to underpin the principal protection. This means 40% of net asset value is available to obtain

1 April 1996 to 31 March 2002

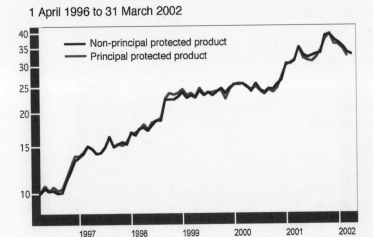

FIGURE 10.2 Comparison of open ended and principal protected product performance. *Source:* Man database. There is no guarantee of trading performance and past performance is not necessarily indicative of future results. Non-principal protected product represented by AHL Diversified plc., which is valued weekly. The inception date of this product was 26 March 1996. Principal protected product represented by AHL Diversified Guaranteed Limited, which is valued monthly. The inception date of this product was 2 January 1996. This is for informational purposes only and is not an offer to sell, or a solicitation of an offer to buy, interests in either or both of these products or any product utilizing the Man-AHL Diversified program. Neither of these products are available to US persons.
[1]Other than in periods of sustained material drawdown.

the required market exposure. As the required level of market exposure is the same for the principal-protected structure as for the nonprincipal-protected structure, the two structures' return potential is the same. The only difference is that instead of having a relatively large cash reserve on short-term deposit, the principal-protected structure has a cash reserve or trading capital reserve of 15–20%, which is the balance of the 40% trading capital portion not applied to futures margin. The additional costs of structuring and providing the principal protection are partially mitigated because the yield on the zero-coupon bonds in the principal-protected structure is usually greater than the risk-free rate applicable to the additional cash in the nonprincipal-protected structure.

The disadvantage of a principal-protection arrangement is that, if the product were to suffer a very significant drawdown, its trading capital would be depleted more quickly than the equivalent nonprincipal-protected structure. To minimize this risk, the investment manager must carefully

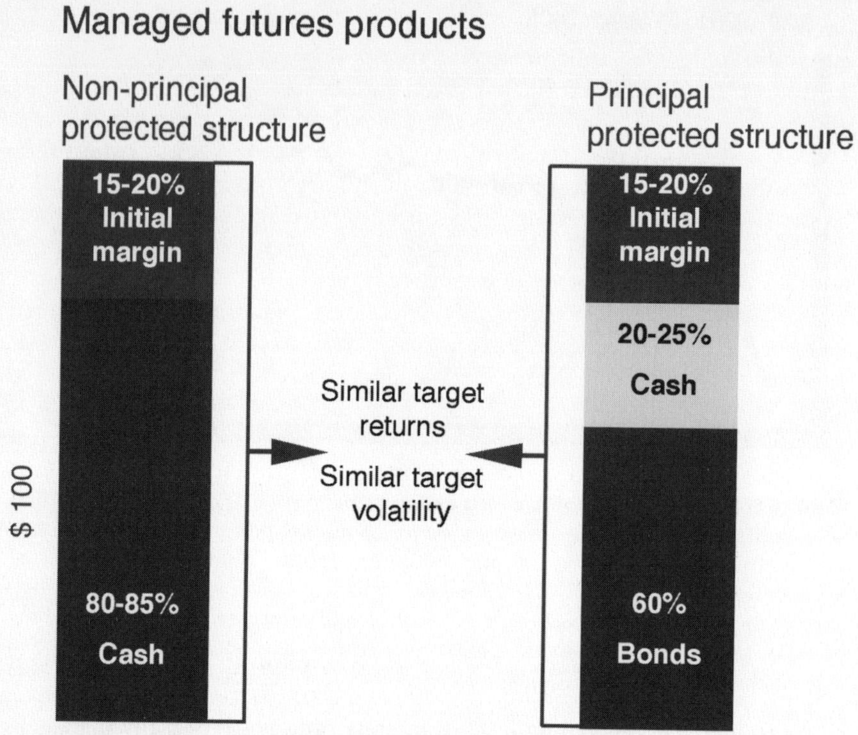

Managed futures products

Non-principal
protected structure

Principal
protected structure

Schematic Illustration.
Past or projected performance is not necessarily a guide to future results.
This is for informational purposes only and is not an offer to sell, or a solicitation of an offer to buy, interests in any account or product utilizing the Man-AHL Diversified Program.

FIGURE 10.3   Effective utilization of investment capital.

determine the optimal split between the trading capital portion and the principal-protection portion. If a manager allocates too much capital to the trading portion, reducing the amount available for the principal-protection portion, the zero-coupon bonds he is able to buy will take longer to reach a value equal to the principal. Conversely, if a manager allocates too much to the zero-coupon bonds, he will be left with insufficient capital to generate the targeted return.

ENSURING ROBUSTNESS AND THE PROBLEM WITH SHORTER TERM MATURITIES

Another important goal in structuring principal-protected products is the assurance of a robust structure. For the purposes of this chapter, robustness implies an investment product that can withstand market shocks at any point during its life, while preserving the trading capital it needs to meet its targeted risk-adjusted return. The robustness of a structured product can be compromised if the manager does not make the optimal allocation between trading capital and the principal-protection portion. It is imperative for the investor and/or consultant to evaluate the manager's experience and ability in constructing, stress testing, monitoring, and rebalancing the structured product, to ensure that the manager can create and maintain a robust structured product during varied market conditions.

In the mid-1980s, when many of the first generation of these products were launched, interest rates were around 15%. Because of these high rates, many of the first principal-protected products had short-term maturities—as short as 5 years. As interest rates fell over the years, the managers had to keep increasing the maturity terms of the funds to keep the split between the guarantee and trading-capital components constant. There was a lot of market pressure to create products with shorter term maturities. Some managers responded by producing products with maturities that were significantly shorter. This involved increasing their exposure to zero-coupon bonds, which meant reducing the trading-capital portion, the trading-capital reserve, or both.

Shorter term guarantees require an environment of high prevailing interest rates or a greater allocation of capital to the guarantee component of a product. The prevailing level of interest rates is beyond any manager's control.

Allocating more capital for purchasing zero-coupon bonds involves two choices. One is to hold the same level of market exposure, thus maintaining the return potential but reducing the amount of funds in the trading-capital reserve below the 15–20% outlined in the example. This increases the risk that the product goes into what is known as guaranteed mode if a major drawdown occurs. Guaranteed mode occurs when capital is no longer available to the manager to generate trading returns, and the investors have to wait out the remaining years until the product matures to regain their principal. This increased risk of entering guaranteed mode arises because there is less of a cushion or trading capital reserve to meet margin calls in a serious drawdown.

The second choice is to reduce market exposure. This diminishes performance potential but makes the portfolio safer by maintaining the trading-capital reserve constant at 20–25% of NAV.

A number of managers have opted to retain their focus on ensuring investment management quality, rather than providing reduced-maturity periods. These managers have tried to ensure that their structured products remain robust, their target returns continue to be competitive, and clients' risk/return parameters are met. The logic that gave rise to principal-protected products in the first place was that a principal product format only makes sense if it allows investors to gain exposure to an investment approach in a form that is robust and also does not compromise performance potential. This logic tends to get subverted when managers offer products with shorter term maturities.

The market pressure to offer shorter maturities has abated significantly in recent years. In part this is because many long-term products focused on investment management quality have delivered returns broadly in line with their targets. It is also because some of the shorter term products offered over the years have lost their trading capital and gone into guaranteed mode. When a product has entered guaranteed mode, an investor may receive significantly less than the amount invested if he or she were to redeem before maturity. Under normal circumstances, structured products typically offer monthly or quarterly liquidity, depending on the investment strategy or strategies in the portfolio, which allows investors to redeem part or all of their holdings before maturity.

PROTECTING INVESTORS AND THE GUARANTOR

Another core requirement in developing structured products is to ensure that the mechanics and details of any principal-protection arrangement preserve the integrity of the principal protection. Therefore, investors who purchase the principal-protected equity or note and the guarantor bank or insurance company that provides the principal protection are not compromised if a product suffers an unexpectedly large drawdown and goes into guaranteed mode.

An effective way to protect investors and the company providing the principal protection is to conduct trading operations through a limited-liability trading subsidiary of the investment company. Because the zero-coupon bonds are purchased and pledged to a bank in exchange for issuance of the principal protection at the investment company level, the investment manager and broker can make a claim against those assets only within the limited liability trading subsidiary. Contractual arrangements can ensure that neither the investment manager nor the broker can claim assets of the product, except for those assets within the limited liability trading subsidiary. This type of arrangement is imperative because if a large drawdown were to occur, and margin calls were triggered, the investment manager and/or broker could not use the zero-coupon bonds as collateral to meet the margin call. The zero-coupon bonds are protected to ensure the principal protection to the client. This is an important distinction. Some advisors have bought zero-coupon bonds for clients to provide principal protection on a leveraged investment. However, once margin calls occur, the broker can sell those securities to meet the margin call if the structure noted above is not in place.

INCORPORATING CASH-INTENSIVE HEDGE FUND STRATEGIES

By the mid-1990s, principal-guaranteed products structured around managed futures programs had become extremely popular. This coincided with a significant broadening of investor interest in principal-protected structures that include different investment styles and approaches.

Clearly, it was highly desirable to bring diverse hedge fund strategies into principal-protected product structures. By combining a number of low-correlation alternative strategies and managers in a structured product, the investment becomes more diversified, leading to better risk-adjusted returns. The problem for investment managers was that while managed futures have inherent leverage, hedge fund styles, such as arbitrage, equity hedge, equity long/short, event-driven, and funds of hedge funds, are cash intensive; the advisors of these strategies generally require most, if not all, of the cash invested to effectively implement their strategies.

To address the cash intensiveness of other alternative investment strategies, several modifications were made to the original structure in Figure 10.1. These modifications are illustrated in Figure 10.4.

The structure depicted in Figure 10.4 is still used today. The left lower portion of the diagram shows the $100 invested in the same way as it is for the early principal-guaranteed product in Figure 10.1. In the new structure, the manager arranges for the product company, not the investor, to borrow $60 to invest in the cash-intensive hedge fund strategies—a diversified fund of hedge funds, for example. With the increased leverage and the investment in a fund of hedge funds, the product is positioned to provide better diversification and target a higher absolute return, after payment of the financing costs associated with the line of credit established to fund the investment in the fund of hedge funds.

This loan, though not a feature of all structured products, is structured as a nonrecourse loan to the principal-protected product. Thus, it is another important step toward ensuring that the principal guarantee remains sacrosanct. However, as an investment manager launches more of these structures, finding sources of lending begins to place a greater burden on the manager. Consequently, financial institutions are exploring innovative ways to structure financing arrangements that provide managers greater flexibility and allow them to offer new combinations of cash-intensive hedge fund strategies within structured-product portfolios. The financing arrangements that have been developed include straightforward bank lending, total return swaps, nondefeased structures, and, more

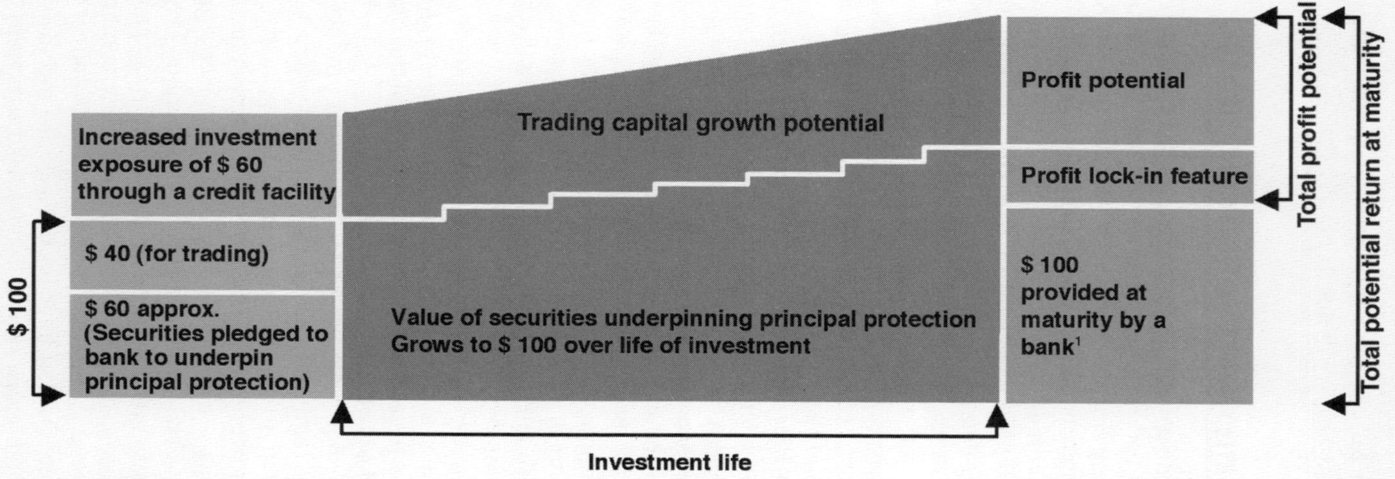

Total potential return at maturity

Total profit potential

Profit potential

Profit lock-in feature

$ 100 provided at maturity by a bank[1]

Trading capital growth potential

Value of securities underpinning principal protection
Grows to $ 100 over life of investment

Investment life

Increased investment exposure of $ 60 through a credit facility

$ 40 (for trading)

$ 60 approx. (Securities pledged to bank to underpin principal protection)

$ 100

Schematic Illustration.
There is no guarantee that a fund will experience a profit as depicted above.
[1]Subject to the terms and conditions of the protection arrangement, payable on the Maturity Date for the Face Value of each Bond outstanding and redeemed on the Maturity Date.

FIGURE 10.4 Example of an enhanced structured product.

recently, collateralized fund obligation (CFO) structures, which are discussed later in this chapter.

THE PROFIT LOCK-IN FEATURE

Another significant product-structuring development has been the provision of a profit lock-in feature, the effect of which is demonstrated schematically by the step line in Figure 10.4. Under the terms of a principal protection, principal can be repaid to investors only when a product reaches maturity. This means that if a product doubled or tripled in value, all the gains over the principal would be at risk thereafter. By building profit lock-in features into structured products, managers have substantially mitigated this risk for the client, however low the probability of it actually happening might be.

The profit lock-in feature makes provision for a portion of net new trading profits to be secured after a product has enjoyed a period of significant profitability. In the same way that principal-protection structures aim to provide an extra level of security without impacting performance, profit lock-in features are designed to raise the level of principal protection at maturity without materially affecting performance.

Each profit lock-in feature has its own particular specifications. In this example, the basic concept is that each time a product attains net new trading profits amounting to about 10% of net asset value, it triggers a profit lock-in. The product company purchases securities, usually U.S. Treasury zero-coupon bonds, so that at maturity an amount equivalent to approximately 50% of the net new trading profits is secured. The manager adds these to the fixed-income securities that have already been purchased and pledged to the guarantor bank, thus raising the principal-protection amount at maturity. The remainder of the net new trading profits is maintained within the trading capital component of the portfolio, and the level of gearing applied to the portfolio remains unchanged.

RISK MANAGEMENT

If risk management is a stabilizing force in the investment industry at large, it is the foundation of success in the structured-products arena. Any investor's primary focus should be the risk associated with an investment. A manager's provision of a principal-protection arrangement, and an investor's decision to opt for a principal-protected product, should be dependent on the manager fulfilling all necessary risk management criteria. In other words, the provision of principal protection should not be the overriding reason why an investor chooses an investment product; principal protection should be regarded as an added feature.

By way of analogy, when you decide to purchase a car, your choice is likely to be governed by a number of critical considerations—size, miles per gallon, performance, reliability, etc. One feature that car manufacturers might offer is an airbag. If the chassis is strong, and you can succeed in driving the vehicle safely, the airbag—which we can liken to a principal-protection arrangement—is largely redundant. However, it is nice to have. In fact, many institutional investors view the principal protection strictly as a relatively inexpensive put option for the segment of their portfolio dedicated to alternative asset management strategies. From a fiduciary standpoint, it is another form of protection after due diligence has been conducted on the manager, the strategies, and the manager's risk-control process.

The risk management framework for structured products usually comprises 2 levels of control. First, risk is controlled at the product portfolio level, and second, on an individual advisor level for multimanager/multi-strategy structured products. The risk management process is driven by three objectives: to identify sources of potential risk; to quantify and analyze these risks in relation to measured criteria; and to manage the rule-based decisions which are executed when predetermined parameters are breached.

At the product portfolio level, the investment manager establishes tolerance bands in accordance with the product's and client's target risk. Ongoing risk-monitoring enables the manager to detect whether the implied risk of the portfolio at any stage diverges from the tolerance bands. Risk measurement tools, such as value at risk (VaR), standard deviation, and correlation, are used in this monitoring process. If, on any day, the risk report identifies a product breaking its limits, there is an immediate evaluation of the advisors and of the more detailed aspects of the risk-analysis process. This means the manager can identify whether the divergence is the result of a change in market dynamics or something else. Then the manager takes appropriate action to bring the portfolio risk back in line with its target level.

At the level of individual advisors, the initial due diligence process takes into account each advisor's risk management systems and ensures that they function to certain standards. Once trading starts, daily risk reports are generated for each advisor, and these cover, among other factors, portfolio volatility, margin-to-equity requirements, leverage, portfolio risk, and turnover. Finally, monthly reviews identify any divergences from target levels. These measures enable the investment manager to monitor daily position and performance information, and the overall risk impact of performance divergences by individual advisors on the product portfolio.

A key priority is to monitor the trading exposure relative to the amount of available trading capital for any product. For each strategy or advisor there is a clearly defined assumption of the worst risk of loss. This worst-risk assumption enables the manager to calculate which levels of trading capital and trading reserve are required to create a comfortable cushion in the event of a deep loss. This helps to determine the level of gearing and implement the risk controls. Part of the daily risk management process is determining the level of gearing that is appropriate to ensure that the level of trading capital and reserve is high enough to cushion a product in a deep loss.

INNOVATIONS IN FINANCING STRUCTURES

Given the present demand for structured products, many of the more recent innovations in this realm have focused on creative ways to structure financing to allow a variety of hedge fund styles to operate in a principal-protected format.

Some of the initiatives seek favorable principal-protection arrangements that allow investment capital to be employed more flexibly and efficiently, to maximize exposure to investment strategies, especially cash-intensive strategies, as indicated in Figure 10.4. Others involve gaining leveraged exposure to investment strategies while utilizing a minimum of capital.

These innovations have benefited the development of the structured products in 2 ways. First, they have provided alternative sources of borrowing, potentially creating better terms and rates for the manager and the underlying investor. Second, they have provided a new spectrum of opportunities for investors who may want to diversify the debt exposure of their portfolio away from traditional forms of debt.

One way to facilitate more efficient financing for structured products is through total-return swaps with banks, as depicted in Figure 10.5. By way of example, the bank buys shares in a fund of funds from the product company. The bank and the product company then enter a swap. Through the swap, the bank offers exposure to the total return on the shares of the fund of funds to the product company. In exchange, the product company pays the bank financing costs and deposits cash with the bank as collateral to protect against adverse market movements. The product company benefits because it can use less cash to get the desired exposure to the fund of funds portfolio. Investors in the product company benefit from the favorable spread between the return on the fund of funds and the costs of the bank financing (see Figure 10.5).

Another financing arrangement is a nondefeased principal protection structure. In contrast to a fully defeased structure described earlier, in which

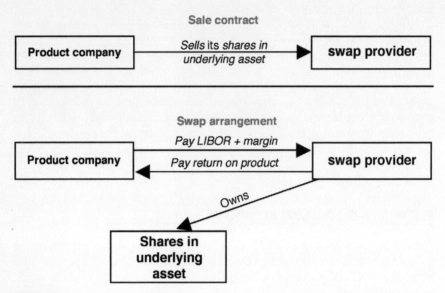

FIGURE 10.5 Example of a total return swap arrangement for a structured product.

a portion of NAV is always invested in securities (such as zero-coupon bonds) that underpin the principal protection, a nondefeased structure does not need the initial purchase of collateral to underpin the principal-protection. The risk management process is very similar to that of a conventional fully defeased principal-protection structure. In this instance, the bank and the product company apply an agreed formula, whereby, should the portfolio decline in value, the product company will utilize investment capital to purchase zero-coupon bonds to secure the principal protection. The willingness of banks to enter into this type of arrangement with an investment manager reflects the degree of their confidence in the manager's risk management capabilities. This type of structure is sometimes referred to as Constant Proportion Portfolio Insurance (CPPI).

Depending on its maturity, a CPPI structure generally starts trading at the same level of investment exposure at which the underlying investment vehicle or portfolio would trade. Subsequent investment exposure levels are calculated as a multiple of the difference, expressed as a percentage of NAV, between the product NAV and the theoretical bond floor, which is the present value of the cost of the bonds required to fully collateralize the principal-protection. Effectively, this means that if the CPPI structure performs well, the portfolio might have no bonds or securities in it to underpin the principal-protection and the leverage applied to the portfolio can increase, often beyond that of a fully collateralized principal-protection structure. Conversely, if performance weakens, the risk of payment under the terms of the principal-protection agreement increases, and so the CPPI structure will de-leverage its investment exposure to the underlying investment portfolio and purchase zero-coupon bonds as collateral for the principal-protection. This can be likened to a "buy bonds as required" collateral arrangement.

By being able to leverage up when performance is strong, the CPPI structure can generate increased returns, yet the borrowing that is required to achieve greater leverage is less than for a fully defeased structure, if anything at all, and can be obtained at very attractive rates from the principal-protection provider. Another characteristic of the CPPI structure is that during periods when there are no bonds in the CPPI portfolio, there are no oscillations in the NAV caused by interest-rate volatility. The NAV of fully defeased structures can experience small short-term oscillations because interest-rate volatility will affect the price of the underlying zero-coupon bonds. To reduce this volatility, interest-rate hedging on the zero-coupon bonds can be used by the product company. Over the long term, any such oscillations are inconsequential if the product is held until maturity.

One of the more recent innovations in financing arrangements is the Collateralized Fund Obligation (CFO), as outlined in Figure 10.6.

The CFO product company issues notes (floating and fixed debt tranches) with various credit ratings, as well as an equity tranche in the form of preference shares. Credit ratings on the debt are awarded by the investment ratings services, such as Standard & Poor's and Moody's, based mainly on the concept of expected loss at the quantitative level, but also on

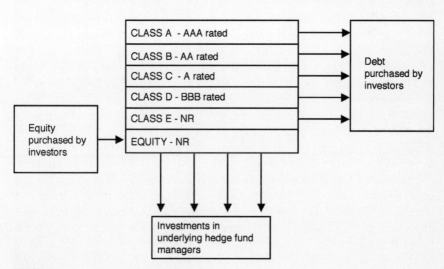

FIGURE 10.6 Example of CFI structure.

qualitative considerations, such as the experience and integrity of the investment advisor and the managers of the underlying strategies.

The proceeds of the issuance of the notes and preference shares are invested in, for example, a portfolio of hedge funds. The notes are collateralized by the issuer's assets—the portfolio of hedge funds, in this case. If the NAV of the CFO portfolio falls below certain levels, and it does not recover within specified times, assets need to be redeemed and leverage reduced by paying down the liabilities. Thus, debt investors have the security of predefined structural protection levels, while the terms of the arrangement mean that the equity investors benefit from greater leverage and longer term committed financing.

The risk associated with the CFO structure is that the returns on the fund of funds may be less than the coupon on the debt. In this case, both debt- and equity-holders' returns could be marginalized.

CONCLUSION

Amid weakness in equity markets and low yields from fixed-income assets, private and institutional investors around the world are rethinking their asset-allocation strategies. Interest in hedge funds and alternative investment styles is surging, driven by a growing recognition that these investments are capable of delivering strong risk-adjusted performance with relatively low correlation to traditional asset classes. Structured products are proving to be an increasingly popular way of gaining exposure to hedge fund strategies.

For those taking their first steps into the world of alternative investment, the security of principal-protected structures is a major attraction. Investors are attracted to a significant extent by the prospect of exposure to alternative investment strategies that are largely uncorrelated to each other and to traditional asset classes, and which are being offered with the security of a principal-protection arrangement.

Although contemporary structured products appear in a variety of forms, each seemingly accompanied by an acronym, many of the ideas on which today's securitized structures are built have been applied as far back as the 1980s. Structured products have evolved and developed in an iterative fashion. Early principal-guarantee structures were applied to managed futures funds, taking advantage of the intrinsic leverage these offered and putting available investment capital to better use. Subsequently, principal-protection arrangements were applied to composite or multistrategy portfolios that borrowed capital to provide greater leverage and exposure to more cash-intensive hedge fund strategies. Profit lock-ins were introduced to create rising guarantees. More sophisticated financing arrangements were developed to optimize cash usage, create even greater flexibility, and add to the diversity of portfolio types and risk/reward outcomes from which investors can choose. Each stage in this development has been a logical extension of the previous one, each progression the result of cumulative insights gained over the years.

Despite the apparent complexity of many structured products, and notwithstanding the sophisticated financial engineering and legal expertise needed to create them, the authors believe that designing and managing successful structured products depends on how successful a manager is at following 4 rather elementary guidelines.

First, any structured product is only as good as its underlying investment management and risk control. Second, every structuring and investment management decision should be aimed at ensuring robustness. Third, where a structured product provides principal protection, the manager should ensure that the provision for principal protection should not be at the expense of trading performance. Fourth, every precaution should be taken to ensure that nothing can compromise the principal-protection arrangement or impinge upon investors or a guarantor bank.

If high-caliber alternative investment strategies are successfully blended, and the quality of product structuring and investment management is of an equally high standard, the structured product will appeal to both new and experienced investors, as well as private and institutional.

The Hedge Fund Difference

Todd Goldman

OVERVIEW

A major difference between hedge funds and mutual funds is the frequency of cash flows in and out. Mutual fund cash flows occur daily. One can do a return calculation for every single trading day of the year. Most hedge funds only allow liquidity events once a month. This makes many of the return-approximation methods discussed within the AIMR guidelines (such as the Modified Dietz Method) irrelevant in computing hedge fund returns.

It is possible to break down the components of a return calculation by focusing separately on the denominator and the numerator.

The denominator can be expressed as "adjusted beginning capital" for a given period. For the month of March 2002, adjusted beginning capital would be derived as follows: ending capital on February 28, 2002 plus March 1, 2002 contributions less March 1, 2002 withdrawals.

The numerator is based on a fund's income or loss. It varies depending on whether or not the measured return is gross or net. A fund's income or loss can be broken into 3 components:

1. Income earned from trading and from cash or debit balances. For funds that have all assets at one prime broker, this number will typically match the income for the month shown on the last day of a month.
2. Expenses other than those charged by the general partner. These include professional fees and state franchise taxes.
3. Expenses and allocations that compensate the general partners and/or investment advisors, mainly the management fee and incentive allocation.

How does one calculate ABC when in theory no capital, or negative capital, is required, as it would be in dollar neutral, short selling, net short, uncovered option writing, etc.? Return calculations are independent of

	Fund #1 Full Expenses	Fund #2 Expenses Reimbursed
Adjusted Beginning Capital	$4,000,000	$4,000,000
Income in primebrokerage account	400,000	400,000
Professional fees	(40,000)	
Ending Capital	$4,360,000	$4,400,000
Annual return	9.00%	10.00%

FIGURE A1.1   Partnership expenses.

strategy. No matter what the strategy, the money invested and used by the fund manager is the same. There can never be negative capital or no capital, as any strategy, at a minimum, needs amounts put up on margin. Some managers present hypothetical stand-alone results. These results are unrealistic and misleading, as they generally assume the smallest possible amounts as margin with little or no cushion. One should still measure actual results with ABC as the denominator.

GROSS RETURN

In calculating the gross return for the fund, the numerator is based on A less B (as defined above). Many people confuse this point as they believe that gross does not include the effect of fund expenses (B above).

Returns can be "massaged" when a general partner reimburses the fund for expenses. This may occur in the early years of a fund's existence when the fund's total capital has not yet reached a critical mass. Figure A1.1 shows an example. This fund has started small, and expenses have a material impact. In this example, the general partner can increase the gross return by 100 basis points by reimbursing the fund for its expenses. The general partner reimbursement would be reported in the footnotes of an audited financial statement but would probably escape attention when numbers were reported to the various indices.

NET RETURN

The net return is the gross return reduced by general partner/advisor compensation, item C above. This computation would be simple if all partners within a fund were subject to the same fee structure. This is rarely the case, as most funds have some investors who pay reduced fees, or none. Some of

	GP & Friends	Limited Partners	Total	
Opening Capital	$500,000	$500,000	$1,000,000	
				120,000
Management fee at 1%	0	(5,000)	(5,000)	
				300,000
Gross income	50,000	50,000	100,000	147,000
Incentive fee at 20%		(9,000)	(9,000)	1.080
Ending Capital	$550,000	$536,000	$1,086,000	136,111
Annual return	10.00%	7.20%	8.60%	

FIGURE A1.2   Management fees.

these issues are displayed in Figure A1.2 For this simple example, assume that the general partner has no direct investment in the fund. Half of this hypothetical fund's investors are friends of the general partner who pay no management fee or incentive allocation. There is a 280-basis point difference between their returns and those of the other investors. Some funds would report this net result at 8.60%, the return for the limited partner group as a whole. While financial highlights computed under AICPA standards require a fund to disclose the return for the limited partner class as a whole (in this case, the 8.60% return), most investors would want to know the 7.20% return of the fee-paying partners.

Figure A1.3 highlights another issue. In this example, the original investor in year 1 has a loss. In year 2 she has enough income to get back to the high watermark but not enough to pay an incentive fee. The new investor, without losses carried from year 1, pays the incentive fee. In this scenario, some funds would report the 8% return and others the 10% return.

OTHER CONSIDERATIONS

People have a lot of misconceptions about return computations with various forms of leverage. AIMR guidelines require that margin borrowings be treated as cash flows into an account. Most analysts would agree that hedge funds would not compute returns differently if they used leverage. Funds should disclose the use of leverage or options strategies, but the return is still based on the numerators and denominators discussed above.

A fund should not break out different investment components in reporting its returns. Some funds have reported the return on their equity investments without reflecting the portion that is in cash. This is clearly misleading, as it doesn't penalize a fund that is overly weighted in cash during a rising market. Once again, returns should be based on the numerators and denominators shown above.

Year 1	Initial Partners	Year 2 Partners	Total
Initial contribution	$1,100,000		$1,100,000
Loss	(100,000)		(100,000)
Ending Capital year 1	$1,000,000	$0	$1,000,000
Annual return	-9.09%		-9.09%

Year 2	Initial Partners	Year 2 Partners	Total
Opening balance	$1,000,000		$1,000,000
New contributions		1,000,000	1,000,000
Income before incentive fee	100,000	100,000	200,000
Incentive fee		(20,000)	(20,000)
Ending capital year 2	$1,100,000	$1,080,000	$2,180,000
Annual return	10.00%	8.00%	9.00%
2 Year Total Return	0.00%	8.00%	-0.91%

FIGURE A1.3 Incentive allocation.

Some Helpful Links

Strategic Financial Solutions, LLC / PerTrac: www.pertrac2000.com
Barclay Global Hedge Source: www.barclaygrp.com/data/index.html
Hedge Fund Research: www.hfr.com
MAR Hedge: www.marhedge.com
CISDM: www.umass.edu/som/cisdm/index.htm
MSCI: www.msci.com/hedge
HedgeWorld: www.hedgeworld.com
Tremont TASS (Europe) Ltd: www.tassresearch.com
The Hennessee Group: www.hennesseegroup.com
Van Hedge Fund Advisors International, Inc: www.hedgefund.com
Zephyr: www.styleadvisor.com
Ibbotson: www.ibbotson.com
AIMA: www.aima.org
HedgeFund.net: www.hedgefund.net
U.S. Offshore Funds Directory: www.hedgefundnews.com
Infovest 21: www.infovest21.com
Eurohedge: www.eurohedge.com
Hedge Fund Intelligence: www.hedgefundintelligence.com
EurekaHedge: www.eurekahedge.com
Albourne Village: www.albounevillage.com
Hedge Fund Alert: www.hedgefundalert.com
Information Management Network: www.imn.org
Institute for International Research: www.iirusa.com
Financial Research Associates: www.frallc.com
Opal Financial Group: www.opalgroup.net
Hedge Fund Association: www.thehfa.com
Hedge Fund Resources: www.hedgefundresources.com
Strategic Research Institute: www.srinstitute.com
Alternative Investment News: www.iialternatives.com

Value at Risk and Probability of Loss

OVERVIEW

Whether investing in traditional securities portfolios or in hedge funds, an investor should have some idea of how much risk of capital loss may exist and how to quantify it. This risk of loss can be measured as the potential loss in the value of a portfolio for a stated probability over a particular time horizon, or it can be the probability of a specific loss over the time horizon. The first measure, amount of potential loss, is called *value at risk*, and the second measure is simply called *probability of loss*.

Value at risk, or VaR, is the "*V*" in the following statement: "Over the following time period, *t*, the portfolio will lose no more than *V*. I am *p* percent confident in this." VaR can be stated as a dollar amount, or as a percent of the portfolio. Stating it as a percent provides for comparability across portfolios of different sizes. To fully understand a particular VaR number you need to know the *t* and *p* above; in other words, you need to know the time period over which this potential future maximum loss is being estimated, and the level of confidence that the loss could be no worse.

Probability of loss is similar to VaR

In this case, you specify the *t*, or time period, and the *V*, or amount of loss you're concerned about, and the measure delivers the *p*, or probability. Both VaR and probability of loss can be calculated using the assumption that returns are normally distributed. With this assumption, the risk measures are calculated by first converting the loss into the number of standard deviations way from the mean, and then calculating the probability of exceeding this number in a normal distribution.

When seeking to measure VaR and probability of loss for hedged portfolios, however, the assumption of normally distributed returns often fails because of the presumption that most absolute return strategies largely eliminate downside volatility (hence, the word "hedge"). Instead, distributions for hedged portfolios can be empirically derived through the use of

Monte Carlo simulations, including bootstrap, non-normal, and GARCH (general autoregressive conditional heteroschedascticity) methodologies. VaR can also be calculated using the Parametric Methodology or historical simulations. Input for these models are generally based on the actual historic returns of each of the hedged portfolios being evaluated, including the periodic returns of diversified Fund of Hedge Fund portfolios. Monte Carlo methodology is preferable when non-linear instruments, including derivatives, are used. It is also useful to estimate the historic correlation and volatilities for the underlying component investments.

RISK BUDGETING

Risk budgeting is a control mechanism for keeping an overall portfolio within acceptable and pre-defined risk limits. Sometimes called *risk allocation* (in contrast to *asset allocation*) the idea is to monitor overall portfolio risk, rather than allocations to asset classes. If risk falls outside the acceptable range—above or below—assets are re-allocated among asset classes and managers. Particular attention is focused on contemporaneous estimates of future risk, usually estimated as future standard deviations and, most importantly, future interactions, measured as correlations. It is this interaction piece that brings home the benefits of diversification. An asset class or investment approach that is very risky may not affect the risk budget much at all if it is uncorrelated with other assets in the protfolio. Instead, such an allocation may actually introduce elements of stability to the portfolio. Risk budgeting, as an investment management practice, is greatly enhanced when a large number of low or negatively-correlated investment options are available, especially if the focus of these strategies is absolute return.

Sometimes risk budgets are monitored by using both VaR and *marginal VaR*, which measures the marginal contribution of each manager to downside exposure. The idea here is to calculate VaR on the entire portfolio, and the portfolio without a particular manager. The difference is that manager's marginal VaR.

A detailed explanation of the uses of VaR and its calculation is beyond the scope of this appendix. A good source for those seeking to delve further is *Value at Risk: The New Benchmark for Managing Financial Risk* by Philippe Jorion.[1]

---

[1] Philippe Jorion, *Value at Risk: The New Benchmark for Managing, Financial Risk*, 2nd ed. 2000, McGraw-Hill.

Resources

FOR FURTHER INFORMATION

ABSOLUTE RETURN PRODUCTS

Agarwal, Vikas, and Narayan Y. Naik. Spring, 2000. "On Taking the 'Alternative' Route: The Risks, Rewards, and Performance Persistence of Hedge Funds." *Journal of Alternative Investments*.
Synopsis: Article discusses that combination of alternative investments and passive indexing which provides a significantly better risk/return trade-off than passively investing in the different asset classes.

Alternative Asset Center web site, May 9, 2001 http://www.aa-center.net.
Synopsis: Web site provides discussions on various aspects of alternative investments, such as typical allocations and investor qualifications as well as advantages and disadvantages.

Alternative Investment Management Association web site, May 29, 2001 http://www.aima.org.
Synopsis: In-depth articles from industry leaders on managed futures, hedge funds, and currency management as well as regulations, marketing, technical issues, and investor viewpoints.

Capital Market Risk Advisors, Inc., 2000. "Hedge Fund Survey: Risk Management Overview." *Journal of Alternative Investments*, Fall.
Synopsis: Article discusses results of survey on issues related to risk management in hedge funds. Survey results provide insights into actual use of various risk management approaches employed by the hedge fund community.

Diamond, Peter A., 2000. "What Stock Market Returns to Expect for the Future?" *Social Security Bulletin*, Vol. 63, No. 2.
Synopsis: Research explores 2 equity premium concepts: realized equity premium and required equity premium.

Edwards, Frank R., and Jimmy Liew, September 14, 1998. "Hedge Funds and Managed Futures as Asset Classes." Graduate School of Business, Columbia University.
Synopsis: Study examines the performance of hedge funds and managed futures through 1996, concluding that they are attractive as stand-alone and performance-enhancing investments.

Engelmann, Knut, October 3, 1999. "LTCM May Be Out of Business, Fed Says." *Time Magazine*/Time.com 128.
    Synopsis: Article reports status of Long Term Capital Management LC as it folds.

Fung, William, and David Hsieh, 1997. "Empirical Characteristics of Dynamic Trading Strategies: The Case for Hedge Funds." *Review of Financial Studies*.
    Synopsis: Academically based presentation of strategy groupings and differences in the market factors affecting the basis of relative groupings.

Fung, William, and David Hsieh, Summer 2001. "The Risk in Hedge Fund Strategies: Theory and Evidence from Trend Followers." *Review of Financial Studies*.
    Synopsis: Article shows how to model hedge fund returns by focusing on the trend-following strategy.

Fung, William, and David Hsieh, September 2000. "Performance Characteristics of Hedge Funds and Commodity Funds: Natural Versus Spurious Biases." *Journal of Financial and Quantitative Analysis*.
    Synopsis: The organizational structure of hedge funds makes data collection an onerous task, amplifying the impact of performance measurement biases. This paper reviews these biases in hedge funds and proposes using funds of hedge funds to measure aggregate hedge fund performance.

Goldman, Sachs & Co. and Financial Risk Management Ltd, January 2000. "Pension & Endowment Forum: Hedge Funds Revisited."
    Synopsis: Report examines hedge fund returns through the first half of 1999. It seeks to support the conclusion that because of their returns, low volatility, and low correlation to traditional benchmarks, hedged strategies should play a role in a diversified portfolio.

Hedge Fund Center web site, May 2, 2001 http://www.hedgefundcenter.com.
    Synopsis: Web site provides objective, educational information on hedge funds. Includes news articles, bookshop, industry debacles, regulatory changes, employment opportunities, and academic work.

Hedge Fund Research web site, July 18, 2001 http://www.hfr.com.
    Synopsis: Web site provides research and information on industry and specific fund news.

Hedge Fund Research, 1999. "The Evolution of Hedge Fund Investing by Institutional Investors. Alternative Asset Management Association (AIMA) web site http://www.aima.org. 129.
    Synopsis: Report examines growth of hedge fund industry by institutional investors from 1990 through 1999.

Hedge World web site, May 29, 2001 http://www.hedgeworld.com.
    Synopsis: Web sites provides industry news and information, research, and academic reports.

Henker, Thomas, 1999. "Naïve Diversification for Hedge Funds." *The Handbook of Alternative Investments*. New York: Institutional Investor.
Synopsis: Article evaluates the reduction of risk of individual hedge funds when they are held in portfolios.

Hopkins, Simon, June 2000. "On Phenomenal Growth Track," *Investment and Pensions Europe*.
Synopsis: Article discusses shift on the part of pension funds to alternative investment allocations.

International Monetary Fund web site, July 3, 2001 www.imf.org.
Synopsis: The IMF is an international organization of 183 member countries, established to promote international monetary cooperation, exchange stability, and orderly exchange arrangements; to foster economic growth and high levels of employment; and to provide temporary financial assistance to countries to help ease balance of payments adjustments.

Jaeger, Dr. Lars, November 28, 2000. "Risk Management for Multi-Manager Portfolios of Alternative Investment Strategies." Switzerland: Swiss Alternative Investment Strategies Group AG.
Synopsis: Article is a general discussion of risk management issues related to hedge funds and managed futures from the perspective of a multimanager fund. Particular emphasis is given to post-investment risk management.

Jorion, Philippe, January 2000. "Risk Management Lessons From Long-Term Capital Management," Graduate School of Management, University of California at Irvine.
Synopsis: Article discusses 1998 failure of LTCM, showing that the fund severely underestimated its risk due to its reliance on short-term history and risk concentration.

Lake, Ronald A., 1996. *Evaluating and Implementing Hedge Fund Strategies: The Experience of Managers and Investors*, 2d ed. London: Euromoney Institutional Investor PLC.
Synopsis: Book consists of a collection of essays covering the trends, developments, and issues facing hedge funds. The introduction has definitions and summaries of strategies in an essay titled "Spectrum of Hedge Funds."

Liang, Bing, 1999. "On the Performance of Hedge Funds." Weatherhead School of Management at Case Western Reserve University.
Synopsis: Article investigates hedge fund performance and risk.

Managed Accounts Report web site, May 2, 2001, http://www.marhedge.com.
Synopsis: Web site includes benchmark returns, conference information, industry news, background articles, and newsletters. Performance and Evaluation Directory is published twice a year, providing detailed statistical and contact information on the performance of more than 500 hedge funds.

McCarthy, David and Richard Spurgin, 1999. "A Review of Hedge Fund Performance Benchmarks." *The Handbook of Alternative Investments*. New York: Institutional Investor.

Synopsis: Article reviews the relative performance of a wide range of alternative, manager-based hedge fund indexes.

Morley, Ian, and Dawnay, Day Olympia Ltd. "Perception and Reality in the Alternative Investment Market." December 2000. *Alternative Investment Management Association (AIMA) Newsletter*.

Synopsis: Article regarding misconceptions related to hedge fund investments, including such issues as leverage, benchmarks, and consultants.

Nicholas, Joseph, 1999. *Investing in Hedge Funds: Strategies for the New Marketplace*. Princeton: Bloomberg Press.

Synopsis: Book provides a financial road map of the hedge fund universe. Explains hedge fund strategies with clear, concise descriptions, including how to access these funds and where they are headed in the future.

Rao, Rama, and Jerry J. Szilagyi, March 1998. "The Coming Evolution of the Hedge Fund Industry: A Case for Growth and Restructuring." RR Capital Management Corp. and KPMG Peat Marwick LLP.

Synopsis: Report analyzes fundamental changes the hedge fund industry is undergoing and predicts its structural evolution for the next decade.

Risk Institute Glossary, July 17, 2001, http://newrisk.ifci.ch/

Synopsis: Web site provides comprehensive glossary of industry terms.

Rosenbaum, Robert I., September/October 2000. "Fund of Funds: The Right Choice for Your Clients' Allocations to Hedge Funds." Investment Management Consultants Association.

Synopsis: Article makes case for hedge funds and discusses diversification benefits.

Schneeweis, Thomas, October 5, 1999. "Alpha, Alpha, Who's Got the Alpha?" University of Massachusetts.

Synopsis: Explores the definition of alpha and the best way to measure the alpha of an investment strategy.

Schneeweis, Thomas, June 20, 2001. Presentation at Undiscovered Managers Wealth Management Symposium.

Synopsis: Discusses the challenges of performance measurement and risk analysis for alternative investments.

Schneeweis, Thomas, and Joseph Pescatore, 1999. *The Handbook of Alternative Investments*. New York: Institutional Investor.

Synopsis: A collection of essays examining hedge funds and managed futures. Includes in-depth essays regarding benchmark comparisons, diversification data, skewness in returns, and how these alternative investments fit into an institutional portfolio.

Schneeweis, Thomas, and Richard Spurgin, 1999. "Alternative Investments in the Institutional Portfolio." *The Handbook of Alternative Investments.* New York: Institutional Investor.
Synopsis: Article presents empirical evidence of the potential risk and return benefits of a wide range of alternative investments.

Schneeweis, Thomas, and Richard Spurgin, 1999. "Benefits of Managed Fund Strategies: Managed Futures and Hedge Funds." *The Handbook of Alternative Investments.* New York: Institutional Investor.
Synopsis: Article focuses on the benefits of adding managed futures and hedge funds to a portfolio.

Schneeweis, Thomas, and Richard Spurgin, 1999. "Multi-Factor Analysis of Hedge Fund, Managed Futures, and Mutual Fund Return and Risk Characteristics." *The Handbook of Alternative Investments.* New York: Institutional Investor.
Synopsis: Article examines the factors that explain the performance of hedge funds and managed futures.

Schneeweis, Thomas, Richard Spurgin, and Mark Potter, 1999. "Managed Futures and Hedge Fund Investment for Downside Equity Risk Management." *The Handbook of Alternative Investments.* New York: Institutional Investor.
Synopsis: Article argues that managed futures and hedge funds investments offer unique risk and return opportunities in downside risk control.

Spurgin, Richard, "How to Game Your Sharpe Ratio." Clark University, Worcester, Massachusetts.
Synopsis: Article describes a derivative structure that can induce an upward bias in the measurement of the Sharpe Ratio.

Swensen, David F., 2000. *Pioneering Portfolio Management: An Unconventional Approach to Institutional Investment.* New York: The Free Press.
Synopsis: Pages 205-216 discuss role of absolute-return strategies in a portfolio. Examines risk and return, asset characteristics, and survivorship bias.

Tannenbaum, Michael G. "U.S. Regulation of Offers of Investment and Advisory Services and Hedge Fund Marketing Over the Internet." Tannenbaum Helpern Syracure & Hirschtritt LLP, New York.
Synopsis: Excerpt addresses the legal ramifications of Internet marketing by investment advisers, and the use of the Internet to distribute hedge fund products.

Tremont Partners Inc., and TASS Investment Research, June 1999. "The Case for Hedge Funds."
Synopsis: Report examines a broad spectrum of areas and issues including industry history, primary investment categories, transparency, capacity, and statistical analysis. The report is particularly focused on the intellectual case for hedge fund investments, and makes the case

that hedge funds offer an "inherent" return separate from the return generated by manager skill.

Tremont Partners Inc., September 2000. "Convertible Arbitrage: Opportunity and Risk." N.p.

Synopsis: White paper focuses on principal strategies used by Convertible Arbitrage Hedge Funds, and examines the evolution and current condition of the convertible bond marketplace.

UBS Warburg/Global Equity Research, October 2000. "In Search of Alpha: Investing in Hedge Funds."

Synopsis: Study focuses on the future of hedge fund investing. Includes summary on the sustainability of attractive risk/return and correlation characteristics of hedge funds.

U.S. Trust Corp., May 2, 2001. Survey of Affluent Americans. http://www.ustrust.com.

Synopsis: The U.S. Trust Survey of Affluent Americans periodically polls the top 1% of wealthiest Americans about financial issues. Survey results include behavior of the affluent, retirement planning, financial and economic worries and concerns, and the impact of the 1990s bull market.

Various contributors, "LTCM to Pay Back Investors: $300mm to Investors, $1B to Banks," *Indian Express Newspapers,* July 8, 1999.

Synopsis: Article reports Long Term Capital Management LP's plan to repay investors and consortium involved in bailout.

Weiss, Peck & Greer Investments Glossary, July 17, 2001, www.wpginvest.com

Synopsis: Investment counsel's web site includes glossary of industry terms.

Zask, Ezra, Winter 2000. "Hedge Funds: An Industry Overview." *Journal of Alternative Investments.*

Synopsis: Discusses increase in traditional institutional investors' use of alternative investments, the structure of the industry, and its relationship to private equity.

Zask, Ezra, Winter 2000. "Hedge Funds: A Methodology for Hedge Fund Valuation." *Journal of Alternative Investments*, pp. 43–46.

Synopsis: Article discusses issues in hedge fund valuation, such as variability of hedge fund revenues and independence of managers, and suggests approach to valuing such funds.

MANAGED FUTURES

Alternative Investment Management Association web site, May 29, 2001, http://www.aima.org.

Synopsis: In-depth articles from industry leaders on managed futures, hedge funds, and currency management as well as regulations, marketing, technical issues, and investor viewpoints.

Carrick, B. Lane (Sovereign Alternative Investment Management, LLC). "Managed Futures: The Grandfather of Alternative Investment Strategies Remains an Attractive Portfolio Diversification Tool." Alternative Investment Management Association web site, May 2, 2001, http://www.iama.org.
Synopsis: Research examines possible reasons the managed futures industry's assets remain small, and why institutional investors have not embraced them in any significant fashion. Summarizes industry growth, return data, and other statistics.

Chicago Mercantile Exchange web site training lessons, May 2, 2001, www.cme.com/educational/lessons/les1.htm
Synopsis: Web site training program provides basics on commodities, such as risk management, speculators and hedgers, technical analysis, and fun facts.

Diz, Fernando, Summer 1999. "CTA Survivor and Nonsurvivor: An Analysis of Relative Performance." *Journal of Alternative Investments*, 134.
Synopsis: Part 1 of 2 discusses debate over impact of survivor bias on CTAs. In this first article, actual performance of survivor and nonsurvivor samples is analyzed.

Diz, Fernando, Fall 1999. "How Do CTAs' Distribution Characteristics Affect Their Likelihood of Survival?" *Journal of Alternative Investments*.
Synopsis: Report suggests that survival is associated with performance, but performance is not necessarily associated with survival. As a result, ignoring survival issues when selecting managed futures programs may result in lower performance.

Edwards, Frank R., and Jimmy Liew, September 14, 1998. "Hedge Funds and Managed Futures as Asset Classes," Graduate School of Business, Columbia University.
Synopsis: Study examines the performance of hedge funds and managed futures through 1996, concluding that they are attractive as both stand-alone and performance-enhancing investments.

Fung, William, and David Hsieh, September 1998. "Pricing Trend Following Trading Strategies: Theory and Empirical Evidence." Foundation for Managed Derivatives Research.
Synopsis: Article reviews the performance of managed futures traders as look-back options.

Fung, William, and David Hsieh, Fall 1997. "Survivor Bias and Investment Style in the Returns of CTAs." *Journal of Portfolio Management*.
Synopsis: Article discusses the impact of survivor bias on CTA performance.

Goldman Sachs Commodity Index (GSCI) web site, May 9, 2001, http://www.gs.com.

Synopsis: Web site discusses the GSCI's economic weighting, liquidity constraints, and construction. Also provides return calculations and index break-outs.

Henker, Thomas, and George Martin, 1999. "Naïve and Optimal Diversification for Managed Futures." The Handbook of Alternative Investments. New York: Institutional Investor.

Synopsis: Article examines the impact of random diversification on randomly chosen and equal-weighted CTA portfolios, and the impact of CTA investment in mixed stock or bond portfolios.

Investorama web site, "What Is Futures Trading All About?" May 9, 2001, http://investorama.com.

Synopsis: Web site includes overview and specifics regarding futures trading. Includes information on cash and forward markets, prices and price factors, discovering prices, hedging, and regulations.

Jaeger, Dr. Lars, and Ross Kestin, March 2001. "The Benefits of Alternative Investment Strategies in the Institutional Portfolio." Swiss Alternative Investment Strategies Group AG.

Synopsis: Research presents empirical study of performance of alternative investment strategies, including return, risk, and correlation characteristics.

Johnson, Robert R., and Gerald R. Jensen, Spring 2001. "The Diversification Benefits of Commodities and Real Estate in Alternative Monetary Conditions." *Journal of Alternative Investments*.

Synopsis: Article demonstrates the implications of monetary was on asset allocation decisions for alternative investments. The argument is made that investors can improve their risk/return profiles in different monetary policy environments by diversifying across both traditional and alternative investments.

Jonkheer, Perry. "CTAs: A Unique, Under-utilized Method to Increase Returns, Reduce Volatility and Raise More Capital," IASG web site, May 9, 2001, http://iasg.com.

Synopsis: Article discusses volatility, returns, and mutual fund timing overlays.

Peters, Carl, and Ben Warwick, editors, 1997. *The Handbook of Managed Futures and Hedge Funds: Performance, Evaluation and Analysis.* Chicago: The McGraw-Hill Companies.

Synopsis: Series of articles dealing with the performance, evaluation, and analysis of managed futures. Articles provide evidence of profitability in technical trading rules and review historical evidence of the case for managed futures.

Schneeweis, Thomas, 1999. *The Benefits of Managed Futures*, 2d Ed., University of Massachusetts and Alternative Investment Management Association.

Synopsis: Summary article is an update of a research study. Presents evidence that CTAs and other managed fund products have the potential to increase the return-to-risk trade-off for investors.

Schneeweis, Thomas and Richard Spurgin, 1999. "Comparison of Managed Futures Benchmarks." *The Handbook of Alternative Investments*. New York: Institutional Investor.

Synopsis: Article reviews the risk/return performance of benchmarks based on commodity prices as well as indices that track various managed futures-based trading products.

Schneeweis, Thomas, and Richard Spurgin, 1999. "Multi-Factor Analysis of Hedge Fund, Managed Futures, and Mutual Fund Return and Risk Characteristics." *The Handbook of Alternative Investments*. New York: Institutional Investor.

Synopsis: Article examines the factors that explain the performance of hedge funds and managed futures.

Schneeweis, Thomas, Richard Spurgin, and Mark Potter, 1999. "Managed Futures and Hedge Fund Investment for Downside Equity Risk Management." *The Handbook of Alternative Investments*. New York: Institutional Investor.

Synopsis: Article argues that managed futures and hedge funds investments offer unique risk and return opportunities in downside risk control.

Spurgin, Richard, Summer 1999. "A Benchmark for Commodity Trading Advisor Performance." *Journal of Alternative Investments*.

Synopsis: Article discusses a passive index, designed to benchmark the performance of diversified trend-followers, which may be used as a benchmark for creating CTAs.

Glossary of Terms

ALPHABET SOUP

CEA	Commodity Exchange Act of 1934
CDO	Collateralized Debt Obligation
CFTC	Commodity Futures Trading Commission
CFO	Collateralized Fund Obligation
CME	Chicago Mercantile Exchange
CPO	Commodity Pool Operator
CTA	Commodity Trading Advisor
ERISA	Employee Retirement Income Security Act of 1974
FCM	Futures Commission Merchants
IAA	Investment Advisory Act of 1940
ICA	Investment Company Act of 1940
LTCM	Long Term Capital Management
MAR	Minimal Acceptable Return
MFA	Managed Funds Association
NAV	Net Asset Value
NFA	National Futures Association
P/E	Price Earnings Ratio
PWG	President's Working Group on Financial Markets
QEP	Qualified Eligible Participants
SEC	Security and Exchange Commission
UBTI	Unrelated Business Taxable Income
VaR	Value at Risk

TERMS

Administrator	Entity that manages the hedge fund operations.
Alpha	Represents the return the investor would receive if the benchmark had a zero return. Can also be thought of as a metric for measuring the risk-adjusted performance based on the fund's average performance distinct from the market.
Arbitrage	Investment that takes advantage of the differences in prices between two like securities.

Beta	Represents the volatility in the return the investor would receive in relationship to the benchmark used in the market.
Calmar Ratio	Compound annualized rate of return over the last 3 years.
Convertible Arbitrage	Investment that takes advantage of the difference in pricing between the value of convertible bonds and common stocks issued by the same company.
Contrarian Approach	Adds to position as prices decline.
Derivative	A financial instrument used to transfer the risk of an investment. The performance of the instrument is tied to a particular benchmark.
Drawdown	Maximum amount of loss from an equity high until a new equity high is reached.
Downside Deviation	Statistical measure that ignores upside volatility and only considers returns below the MAR.
Fully defeased	Setting aside sufficient cash or bonds to service debt.
Hurdle Rate	Minimum return needed for the manager to receive any incentives. It is normally tied to a benchmark in the market.
Liquidity	The ability of the manager to sell investments without affecting the price.
Long Biased	When the manager holds substantially more long positions than short ones.
Long Only	The manager holds no short positions.
Margin Call	Ensure that the margin deposits are at a required minimum.
Merger/Risk Arbitrage	The expected price convergence of two distinct securities.
Net Asset Value	Market value of a fund based on total assets, minus liabilities, and divided by the outstanding shares.
Neutral	Combination of long and short positions to neutralize risk.
Nonaccredited Investor	Net worth is less than $1,000,000, as defined in Regulation D.
Nondefeased Structures	No initial setting aside of collateral.
Options Arbitrage	Investment that takes advantage of the pricing differences between like options contracts or related instruments.

Regulation D	The portion of the Securities Act of 1933 affecting whether a security transaction must be registered or not.
Section 3(c)(1)	Section of the Investment Company Act (ICA) of 1940 that defines which hedge funds must be registered as investment advisors.
Sharpe Ratio	Risk-adjusted statistic.
Sortino Ratio	Alternative to Sharpe Ratio that uses a downside deviation instead of a standard deviation in the formula.
Standard Deviation	Statistical measure for predictability. The higher the deviation, the more volatile the manager and the lower the deviation, the more consistent the manager.
Sterling Ratio	Measures the annualized rate of return over the last 3 years.
Structured Products	Securities that are customized.
Tranches	Related securities that are offered at the same time.
Uptick	Purchase of security occurs at a higher price than the preceding transaction.
Value at Risk (VaR)	Metric for determining the confidence level that a change in value of a portfolio may potentially change.
Volatility	The change in price over a specified time.

Milton Baehr is a co-founder and director of technology at Strategic Financial Solutions (SFS), LLC, a software company founded in 1996, whose mission is to provide solutions to the technological needs of the financial industry. He received his BSEE in computer science from Case Institute of Technology in 1968, and has over 35 years of experience in the computer field, as well as over 25 years in the financial industry. In 1995, he began initial development of PerTrac, a state-of-the-art asset allocation and statistical analysis system, to meet the needs of the increasingly complex financial services industry. In August 1996, he co-founded SFS to further the development and marketing of PerTrac, and to create additional software solutions for the financial industry. As principal and director of technology, he is responsible for the creative development and consulting services activities for SFS. He founded The Derivative Management Group, Inc. in 1991. DMG provided investment management services to institutions and high net-worth investors. The company designed and used real-time and artificial intelligence-based software for the trading of S&P 500 Index Futures. As the Internet developed, DMG was one of the original companies to host its own website.

Steven D. Berkshire, EdD, CHE, SPHR Steven Berkshire currently serves as the Associate Academic Dean for Graduate Programs in the School for Professional Studies (SPS) at Regis University in Denver, Colorado. The Graduate Programs division of SPS represents over 5,000 students in five programs including Masters of Business Administration, Masters of Science in Management, Masters of Science in Computer Information Technology, Masters of Nonprofit Management, and Masters of Arts in Liberal Studies. Approximately half of the students participate in the online degree versions. Prior to Regis, Dr. Berkshire was the Associate Dean for Adult Programs at Alaska Pacific University in Anchorage, Alaska. Adult Programs included the Degree Completion Program and its three majors, the Rural Alaska Native Adult (RANA) online program, corporate education, and the Masters of Arts Program, a self-directed interdisciplinary program. Steve has also taught at the University of LaVerne Alaska Center, University of Massachusetts Lowell, and Emmanuel College in Boston.

Prior to coming to academia, Dr. Berkshire was a healthcare executive for more than twenty-five years including assignments in hospital administration, government affairs and lobbying, advocacy organizations, medical school administration, and managing hospital associations. He also is the principle in his own management and human resources consulting firm, Steve Berkshire Associates.

Steve earned his doctoral degree from Boston University in human resource education and organizational behavior, his Masters in Healthcare Administration from Indiana University, and his BA degree in political science from the University of Colorado. He attended the University of Alaska Fairbanks prior to transferring to Colorado and participated in the MPA program at Boise State University in Idaho. Dr. Berkshire holds certifications as a Senior Professional in Human Resources and as a Certified Healthcare Executive. Steve is active in the Society for Human Resource Management (SHRM), American Society for Training and Development (ASTD), American College of Healthcare Executives (ACHE), Academy of Management, and other professional and civic organizations.

Todd Goldman specializes in serving clients in the investment partnership and broker–dealer segments of the financial services industry and is the managing principal of the Walnut Creek office of Rothstein, Kass & Company, P.C. & RK Consulting, LLC. He has extensive expertise in consulting on issues common to the financial services industry.

Mr. Goldman's experience includes advice on initial hedge fund and broker–dealer organizational structure, supervision of audits, and ongoing consultation with management regarding many diverse operational and tax matters. Mr. Goldman is a frequent speaker on various securities industry topics including performance reporting issues for investment partnerships. Mr. Goldman is a certified public accountant in the States of California, Texas and New York and is a member of the American Institute of Certified Public Accountants.

Dr. Gary T. Hirst is the Founder and Chairman of Hirst Investment Management Inc, a Partner in Margate Management LP, and a member of the Board of Directors of several financial and investment companies. Dr. Hirst has over twenty-eight years of experience in alternative investments as a money manager, asset allocator, and researcher. His educational background includes an Honors Degree in Computer Science and Physics from the University of Miami, and Doctorates in Law and Medicine.

Meredith Jones joined Strategic Financial Solutions in December 2001 as the director of market research. In that capacity, she is responsible for researching, speaking, and writing about alternative and traditional investments as well as developing and implementing marketing initiatives and strategic partnerships for SFS. Prior to joining SFS, she was vice president and director of research for Van Hedge Fund Advisors International, Inc., a global hedge fund consultant with more than $500 million under management. There, she led a staff of 10 research analysts in manager selection, evaluation, and ongoing monitoring. She conducted quantitative and qualitative due diligence, onsite visits, and portfolio construction, as well as a number of other research functions. She graduated from Centre College *cum laude* and *Phi Beta Kappa* in 1993.

John M. Kelly is the President and Chief Executive Officer of Man Investments Inc., and is Director of the Man Investments Inc. division of Man Group plc.

Mr. Kelly graduated from Southampton College of Technology and then went on to work for various industrial companies, attaining general manager and directorship positions. In 1978, he joined a business consultancy service specializing in investment, finance and aviation in the Gulf Region. In 1987, he joined the Man Group of companies as a Regional Manager in Bahrain where he was responsible for negotiations, corporate finance and marketing support for specialist financial products promoted jointly with major institutions in the region.

In 1991, he became the Sales and Marketing Director of Man Investment Products Limited and was responsible for managing sales and marketing globally until he moved to Chicago in 2001 to establish Man's presence in the United States.

Kenneth S. Phillips is the Managing Principal of RCG Capital Partners, LLC, a New York based investment management and consulting firm specializing in alternative investment strategies and hedge funds. He has more than twenty years of experience in the design and management of complex, multi-manager investment strategies. In 1984 he founded PMC International, Inc, an investment advisory firm that pioneered the multi-manager, segregated account industry. By 1998, when PMC was sold, firm assets had grown to nearly $12 billion including institutional and high-net-worth clientele.

As a leader in the development of multi-strategy/multi-manager portfolios, Mr. Phillips has been deeply involved in the evaluation and due diligence of non-proprietary investment management companies and private funds. The success of his former firm, PMC, and its concepts was reflected by the comprehensive assignments it executed for a broad range of prestigious US and International financial institutions.

Mr. Phillips founded RCG Capital Partners in 2001, three years after the sale of his former firm and after completing a three-year covenant not to compete. In 1984 Mr. Phillips was also a founding participant in the Wilshire Cooperative. He has been an active member of the Investment Management Consultants Association ("IMCA") where he has served as a Member of its Advisory Board for more than ten years. He also has served IMCA as Chairman of its Educational Publications Committee, Chairman of its Public Relations Committee, and as a Member of its Editorial Board.

Frank S. Pusateri is the President of Adirondack Portfolio Management, Inc., a consulting firm that specializes in managed futures.

Until August 2002, he also provided consulting on managed futures as an associated person of The Price Futures Group, Inc., a Guaranteed Introducing Broker. Prior to joining Price in, he was a Senior Vice President at Index Futures. He was previously Managing Director of a Commodity Trading Advisor, LaSalle Portfolio Management Inc., where he also helped establish and register an affiliate, Sheridan Investments Inc., as an Investment Advisor to offer yield enhancement programs and Marketing Director of Sheridan.

Prior to 1994, Mr. Pusateri was Managing Director of Cotswold Management Inc., a provider of multi-advisor managed futures program; Publisher of *Managed Futures Today;* and Vice President (later Senior Vice President) of Investments for Prudential Securities Inc., where he specialized in the selection of trading advisors for multi-manager futures portfolios for large sophisticated clients.

He was president of Pusateri Associates, a consulting firm that specialized in providing expertise in the evaluation and selection of commodity trading advisors.

Mr. Pusateri also worked for E.F. Hutton where he was in charge of performance analysis was also Director of Managed Commodity Accounts.

His written contributions to the industry include articles in *Managed Futures Today, the Managed Account Report Yearbook,* and two chapters for *The Commodity Futures Handbook.* He has been a guest speaker on the topic of managed futures on numerous occasions. He is the past president of the Managed Futures Trade Association, the past treasurer of the Managed Futures Association, past director of the Rose-Baratz Literary Foundation, and past director of the Foundation for Managed Derivatives Research. He is actively involved in rasing funds from the investment industry for charities was chairman of the Brazillion Dollar Bash, and co-chairman of, the CTA/CPO Advisory Committee for CARE's World Trading Day., In January 1991, he received the Donchian Award in recognition of his contributions to the managed futures industry.

Mr. Pusateri earned his Masters of Business Administration in Accounting and Finance from the Amos Tuck School of Business Administration, Dartmouth College, and his Bachelor of Arts in Mathematics from Colgate University.

Leslie Rahl founded Capital Market Risk Advisors, Inc. (CMRA) in 1994. In 2003, Leslie Rahl, with Lisa Polsky, formed L^2 = Exponential Synergy.

Mrs. Rahl was a pioneer of the swaps and derivatives business and was the originator of the interest rate cap, collar, and floor business. Prior to forming CMRA, she was President of Leslie Rahl Associates, Inc., a consulting firm specializing in swaps, options and derivative products.

Mrs. Rahl spent 19 years at Citibank, including nine years as co-head of Citibank's Derivatives Group in North America. She launched its caps and collars business in 1983 as an extension of the proprietary options arbitrage portfolio she ran and was a pioneer in the development of the swaps and derivatives business.

Mrs. Rahl was named one of the Top 50 Women in Finance by *Euromoney* in 1997 and was profiled in both the fifth and tenth anniversary issues of *Risk Magazine*. She was listed in "Who's Who in Derivatives" by *Risk Magazine* and was profiled in *Fortune Magazine's* "On the Rise" and *Institutional Investor's* "The Next Generation of Financial Leaders".

Mrs. Rahl was a Director of the International Swaps Dealers Association (ISDA) for five years. She is currently on the Board of Directors of the International Association of Financial Engineers (IAFE) and the Fischer Black Memorial Foundation. Mrs. Rahl chairs the IAFE's Investor Risk Committee (IRC) and the Philanthropy Committee of 100 Women in Hedge Funds. She is a member of the hedge fund committee of the Alternative Investment Management Association (AIMA); a member of the Board of Advisors of The Financial Engineering program at the MIT-Sloan School; a senior advisor to the MIT Club of NY's partnership with the New York City Public Schools and Intel Computer Clubhouses, and is active in all key areas of the industry.

Mrs. Rahl is the author of *Hedge Fund Transparency: Unravelling the Complex and Controversial Debate* published in March 2003 by Risk Books and the editor of *Risk Budgeting—a New Approach to Investing* published in November 2000 by Risk Books. Her articles have appeared in a wide range of publications.

Mrs. Rahl earned her undergraduate degree in Computer Science from MIT and her Masters of Business Administration from the Sloan School at MIT.

Thomas Schneeweis is the Michael and Cheryl Philipp Professor of Finance at the School of Management at the University of Massachusetts in Amherst, and director of the school's Center for International Securities and Derivatives Markets. He received his PhD in finance from the University of Iowa in 1977. He is author of the Alternative Investment Management Association publications, *The Benefits of Managed Futures Alternative Investments in the Institutional Portfolio;* co-author of *Financial Futures: Fundamentals, Strategies, and Applications (Richard Irwin);* and co-editor of *The Handbook of Alternative Investments: An Investor's Guide* (Institutional Investor); and co-editor of *Applications in Finance, Investment and Banking (Kluwer).* He is on the board of directors of the Managed Funds Association and is editor of *The Journal of Alternative Investments.* He has published over 50 articles in academic finance and management journals, in the areas of traditional and alternative investment management and asset performance. He has been a Fulbright Research Fellow in France, taught at ESSEC in France, and is an adjunct professor of finance at Lund University, Sweden. He is an outside director for the Managers Funds, a no-load, open-end, management investment company with over 10 different funds.

Richard Spurgin has been assistant professor of finance at Clark University since 1995. He is also associate director of the Center for International Securities and Derivatives Markets at the University of Massachusetts. He holds a bachelor's degree in mathematics from Dartmouth College and a PhD in finance from the University of Massachusetts. He has published research in academic journals, such as the *Journal of Futures Markets* and the *Journal of Derivatives,* and has also written articles for practitioner journals and trade magazines, such as *Derivatives Quarterly* and *Futures Magazine.* Previously employed by Technical Data in Boston as director of fixed-income research, he now manages analytical support for passive-index replication and active investment strategies.

Kirk C. Strawn joined Man Investments Inc. in 2001 with a particular responsibility for development and service of Man's broker–dealer network. He graduate cum laude from George Washington University with a Bachelor of Arts in Finance. Mr. Strawn is a Certified Investment Management Analyst, certified by the Investment Management Consulting Association. He is also a CFA charter holder. Mr. Strawn gained financial experience when he joined Lehman Brothers, New York in 1989, where he provided financial services to institutional accounts, hedge funds and private investors. In 1996, he joined ING Furman Selz

Capital Management where, as Managing Director of its Institutional Marketing and Sales Division, he was responsible for raising capital for a variety of asset classes and for managing the sales team for the Investment Management Accounts Program.

Ronald J. Surz is president of PPCA, Inc., an investment technology firm in San Clemente, California, specializing in performance evaluation and attribution. He also serves on the following boards and councils: Investment Management Consultants Association (IMCA) board of directors; IMCA *Monitor* (newsletter) editorial board; IMCA standards of practice board chair; City of San Clemente, California Investment Advisory Council; FinanceWare.com Advisory Board; Association for Investment and Research AIMR Investment Performance Council; AIMR After-tax Subcommittee; *Journal of Performance Measurement* Advisory Board; and the RCG Investment partners Advisory Board. He holds an MBA in finance from the University of Chicago, an MS in applied mathematics from the University of Illinois, and a CIMA (Certified Investment Management Analyst) designation. He is published regularly in *Pensions and Investments, Senior Consultant,* the *IMCA Monitor.*

Alfredo Viegas is a Principal and Director of Investment Strategy at RCG Capital Partners, an investment management company specializing in alternative investments and funds of hedge funds. Mr. Viegas was formerly head of ADR arbitrage and international equity trading at Tullet Liberty in New York. Previously he managed a $100M hedge fund and three mutual funds with assets of nearly $500M, from 1995 through 2001. As a money manager, Mr. Viegas has primarily specialized in equity arbitrage, international relative value, emerging markets equities, and global macro trading strategies. In 1999 he ran the #1 global emerging markets fund according to MorningStar, and in 1996 through 1997 he ran a top performing international macro hedge fund. Prior to his asset management experience, Mr. Viegas was an institutional investor-ranked analyst and strategist at Salomon Brothers where he was Director of Latin American Strategy. He also worked closely with the proprietary trading desk to source trading ideas. Mr. Viegas has an Honors Bachelor of Arts from Wesleyan University in Classics and History, and a Masters of Science in Astronomy.

Samuel S. Weiser is the President and CEO of Foxdale Management, a consulting firm specializing in hedge funds and hedge fund-related services. Mr. Weiser is also Chairman of the Managed Funds Association, the representative association for hedge fund managers and their voice in

Washington. The Association currently has more than 500 members. The MFA performs lobbying activities and promotes a legislative and regulatory agenda to support the hedge fund industry.

Mr. Weiser was previously a Managing Director with Ranger Capital Group, and a member of the firm's investment committee; Director and Head of Sales and Marketing for the prime brokerage group within the Pershing Division of Credit Suisse First Boston (formerly Donaldson, Lufkin and Jenrette); Administrative Principal with the asset management firm of Sonsoff, Sheridan, Weiser; and a Partner with Ernst & Young LLP Where he served as the National Director of Investment Consulting and was an active member of Ernst and Young's global funds group coordinating the firm's international hedge fund industry activities. He also served in a similar capacity as a Senior Manager for Arthur Andersen LLP Mr. Weiser was President of Virginia Futures Management Corporation, a division of Quantum Financial Services, and Chief Financial Officer of Glenwood Financial Group Mr. Weiser earned a Bachelor of arts in Economics from Colby College and a Master of Arts in Accounting from George Washington University.

Brian A. Wolf joined Grosvenor Capital Management, L.P., in 1995, and is one of five investment principals of the firm. In this capacity, he shares responsibility for portfolio management of various Grosvenor entities and leads the evaluation, selection, and monitoring efforts of equity-oriented hedge fund strategies and managers. From 1993 to 1995, he was an analyst and trader for M&M Financial, a Chicago-based money management firm. He received a BS *summa cum laude* in finance from Bradley University in 1992 and an MBA *magna cum laude* from the University of Notre Dame in 1993. He is a chartered financial analyst and a member of the Investment Analysts Society of Chicago.

Thomas Zucosky, President, Discovery Capital Management As the Chief Investor Officer of Discovery Capital, a fund of hedge funds he started in 1997, Tom oversees manager selection, portfolio management, and fund monitoring.

Previously, as Senior Vice President in charge of alternative investments for InvestorForce, Tom oversaw all hedge fund and private equity manager searches done through the InvestorForce Internet platform. He was also responsible for creating structured products, investment risk monitoring and interactions with investors and managers regarding alternative investments.

Since 1981, Tom has been involved in alternative investments as an institutional salesman, investment strategist and hedge fund operator.

Since 1991, he has analyzed and allocated assets to managers of alternative investment strategies. Prior to joining InvestorForce, Tom was the Head of Marketable Alternative Investments for Strategic Investment Group. In this capacity, Tom oversaw all due diligence, portfolio management and business development as it pertained to marketable alternative investment strategies. Prior to joining SIG, Tom founded Discovery Capital Management, a Registered Investment Adviser and Commodity Trading Advisor focusing on consulting to institutions worldwide regarding hedge funds. Previously, he was in charge of Manager Due Oiligence for Olympia Capital Management, a Europeanbased asset allocator. In 1985, he co-founded Aegis Capital, a hedge fund manager and Registered Investment Adviser.

Tom graduated with a Master of arts from Montclair State University, where he was awarded a full scholarship and graduated magna cum laude. He received his Bachelor of Science in Business Administration from The College of New Jersey. He is a member of the National Futures Association, was founding member of the Managed Funds Association, is registered with the NASD and CFTC (Series 24, 7, 63, 6, and 3) and has served on the Board and Investment Committees of a number of multi-manager funds that concentrate on alternative investment strategies.

Index

A
Active manager index, 19
Adjusted beginning capital, 176
Administrator, definition, 190
ADR arbitrage. *See* Alternative dispute
    resolution (ADR) arbitrage
Alpha
  active manager index, 19
  alternative investments as sources,
      12–14
  Capital Asset Pricing Model
      equation, 11–12
  definition, 190
  determination, 11–12
  hedge fund addition to traditional
      asset portfolios, 21–22
  hedge fund performance compared
      with traditional investments,
      10–11, 14–17, 26–27
  portfoliio creation with alpha-
      generating strategies, 20–21
  prospects for determination, 15, 17
Alternative dispute resolution (ADR)
    arbitrage, 80
Arbitrage. *See also* Contrarian
    arbitrage; Convertible arbitrage;
    Fixed income arbitrage;
    Merger/risk arbitrage
  advantages, 80–81
  alternative dispute resolution (ADR)
      arbitrage, 80
  asset distibution in hedge funds,
      65–66
  capital structure arbitrage, 78
  closed-end fund arbitrage, 79
  convergence of prices, 65
  definition, 65, 190–191
  historical perspective, 65

index arbitrage, 78–79
leverage, 129
multistrategy arbitrage, 80
options arbitrage, 79
relative-value arbitrage, 76–77
restructuring arbitrage, 78
returns of hedge funds, 66
statistical arbitrage, 76
treasury arbitrage, 74
volatility arbitrage, 79
Asset size
  Commodity trading advisor (CTA),
      97, 100
  effects on performance, 37
  global macro funds, 84
  management of large accounts, 131
Audit, 130–131

B
Berger, Michael, 130
Beta, definition, 191
British pound, imbalance, 90–91
Business risk, funds of hedge
        funds, 41

C
Calmar ratio
  definition, 191
  fund manager screening, 124
Capital Asset Pricing Model (CAPM),
        alpha determination, 11–12
Capital structure arbitrage, 78
CAPM. *See* Capital Asset Pricing
        Model (CAPM)
Cash/futures basis trading strategies,
        74–75
CEA. *See* Commodity Exchange Act
        (CEA)

CFO. *See* Collateralized fund
   obligation (CFO)
CFTC. *See* Commodity Futures
   Trading Commission (CFTC)
Chicago Mercantile Exchange
   (CME), 96
Closed-end fund arbitrage, 79
CME. *See* Chicago Mercantile
   Exchange (CME)
Collateralized fund obligation (CFO),
   173–174
Commodity Exchange Act (CEA),
   registration of managed
   futures, 5
Commodity Futures Trading
   Commission (CFTC)
  registration of managed futures, 2
  regulation of managed futuress,
   7–8, 94
Commodity pool operator (CPO)
  advisor selection, 94, 104
  Commodity Futures Trading
   Commission regulations, 7
  liquidation, 103–104
  multiadvisor pools, 104
  structure, 103
Commodity trading advisor (CTA).
   See also Commodity pool
   operator (CPO)
  account sizes, 97, 100
  capital preservation, 99–100, 104
  Commodity Futures Trading
   Commission regulations,
   8, 94, 102
  fees, 101, 106
  fundamental analysis, 98–99
  hypothetical performance, 98
  limited power of attorney, 101
  National Futures Association (NFA)
   membership, 102–103
  performance monitoring, 111
  portfolio diversity, 100–101
  risk management, 99–100
  selection criteria
    data vendors, 107
    investor objectives, 105
    qualitative analysis, 108–110

  quantitative analysis, 106–108
  track record, 104–108
  solicitation, 102
  spread trading, 101
  technical traders, 98–99
  turnover of trades, 101–102, 108
Compliance, 142
Constant Proportion Portfolio
   Insurance (CPPI), 172–173
Contrarian arbitrage, definition, 191
Convertible arbitrage
  advantages, 67–68
  definition, 191
  leverage, 69
  principles, 67
  return dynamics, 68–69
Convertible securities/capital structure
   arbitrage, funds of hedge
   funds, 32
Counterparty risk, funds of hedge
   funds, 41
CPO. *See* Commodity pool operator
   (CPO)
CPPI. *See* Constant Proportion
   Portfolio Insurance (CPPI)
Credit risk, funds of hedge funds, 41
CTA. *See* Commodity trading advisor
   (CTA)

D
Derivative, definition, 191
DiMenna, Joe, 92
Disclosure, Commodity Futures
   Trading Commission (CFTC)
   regulations, 7–8
Downside deviation
  definition, 191
  fund manager screening, 120–122
Drawdown
  definition, 191
  fund manager screening,
   122–123, 126

E
Employee Retirement Income Security
   Act (ERISA), regulation of
   hedge funds, 5, 8

Equity hedge funds
  funds of hedge funds, 31
  investment research process by
      manager, 52–58
  investment strategies
    exposure bias, 52
    geographic market specialization,
      51–52
    sector specialists versus
      generalists, 50–51
  manager evaluation
    overview, 60–61, 63–64
    qualitative analysis, 62–63
    quantitative analysis, 61–62
  popularity, 49–50
  portfolio mangement, 58–60
ERISA. *See* Employee Retirement
      Income Security Act (ERISA)

F
Fixed income arbitrage. *See also*
      Mortgage-backed securities
      (MBS) arbitrage
  cash/futures basis trading strategies,
      74–75
  funds of hedge funds, 32
  government yield curve arbitrage
  index replication trades, 75
  macro convergence trades, 75–76
  principles, 73
  relative swap spread trades, 75
  risks, 73
  spreads, 73–74
  treasury arbitrage, on the run versus
      off the run, 74
FoHF. *See* Funds of hedge funds
      (FoHF)
Fully defeased, definition, 191
Funds of hedge funds (FoHF)
  adminstrator duties, 35
  advantages, 28–29
  advantages, 47
  broker/dealer duties, 35
  consultants, 46–47
  custodian duties, 35
  disadvantages, 28–30
  fees, 38

investment management process,
      39–40
  investment strategies
    convertible securities/capital
      structure arbitrage, 32
    distressed securities strategy,
      32–33
    equity hedges, 31
    event-driven strategies, 31
    futures trading, 33
    global macro strategy, 32
    merger/risk arbitrage, 31
    relative value managers, 32
    short selling, 33–34
  liquidity, 38
  manager, 34–35, 37
  market size, 34
  offshore venues, 39
  popularity, 47–48
  portfolio leverage, 39
  principal protection and guarantee,
      38–39
  registration, 39
  risks, 40–42, 47
  size and experience effects on
      performance, 37
  structure, 36
  volatility, 38
Futures. *See* Managed futures

G
Global macro fund
  advantages, 93
  appropriate investors, 93
  definition, 82–83
  investment strategy, 32, 82
  leverage, 92
  managers
    imbalance analysis, 90–91
    reflexivity, 89–90
    selection, 91–93
    Soros, George, 87–89
  percent of total investor portfolio, 93
  popularity, 83–85
  returns, 85–86
  selection criteria, 91–93
  size, 84

Government yield curve arbitrage
Gross return, 177

H
Hedge fund
  advertising, 138
  cash flows versus mutual funds, 176
  definition, 1
  image, 1, 26
  origins, 49, 82
  performance measurement and
      monitoring
    qualitative monitoring, 137
    quantitative monitoring, 133–137
  popularity, 27, 47–48
  registration, 2–5
  regulations, 5–9, 25
  return approximation
    adjusted beginning capital, 176
    gross return, 177
    income loss components, 176
    net return, 177–179
Hedgefund.net, 114–115, 132
Hedge Fund Research (HFR),
      114–115, 125, 133–135
HFR. *See* Hedge Fund Research (HFR)
Hurdle rate, definition, 191

I
IAA. *See* Investment Advisory Act
      (IAA)
ICA. *See* Investment Company Act
      (ICA)
Index arbitrage, 78–79
Index replication trades, 75
Internet resources, 115–116, 180
Investment Advisory Act (IAA)
  antifraud provisions, 6
  manager registration requirements,
      3–4
  registration of hedge funds, 2
Investment Company Act (ICA),
      registration of hedge funds,
      2–3

J
Jones, Alfred Winslow, 49, 82

L
Liquidity
  definition, 191
  funds of hedge funds, 38
  risk management, 150, 152, 154
Liquidity risk, funds of hedge
      funds, 41
Long biased, definition, 191
Long only, definition, 191
Long Term Capital Management
      (LTCM), 1, 66, 74, 112,
      128–129
LTCM. *See* Long Term Capital
      Management (LTCM)

M
Macro convergence trades, 75–76
Managed Funds Association (MFA),
      commodity trading advisor
      (CTA) performance
      tracking, 107
Managed futures
  advantages, 95
  Commodity Futures Trading
      Commission (CFTC) regulation
      of hedge funds, 2, 7–8, 94
  funds of hedge funds, 33
  futures exchanges, 96–97
  historical perspective, 97
  investment strategy, 110–111
  leverage, 97
  manager. *See* Commodity trading
      advisor (CTA)
  performance monitoring, 111
  principles of futures, 94–95
  taxes, 95
Manager
  active manager index, 19
  equity fund manager evaluation
    overview, 60–61, 63–64
    qualitative analysis, 62–63
    quantitative analysis, 61–62
  equity portfolio mangement, 58–60
  equity selection strategies
    screening, 53–54
    networking, 54–55
    information-gathering, 55–56

equity valuation approaches, 56–57
exposure bias, 52
firing criteria, 137–138
funds of hedge funds, 34–35, 37
futures funds. *See* Commodity
    trading advisor (CTA)
geographic market specialization,
    51–52
global macro funds
    imbalance analysis, 90–91
    reflexivity, 89–90
    selection, 91–93
    Soros, George, 87–89
performance data sources
    administrators, 116
    analytical software, 117–118
    databases, 112–115
    industry publications and
        websites, 115–116
    networking, 116–117
    prime brokers, 116
sector specialists versus generalists,
    50–51
selection process
    comparative statistics, 119–124
    due diligence checklists, 132
    indices for fund screening, 124
    investment mandate development,
        118–119
    on-site visit, 132
    qualitative screens, 128
    quantitative screens, 119–128
    software, 125
    short selling views, 57–58
MAR. *See* Minimal acceptable return
    (MAR)
Margin call, definition, 191
Market risk, funds of hedge funds, 41
MBS arbitrage. *See* Mortgage-backed
    securities (MBS) arbitrage
Merger/risk arbitrage
    definition, 191
    duration of transaction, 71
    funds of hedge funds, 31
    initiation, 72
    leverage, 73
    principles, 69–70

returns, 72
risks, 71–72
stock-for-stock transaction, 70–71
MFA. *See* Managed Funds Association
    (MFA)
Minimal acceptable return (MAR),
    fund manager screening,
    120–121, 125–126
Mobley, David, 130
Mortgage-backed securities (MBS)
        arbitrage
    funds of hedge funds, 32
    spreads, 73

N
National Futures Association (NFA),
        Commodity trading advisor
        (CTA) membership, 102–103
NAV. *See* Net asset value (NAV)
Net asset value (NAV)
    definition, 191
    risk management, 157
Net return, 177–179
Neutral, definition, 191
New York Mercantile Exchange, 96
NFA. *See* National Futures Association
    (NFA)
Nonaccredited investor, definition,
    191

O
Operational risk, funds of hedge
        funds, 41
Options arbitrage, 79, 191

P
Personnel risk, funds of hedge funds,
    41
President's Working Group on
        Financial Markets (PWG),
        hedge fund findings, 1, 2
Principal protection, Principal
        guarantee. (*See* Structured
        products)
PWG. *See* President's Working
        Group on Financial Markets
        (PWG)

Q
Quantum, 128–129

R
Registration, hedge fund requirements, 1–5
Regulation, hedge funds, 5–9, 25
Regulation D
definition, 192
registration of hedge funds, 4–5
Regulation T leverage, 129
Relative swap spread trades, 75
Relative-value arbitrage, 76–77
Reporting
Commodity Futures Trading Commission regulations, 8
risk, 148–150
Reputational risk, 158
Restructuring arbitrage, 78
Return on fund, 12
Return on risk-free asset, 12
Risk
benchmarks, 46
business risk, 41
capacity, 43–44
counterparty risk, 41
credit risk, 41
definition, 139
institutionalization, 42–43
liquidity risk, 41
market risk, 41
operational risk, 41
personnel risk, 41
structure risk, 42
transparency, 44–45, 142–144
Risk arbitrage. *See* Merger/risk arbitrage
Risk management. *See also* Value at risk (VaR)
components, 140–141
due diligence, 154–156
goals, 140
leverage impact, 157
liquidity of portfolio, 150, 152, 154
market risk determination, 156
net asset value (NAV), 157
prioritization of risk, 141

reporting of risk, 148–150
reputational risk, 158
risk-adjusted performance, 156
risk-budgeting, 146–148
stress testing, 144–146
structured products, 169–171
transparency, 44–45, 142–144
Risk-return, hedge fund performance compared with traditional investments, 26–27
Robertson, Julian, 131

S
SEC. *See* Security and Exchange Commission (SEC)
Section 3(c)(1)
definition, 192
registration of hedge funds, 3
Securities Act
antifraud provisions, 5
registration of hedge funds, 4
Securities Exchange Act
antifraud provisions, 6
registration of hedge funds, 4–5
regulation of hedge funds, 9
Security and Exchange Commission (SEC), registration of hedge funds, 2, 4
Sharpe ratio
definition, 192
fund manager screening, 121–122, 125, 136
Shogren, Alex, 113
Soros, George, 82–83, 85, 87–92, 131
Sortino ratio
definition, 192
fund manager screening, 122, 126–127
Standard deviation
annualized, 124
definition, 192
fund manager screening limitations, 119–121
Statistical arbitrage, 76
Sterling ratio
definition, 192
fund manager screening, 123

Stress test
  hedge fund performance
      measurement and monitoring,
      136–137
  risk management, 144–146, 156
Structure risk, funds of hedge funds, 42
Structured products
  cash-intensive hedge fund strategy
      incorporation, 167, 169
  collateralized fund obligation
      (CFO), 173–174
  Constant Proportion Portfolio
      Insurance (CPPI), 172–173
  definition, 192
  features, 159–160
  guarantor protection, 166–167
  innovations, 171–174
  investor protection, 166–167
  manager guidelines, 175
  nondefeased structure definition,
      191
  performance potential preservation,
      160, 162–164
  principal-protection structure, 160,
      162–163, 171–172, 174
  profit lock-in, 169, 174
  risk management, 169–171
  robust structure assurance, 164–165
  shorter term maturities, 165–166

T
Tass, 114–115
Taxes
  fund structure and tax burden, 9

funds of hedge funds, 39
  managed futures, 95
Tiger, 128–129
Total return swap, 171–172
Tranche, definition, 192
Transparency, risk management,
      44–45, 142–144
Treasury arbitrage, on the run versus
      off the run. (*See* Arbitrage)

U
UBTI. *See* Unrelated business taxable
      income (UBTI)
Unrelated business taxable income
      (UBTI), 128
USA PATRIOT Act, antimoney-
      laundering requirements, 6

V
Value at risk (VaR)
  definition, 192
  hedge fund performance
      measurement and monitoring,
      135–136
  risk management, 144, 156
VaR. *See* Value at risk (VaR)
Volatility
  definition, 192
  funds of hedge funds, 38
Volatility arbitrage, 79

Z
Zweig, Martin, 92

Positive Aspect
Skill
Apple Creation
Apple Reference